Big Booze

is

Slowly, Softly,

Killing

Women

Larry D. Reid
Meta L. Reid

with assistance of
Katelyn N. VanderClute

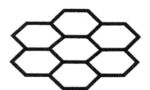

ISBN-13: 978-1981681587

ISBN-10: 1981681582

Library of Congress Control Number: 2015904364

This book is published by Hexagon, Brunswick, NY.

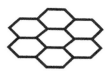

Contents

Chapter 1: Introduction

Our title, *"Big Booze is Slowly, Softly, Killing Women,"* reflects a theme of the book. We assert that there are organizations in the USA, and in similar nations, which are actively, knowingly promoting unhealthy products. There are organizations, for example, that are manufacturing, distributing, and actively selling products known to increase the risk of lung cancer, a deadly disease. Because they can be addictive, these products are relatively easy to sell. Consequently, these organizations' goals are to get people to use their product for a sufficient time to establish an enduring habit of buying and using their products. They do this with the full knowledge that the habitual use of their product can, but perhaps not always, cause a variety of diseases of the lungs. You know about one of these organizations; they are the transnational corporations that sell tobacco products. Collectively, they have been called "Big Tobacco."

Big Tobacco

It is clear: no one prefers to be addicted; no one wants to continually do something leading to disease. Once addicted to a product, however, individuals may express considerable fondness, even love, for the objects of their addiction. Additionally, no one wants to suffer the painful death that is often a consequence of smoking cigarettes. The question is: why would one regularly, habitually, engage the unhealthy act of buying and smoking cigarettes? It just seems irrational that people would pay to do something that is clearly unhealthy. Yet, many millions of people regularly buy cigarettes so that they have, at the very least, a daily supply of them. Millions smoke them.

You might think that an organization devoted to selling an addictive, cancer-producing product would surely be scorned by the larger community. Yet, the people who run these organizations are rewarded very, very well and in accordance of the established norms of their communities. Further, the people who are the companies of Big Tobacco do not think of themselves as agents of disease. They believe what they do is O.K., makes sense, fits into the culture. They surely do not think of themselves as bad people. In many societies in which cigarettes are sold, dealers in illegal drugs such as methamphetamine are scorned and often severely punished for their activity. Those who sell the drug nicotine in the guise of a cigarette, an e-cigarette or a cigar, however, are rewarded. Both nicotine and methamphetamine can become rather easily the focus of an addiction and can have dire effects when taken habitually, yet many societies treat the dealers in these two drugs very differently.

A major reason that smoking cigarettes continues is that the harsh effects of smoking are delayed. Usually, you have to smoke for years before you develop smokers' hack which is a prelude to the very serious lung diseases. The deadly long-term effects are just not easily associated with the immediate effects. Consequently, it is the immediate effects that sustain the habit of smoking even as the disease-producing effects slowly, ever so slowly, accumulate into a serious disease, which is often incurable and deadly.

The "slowly" part of the title reflects the fact that it often takes years for the deadly effects of many bad habits to take hold. What is the idea behind the "softly" part of the title? It takes persuasion to get people to buy and use a product such as cigarettes. It takes advertising and other promotions (e.g., product placements) to get millions to start smoking. For many people, the drug-effects once experienced a number of times, will be sufficient to establish and sustain a pattern of regular use. The drug-effects, then, continually reinforce the maintenance of the habit and often strengthen the habit, i.e., a full-blown addiction is established to tobacco products. No one is forced by Big Tobacco to start smoking. Big Tobacco's job is to persuade you to buy and smoke cigarettes. They know that efficient selling is done softly, almost so softly that you have little awareness of being sold a hazardous product.

Their goal is for you to come to the conclusion that you are doing yourself a big favor by buying their product.

To effectively sell cigarettes, Big Tobacco must also mask, or make irrelevant, the knowledge that smoking produces disease.[1] In a community where there is advertising directed toward getting people to not start smoking or to stop smoking, Big Tobacco counters the messages that smoking is unhealthy. They do this by a variety of means, for example, publishing opinion pieces arguing that the evidence for the unhealthy effects is unclear, perhaps even false. Nowadays, they extensively use the Web to publish their work. They also pay public figures to subtly discredit the public health perspective. In brief, they engage sophisticated public relations and advertising.

In some countries where the government is aligned with Big Tobacco, the message is not subtle: they brand their cigarettes with names such as Good Health and Good Luck. In the past in the USA, when advertising to sell cigarettes was not regulated, Big Tobacco advertised that cigarette smoking was harmless, even actually healthy and surely not unhealthy. For example, a classic ad pictured doctors (guys in white coats with stethoscopes about their necks) with this text: "More doctors smoke Camel cigarettes than any other brand." It may or may not have been true that more doctors preferred Camels as the ad indicated. It surely is a bold-faced lie to promote the idea that smoking is a healthy practice endorsed by the medical profession.

Notice that, currently, the people of Big Tobacco do not directly say "smoking is healthy." They convey that message softly, subtly using well-established knowledge of what kinds of advertising associates a product with health and well-being. Advertising and public relations are skills taught at major universities, and there one can even develop those skills sufficiently to earn a doctorate in marketing. They learn how to sell softly, because they have learned that softly works better than the alternatives. They have learned how to manipulate the messages about cigarettes and smoking to convince many young women that it is O.K. to smoke.

Big Booze

Only a few decades ago, smoking cigarettes by women was socially unacceptable. Only a few decades ago, more men were alcoholics than women, reflecting the fact that women were not large consumers of alcoholic beverages. Big Tobacco and the alcohol-beverages-producing companies (Big Booze) began campaigns to change the custom of limited smoking and limited drinking by women. They have succeeded; now the incidence of addictive use of tobacco products (including e-cigarettes) and alcoholic beverages is similar among women and men, girls and boys.[2]

The rise of women smoking and drinking did not come about by accident or by women demanding the right to smoke and drink. It came about gradually as Big Tobacco and Big Booze manipulated public opinion to make smoking and drinking not only acceptable, but a sign of sophistication.

One way Big Tobacco and Big Booze develop powerful marketing campaigns is to use data collected by government to tabulate the incident rates of smoking, drinking, and use of illegal drugs.[1] A major finding of that data: If adolescents start smoking and drinking, they are likely to continue their habit for decades, often for a lifetime (likely a somewhat shortened lifetime). The same data also indicates that if individuals do not develop the habit of smoking and excessive drinking early in their life, they are unlikely to develop the habits.

The marketers of Big Tobacco and Big Booze are aware of the data concerning adolescents and adults. To ensure a steady, profitable market, they then logically came to the conclusion that they should devote their marketing toward adolescents and young adults. They also know that it is easier to convince adolescents with slick advertising than older people and that adolescents are more prone to becoming addicted to the drugs in their products. Based on the conception that Big Tobacco and Big Booze *should do* any and everything that is legal to increase the sales of their products, they strive to get adolescents and near adults to start using their products. Those interested in public health do not approve of the goals of Big Tobacco and Big Booze. They, along with most everyone, understand that societies would be healthier if individuals never developed the habit of smoking and never developed the habit of drinking large amounts of alcoholic beverages.

The USA has democratically concluded that it is not in the best interests of children and young adults to use tobacco products and alcoholic beverages. The conclusion is made clear by making it illegal to sell tobacco products to minors and to sell alcoholic beverages to anyone under the age of 21. Although many families may think it is O.K. for a minor to have an occasional glass of wine or beer with dinner, we believe that it is only the most perverse, weird parents who would be happy to see their 12-year-old daughter frequently getting drunk and smoking cigarettes. The marketers of Big Tobacco know that parents disapprove of them trying to sell their products to children. Consequently, the people of Big Tobacco say that they do not want to and do not market their products to minors. They say that even while they devise ways of marketing their products to under-aged individuals.

We hope that women between the ages of 15 and 25 will read this book. It was written for them and for those who love them. The focus is on them because we believe that they are particularly at risk for developing alcoholism. That belief was supported by results from some our research. Relatedly, drinking alcoholic beverages may be more toxic to women compared to men. The reasons for these conclusions are explained, in some detail, in the following chapters.

Alcoholism and clinical depression often occur in the same woman. Evidently, alcoholism can contribute to depression and depression can lead to alcoholism. The incidence of depression occurs more often in women than men. Also, depression is affecting younger women more than older women. Unfortunately for the avoidance of these common problems, there are organizations (Big Booze and others) that are marketing products that are particularly unhealthy for young women. We are writing this book to advise young women on how to have a happier life, one free of the avoidable problems of alcoholism and depression. A bit of advice at the outset: Do not believe the messages delivered by Big Booze; they foster lifestyles with unhappy endings.

Some might accuse us of being sexists, because we are stating that young women, in comparison to men, are particularly vulnerable to alcoholism. There is no advantage, however, to women in hiding the recent findings that women are at greater risk of alcoholism than previously believed; or, in hiding the apparent fact that alcoholism is on the rise in young women. There is no advantage in hiding that depression is more common in young women than previously thought or that depression is becoming even more common. There is no advantage to women to obscure the facts that some organizations are exploiting women by marketing products that increase their risk of developing alcoholism and depression. It seems advantageous to point out some of the reasons why women are becoming more alcoholic and depressed.

Women's issues

Women are different than men. Women have the anatomy and physiology to carry developing babies from conception to birth; men do not. We do not believe that this difference should be exploited.[3] We believe that it is particularly awful that women should be exploited by highly profitable organizations in order to merely make more money than they are already making. The people of Big Booze are supported by the larger society in almost uncountable ways, yet they have chosen to encourage young women to drink more and more. They do this even though they know that it might be harmful to women, hence to the very society that supports them.

Let us be clear at the outset. This we firmly believe: In an ideal society, women and men should have equal opportunity to exercise power. Further, we believe that equal opportunity will produce happier men as well as happier

6

women. Further, our beliefs are supported by tabulations of data comparing the well-being among different societies. Such tabulations support the idea that those supporting equal opportunity to exercise power for both sexes are happier; both sexes are happier. It may be necessary for different norms and customs to be incorporated in a society for there to be equal opportunity to exercise power for all citizens. Fairness can be achieved by taking into account individual differences as long as fairness is the paramount goal.

This we also believe: When a society moves toward providing equal access to power for all of its citizens that such a society is more likely to be stable, peaceful, and prosperous. Further, such a society will have happier citizens, and importantly, it is more likely for the individual citizen to respect authority. These are the founding ideas of democracy that are so very contrary to ideas of autocracies. Further, as limited democratic societies have matured they have, although at times slower than ideally, broadened access to power for more and more of their citizens. This broadening of access to privilege and power need not cause chaos and discord. For example, providing women the opportunity to vote did not produce the chaos that some predicted.

There is a flip side to the idea of the previous paragraph. When unfair, corrupt practices pervade societies they become unhappy places. One of us (Larry) ran a quick statistic measuring the relationship between indices of corruption and a measure of happiness across nations. The result was as predicted: The more corrupt the nation, the less happy were its citizens. Societies that foster fairness also foster equal opportunity for access to power. Societies that provide equal opportunity for education and equal pay for equal work set the basis for fair competition. When there is fair competition and many different kinds of opportunities to compete, it is not a tragedy to lose a particular competition. All of us have lost at some sporting event or some game of chance and it has not been a bother. It does become bothersome, however, if the competition was judged to be unfair.

Surely nearly all of us agree: It is unfair for adults sophisticated in the art and science of public relations and advertising to take advantage of children and young people who have yet to become sophisticated consumers. That is why we find it particularly troubling that Big Tobacco developed advertising to persuade children to begin smoking. Eventually, the society as a whole did do something about it (perhaps, not enough, but something). Further, even Big Tobacco now voices the idea that it is improper to advertise their products to children and claim that they do not. If it is unfair for Big Tobacco to advertise to sell to children, it is probably unfair for Big Booze and for those transnational companies to advertise food they know is unhealthy.

We have made some definitive statements. A question of interest: Why should you believe our statements rather than the statements of those who might disagree with us (such as spokespersons for Big Tobacco and Big Booze)? We deal with issues of how to assess the truth value of any proposition in the last chapter of this book; here we provide the short answer. We believe that scientifically derived and supported propositions are more truthful than propositions derived and supported by other means. We believe that many of the preceding statements can be supported by scientific studies. Stated another way, the practice of science tends to sort out true statements from false ones. Also, we have no vested interests: We make no money from reduced sales of tobacco products or alcoholic beverages. Big Tobacco and Big Booze make more money the more they sell their products, hence have vested interests. Unfortunately, the use of their products also tends to induce disease. If we have a vested interest, it is this: We would find it rewarding to see less alcoholism among young women; thereby, eventually fewer alcoholic mothers and grandmothers.

In the next chapters, we discuss alcoholic beverages, alcoholism and more specifically alcoholism and women. We are focusing on alcoholic beverages and young women. We are particularly concerned that young women are being seriously challenged by Big Booze. In the last chapter, we again address the issue of why you should believe our conclusions and then present a simple summary.

Our goal is to provide information for smart choices.

Chapter 2.   Alcoholic Beverages: a Little History

Alcoholic beverages have been a part of human culture since its beginning.[1] To make an alcoholic beverage, all that is necessary is to have a sweet fluid open to the air. Some of the ever-present yeast in air will most likely become part of the fluid. Yeasts convert sugars into ethanol. Ethanol is the active ingredient in alcoholic beverages, i.e., ethanol is the molecule producing the psychological effects sought by those who like to drink alcoholic beverages. We use the term alcohol to designate ethanol in our usual language and beverages containing ethanol are called alcoholic beverages.

Overly ripe fruits contain ethanol, which is a product of the breakdown of some foods. Consequently, we are well-adapted to handling small amounts of it. Our livers process ethanol efficiently using it as a source of energy and protecting us from the potentially toxic effects due to an accumulation of ethanol. However, as we shall see subsequently, the capacity of the liver to protect us from a toxic buildup of ethanol is limited.

Given the ease of making alcoholic beverages, humanity has had plenty of opportunities to experience and experiment with them. Very early in our history, it was discovered that even weak alcoholic beverages were different than fruit juices and water. Alcoholic beverages have the ability to induce pleasure in some people. The fact that alcoholic beverages could also cause drunkenness was discovered very early as well. That some beverages are tastier than others and that some beverages are more likely to induce pleasure than others was surely obvious. Humans' ability to pass information from one generation to the next and the development of the arts and crafts of processing edibles for future use is one of the exquisite manifestations of our exceptional abilities. The development of skill at making beer and wine was honed along with our ability to obtain and prepare other food-stuffs. As knowledge of beer and wine making advanced, alcoholic beverages became a staple in the diets of many emerging cultures.

A depiction of the Greek God Dionysos. A photograph by © Marie-Lan Nguyen / Wikimedia Commons of the statue as it resides in the Musée du Louvre, Paris, France.

Michelangelo's depiction of the Roman God of Wine. A photograph by © Marie-Lan Nguyen / Wikimedia Commons of the statue as it resides in the Musée du Louvre, Paris, France. During the Renaissance, ideas of the ancient Greeks and Romans were revived. In that same spirit, Cardinal Raffaaele Riario commissioned Michelangelo to produce a statue to honor the spirit of Bacchus, not an unusual concept for the Church of the day which was highly involved in the production of alcoholic beverages. Michelangelo' depiction, however, was a bit too realistic for the Cardinal, showing a sadness that is common to those who devote themselves to alcoholic beverages. The Cardinal rejected it, evidently he wished for something more celebratory. Michelangelo eventually sold it to someone else.[1]

Alcoholic beverages became a feature of celebrations in many cultures. Their ability to produce pleasantness and drunkenness (often characterized by apparent modifications of personality) probably gave rise to the idea that a spirit is associated with wine. About 5000 years ago, the Egyptians worshipped Osiris, the god of wine and the Mesopotamians worshipped Siduri, their God of wine.[2] Depicted here are statues depicting two gods associated with wine and celebration. The Greek God was Dionysus; the Roman God was Bacchus.

Notice that the two statues of the god of wine are a bit feminine. Evidently the sculptors were aware that heavy intake of alcoholic beverage had a feminizing effect on men. Compare this statue with the other statues of Michelangelo's which depict males with more pronounced masculine muscles. The feminizations are due to the fact that heavy alcohol-intake interferes with the availability of testosterone leading to a reduction in secondary sex characteristics. Notice, also, that neither statue depicts happiness or joy.

Alcoholic beverages have some advantages over other beverages. The ethanol content of wine-like beverages kills or limits the growth of many germs that cause diseases such as diarrhea. Apple jack, fermented or hard cider, for example, was a common drink of the early years of Europeans on the American continent. This apple jack had sufficient ethanol to retard the growth of some disease-producing germs and was probably safer to drink than much of the available water.

With the advent of having plenty of alcoholic beverages, the dark side of drinking must have become apparent very early in history. From one perspective, beer and wine are not much different than bread; both products of microorganisms working on carbohydrates. Both kinds of food-stuffs provide ready calories and are capable of inducing pleasure. Surely, the smell and taste of warm bread to a hungry person is a pleasurable event as well as its eating. Wine can also taste good, particularly to the experienced drinker and can induce pleasure after its ingestion. Wine and bread can combine to enhance the pleasures of each. Even further, other pleasures can be combined to produce something more than each alone. This was apparent to Omar Khayyam, a scientist and poet whose life spanned the 11th and 12th centuries. His writings became popular when Edward FitzGerald translated his work: "Rubáiyát of Omar Khayyam." The following verse makes the point.

> "A Book of Verses underneath the Bough,
>
> A Jug of Wine, a Loaf of Bread—and Thou
>
> Beside me singing in the Wilderness—
>
> Oh, Wilderness were Paradise enow!

There is a significant difference between bread and wine. One can eat a lot of bread and not exhibit drunkenness. One can drink a lot of wine and exhibit not only drunkenness, but foolishness. Further, drunkenness seems to be associated with other unacceptable behavior. When one eats bread, one becomes sated rather quickly. When one drinks wine, there is a tendency for one glass of wine to lead to the next and so on without apparent satiety until toxicity is reached.

The different consequences between consuming bread and consuming alcoholic beverage have led to the coinage of words to designate the differences. Hence, we have concepts such as being drunk (designating someone with toxic levels of alcohol) and drunkard (one who frequently gets drunk). In our society, we designate the condition of being a drunkard as being an *alcoholic*. An alcoholic is said to have a condition called *alcoholism*. Subsequently, more will be said about labels associated with the intake of alcoholic beverages.

A book endorsed by the World Health Organization has as its title: "Alcohol: no ordinary commodity."[3] It is a reasonable name. Alcoholic beverages are unique food. They can, for many, induce pleasure and considerable harm. Alcohol beverages, aside from tobacco products, induce more adverse effects than any other consumable (some put the costs of alcohol-induced mayhem to be greater than tobacco-induced).

Given the unique nature of alcoholic beverages, every advanced society has tried to regulate the consumption of alcoholic beverages. Every major religion addresses the issues associated with alcoholic beverages. Some ban the use, others advise moderation. Laws and regulations have been written, modified interminably, all with the goal of reducing the harmful effects of drunkenness.

As mentioned, the craft of making alcoholic beverages developed early in our history. Drinking alcoholic beverages similar to modern beers and wines became a staple feature of the very earliest cultures. Early on, farms were developed to produce fruits, such as grapes, for wine-making. There is evidence that wine became a product of trade as soon as cultures developed the technologies for trading.

There were surely slow but steady advances in the making of alcoholic beverages that enhanced their palatability, probably increased their ethanol-content and produced a more standard beverage. Alcoholic beverages were and are characterized by the source of carbohydrates used to make them. Beer and the like are from malted grains. Wine and the like are from grapes and other fruits. The manufacture and distribution of wine and beer became significant parts of many nations' economies.

Two advances in knowledge made monumental changes in the technology of alcoholic beverage production: distillation and understanding the process of fermentation.

Distillation

In about the first century of the modern era, persons living in Alexandria, Egypt, discovered distillation, a process of heating mixtures and collecting the vapors as they condense, thereby allowing the separation and collection of different parts of a boiling mixture. Distillation for the purpose of collecting ethanol was probably first begun in southern Italy during the 12th century. The technology spread rather rapidly and was widespread by the 13th century.

Fermentation is the term used to label the process of producing beer and wine. When the ethanol content of alcoholic beverages becomes 12 to 15%, it tends to kill the yeast that produces the ethanol. That limits the content of ethanol in the beverage. The highest concentrations of most wines are about 14%. Distillation allowed for the creation of alcoholic beverages with much higher concentrations of ethanol.

Alcohol produced by distillation is not created, merely concentrated. A weak alcoholic beverage, for example, wine or beer, is heated to boiling and the vapors collected. The various vapors, for example, water and ethanol, boil (become vapors) and condense (become fluids) at different temperatures thereby allowing them to be separated. Modern distillation can be very precise; pure ethanol is possible. Most alcoholic beverages produced by distillation are a combination of water and ethanol with small amounts of other ingredients. When the distillation process is rather precise, the desired fluid is clear. The distilled spirits with the amber color are associated with the aging process usually in oaken barrels.

When an individual drinks a large amount of an alcoholic beverage, the amount of ethanol in blood overwhelms the body's efficient processing (metabolism) of ethanol. There is some processing of ethanol in the stomach, but generally, ethanol goes from the gut straight into the blood, through the liver where some is processed, then circulated throughout the body over and over again. With each pass through the liver, some of it is metabolized until it is completely gone. The heart pumps blood very efficiently. In about a minute, the entire amount of blood is circulated once. A large proportion of the blood goes to the brain. Consequently, when an alcoholic beverage is drunk, the ethanol that enters the blood stream quickly reaches the brain where it has both its desired and major undesirable effects.

When alcoholic beverages are produced by distillation, the beverages can have a high concentration of ethanol. Consequently, these products can produce intoxication very quickly. Distilled spirits' higher concentration of ethanol seems to distinguish these liquors from ordinary beers and wines. In attempts to control drunkenness and its consequences, often rules were made to control distilled spirits that did not apply to beer and wine.

The most common commercial products of distillation include rum, whiskey, gin, tequila, and vodka. These alcoholic products are usually sold at about 80 proof (or 40% ethanol in water). Some features of the raw material used to make the beverage are also a part of the products and produce the different flavors. Also, flavorful substances are often added to the distilled product to enhance its flavor.

The differences among distilled spirits (also called liquors), beer and wine are reflected in the modern marketing of these products. There are beer related industries, wine related industries and the distilled spirits industries. Each industry has its own trade association that fosters its manufacturing and marketing. They often cooperate to further their common interests, but they also compete for the consumer's money. As will be discussed, governments often have established different rules for each of these classes of alcoholic beverages which, among other things, are characterized by their differences in ethanol content (beer usually being the lowest, up to about 6% ethanol), followed by wine (about 13%) and then distilled spirits (usually 40 to 50%).

There was a time in France (from 1805 to 1914) when an alcoholic beverage, absinthe, was produced and marketed widely with a high ethanol content, sometimes as high as 90%.[4] It was also flavored with herbs, particularly, e.g., wormwood. The absinthe cocktail was often prepared by pouring absinthe over sugar into water which turns the drink milky green; hence the name, the green fairy. Absinthe is very toxic, and it was not allowed to be marketed in most countries. France, however, did not ban it until 1914. At the height of absinthe's popularity, it was drunk considerably more often than wine in France.

Because absinthe was a favorite beverage of a number of impressionist painters and writers of the era, absinthe achieved considerable notoriety, even something of a cult-following in Paris. You will notice the green cocktail in a number of paintings of famous painters.

As noted, absinthe is very toxic and those who regularly consumed it deteriorated very fast in comparison to those who regularly drank large amounts of wine. There was considerable speculation that the flavorings, particularly some ingredient in the wormwood (particularly thujone), caused the toxic effects. On the other hand, there are those who maintain that the toxicity from the regular intake of absinthe is merely due to drinking a product with a very high concentration of ethanol. As will be noted often here and probably in every account of people and alcoholic beverages, the toxicity and the psychoactive effects of alcoholic beverages are directly associated with the dose of ethanol. If one drinks an alcoholic beverage with a high concentration of ethanol quickly, one gets intoxicated quickly; it is that simple. Drinking to drunkenness regularly produces a number of dire consequences; it is that simple. The question is: Why drink a known intoxicating product? The answer is a topic of subsequent chapters.

Stoked by absinthe's association with Paris and its artists, the absinthe cocktail has maintained its mystique, its fascination. Noting a marketing opportunity, there has been a lifting of the regulations against selling absinthe. The USA lifted its ban on absinthe, in 2007, with the regulation that the thujone-content must be less than 10 ppm (equal to 10 mg/kg). It is not uncommon for absinthe, in a variety of brands, to be sold in restaurants. At some places, you can have them mixed into cocktails at your table side.[5] The absinthe sold currently in the USA, however, is not the nearly 90% ethanol sold in some places in Europe; it is more like 60%. The current brands of absinthe may be considerably different that those sold in France during its peak of popularity.

Lead and Methanol Are Neural Toxins

In the USA, unlawful production of alcoholic beverages produces a product called *moonshine,* probably because it was usually produced at night. Lead is the most frequent contaminant in illegal distilled products. The lead can come from lead-based solder used to make a still with copper pipe. Another potential source of lead is using the copper tubing from car radiators which have become contaminated with lead. Lead as well as other heavy metals poison brain cells and, thereby reduce cognitive ability.[3]

Methanol, an alcohol, is a contaminant in illegally produced alcoholic beverages in some poor countries. Methanol is legally available and usually inexpensive. Methanol is toxic at low doses. At low levels of toxicity, it is difficult for the drinker to know if his drunkenness might be due a combination of ethanol and methanol. In very small amounts, methanol might be relevant to the discomfort called a hang-over (an aftereffect of a bout of drinking characterized, mainly, by a throbbing headache). In larger amounts (4 ml), methanol can destroy the optic nerve thereby inducing blindness. The lethal dose is 100 to 125 ml or about 4 oz. Methanol is sometimes called wood alcohol, because it can be a product of heated wood. Methanol is used to spike ethanol used in industry to prevent the ethanol-methanol mixture from being drunk.

Understanding the Process of Fermentation

Prior to the mid-19th century, hardly anything of precision was known of the process of fermentation. Gately (2008) summed the situation thusly: "For all they knew, it might have been the invisible hand of Bacchus or some other form of divine intervention" (p. 301).[1]

Building on the work of Lavoisier and Schwann, Pasteur demonstrated that yeasts were the agents that changed carbohydrates into ethanol. With this basic understanding, he worked out the details for making wine and beer. His knowledge allowed the technology for making wine and beer to go from recipes based on folk knowledge to more precise processes. Pasteur's findings also are relevant to making water and milk safe to drink (i.e., Pasteurization).

The beers and ales currently marketed world-wide have ethanol contents ranging from less than 3% alcohol by volume to around 14% (somewhat larger concentrations can be achieved by using special kinds of yeast). The pale beers familiar to most Americans have ethanol contents that fall in the range of 4–6%. One can freeze the water in beer and have it rise to the top of a container and then lift off the ice, a process known as freeze-distilling. Using freeze distilling, a beer-like product can be made with concentrations of ethanol typical of ordinary distilled spirits.

One can take apple wine (apple jack) and place it in a freezing temperature and institute freeze-distilling. The result will be a drink with a higher concentration of ethanol. This was a practice in colonial America.

With the development of civilization came the development of the alcohol-producing industries. Currently, the alcohol-producing and alcohol-distributing industries are as sophisticated as other major industries. They do research and sponsor research at major universities directed toward all facets of the industry. They do research to enhance the palatability of their products. They are very skilled at marketing. They are very skilled at public relations being ever mindful that the industry has faced and continues to face threats of prohibition and limits on the sale of their products (heavily regulated nearly everywhere).

America's Experience with Alcoholic Beverages

From the time Europeans began settling the Americas, drinking alcoholic beverages was a standard practice. Before the advent of the knowledge of Pasteur and the development of the technology of providing safe drinking water, it was probably healthier to drink alcoholic beverages than water. Drinking to one's health was probably not a bad idea.

Drinking small amounts of beer and wine regularly is not particularly toxic; the liver processes it efficiently and prevents a toxic accumulation of ethanol. Drinking lots of beer, wine or drinking distilled spirits quickly does lead to intoxication (the liver has limited capacity to process ethanol). The intoxication is directly related to the amount of ethanol that gets circulated to the brain. It is the intoxication (drunkenness) that is problematic. A feature of alcoholic beverages is that it produces an effect, particularly in some people, that establishes a habit of drinking intoxicating amounts. When a large proportion of a population regularly drinks to intoxication, the society does not function as well as it might.

When alcoholic beverages are cheap and available in large amounts, overall consumption grows by more people drinking more and more. Consequently, drunkenness becomes more frequent. Since drunkenness is manifest often in asocial behavior, every society that has had the opportunity to produce cheap, reasonably palatable alcoholic beverages also produces rules for governing drinking. These rules are often codified in law. Rules are also established by way of cultural norms and mores. In colonial America, rules were established that limited the opportunities for women to drink large amounts of alcoholic beverages and that kept the consumption of alcohol by women at a much lower rate than men's.

From the perspective of America, alcoholism used to be considered a man's problem, i.e., the incidence of alcoholism was considerably larger among men than women. Throughout America's early history, however, women often suffered inordinately as a result of men's intemperance.[6] Even as late as the mid nineteenth century, nearly every state of the United States had strict laws that united women's legal rights to those of her husband's. With marriage, all property and sources of income automatically became the husband's right to use as he wished. Divorce was socially unacceptable and often legally difficult. The man of the family, therefore, could take the earnings of the family, including those brought to the marriage by the wife and any she earned, and spend it on drinking. Given men's level of drinking at this time and the fact that problems emerge with heavy drinking (e.g., gambling), the women and children of alcoholic men were often left in desperate circumstances. This circumstance was a prime motivation of the temperance movement that eventually led to national Prohibition. The temperance movement involved large numbers of women and was often sustained by women. The temperance movement, by bringing to the fore women's lack of civil rights, was significant in women gaining the right to vote.[6]

Temperance and Prohibition

The temperance movement in the USA was advanced early in the history of the nation. The movement was fueled by the obvious observations that alcoholic beverages were linked to a wide variety of problems. In the new nation, beer, wine and whiskey were plentiful and drunk often. The industries supporting the manufacturing and marketing of alcoholic beverages (Big Booze) prospered.

Big Booze evolved with the development of better ideas for such things as to how to grow grapes best suited to making wine (a particular interest of Thomas Jefferson) or how to produce whiskey so that a more palatable product was produced (an interest of George Washington).

Plentiful grain and the knowledge of distillation combined to produce large amounts of whiskey around the time of the American Revolution from European domination. There were economies associated with producing whiskey. There was a strong market for it; many had a large appetite for more ethanol-concentrated alcoholic beverages fostered by the habits of drinking beer and wine. Shipping grain from the newly settled western frontiers (western Pennsylvania and Kentucky) was cumbersome and costly. Using the grain to produce whiskey provided solutions to problems: (a) shipping whiskey was easier than shipping stores of grain, (b) whiskey was a value-added product producing more profit than selling cheap grain, and (c) whiskey was a taxable product and those taxes helped to finance the new Federal government.

The distillers' product, e.g., raw whiskey, is harsh to the taste and often unpalatable for other reasons. Distilled spirits can be made more palatable by adding sweeteners and other flavors. The culinary art of making cocktails flourished. The result is, as would be expected, an increase in intake of ethanol. To state the evident: drinks that taste good are more readily taken than those that do not taste so good.

By the time there were well-developed cities all along the Atlantic coast and the frontiers were being extended toward the west, the average intake of alcohol had, by almost any standard, reached enormous amounts. The intake of alcoholic beverages produced considerable drunkenness, considerable mayhem. It was noticed, by being obvious, that problems emerged when persons drank too much, too often.

Although women drank, the bulk of this consumption was by men who regularly drank beverages with high ethanol content, e.g., distilled spirits. The negative effects of this level of drinking were surely obvious to many and noted particularly by Dr. Benjamin Rush.[7] He practiced medicine throughout his lifetime while at the same time being an avid contributor to the media of the day (newspapers, the printing of pamphlets, books and letter-writing). Rush was an early advocate for repeal of British taxes and eventually for separation of the colonies from England. He was a signer of the Declaration of Independence.

Rush was a strong advocate for various reforms including better treatment for the insane. His strong advocacy for education led to the establishment of two colleges in western Pennsylvania that continue to this day (Dickinson & Franklin and Marshall). He was a vigorous trainer of young doctors and it has been said that eventually nearly all doctors of the United States were either his students or students of his students. A list of his accomplishments, and his tribulations in trying to get reforms enacted, would take a book-length narrative and that has been done, i.e., Brodsky, 2004.[8]

What interests us here is his views on what has been become known as alcoholism and his work that led him to be the acknowledged father of psychiatry. Through his medical practice and his general observations, Rush came to the conclusion that the habitual intake of distilled spirits caused disease. He wrote about the disease-inducing effects of distilled spirits as well as ways of preventing and curing the diseases induced by the intake of distilled spirits. He may not have been the first to talk about distilled spirits as being a disease-vector, but he was surely among the first (e.g., Thomas Jefferson commented that distilled spirits were harmful and advocated use of wine rather than spirits). Rush indicated that the habitual intake of distilled spirits *was* a disease (a novel idea that most credit the Scottish physician Thomas Trotter with being the very first to advocate).

Rush's conclusion was that distilled spirits were disease vectors, but that cider, wine and beer were not in the same category. In fact, he advocated that cider and wine were often healthy drinks and prescribed them in his practice of medicine. He advocated temperance, not prohibition. He recognized that it was the large doses of alcohol that were the most, if not sole, cause of considerable disease.

The first paper he wrote on the topic of alcoholic beverages was on the wide-spread use of rum during harvest-time. The custom was for considerable rum to be drunk as a way of countering the effects of hard labor in the heat of the day. Rush stated that the rum actually contributed to what we know as heat stroke. He advocated the use of water to counter the effects of hard labor during hot days, a truly revolutionary idea—he was such a rebel. He also advocated against slavery and for prison reform.

He wrote other tracts on the problems associated with drinking distilled spirits and eventually collected them into a larger one, *Essay on the Effect of Ardent Spirits …*, published in 1794. The message was clear. Habitual drinking was damaging to health and moral well-being of the individual as well as the nation. His last major work can be called the first textbook on insanity, i.e., on the psychology of abnormal behavior, the basic science of psychiatry and clinical psychology. He concluded that what we currently call mental illnesses were treatable diseases caused by knowable events. He advocated that those suffering mental problems should be given the same humane treatment afforded to those with obvious physical problems. He stated again his conclusion that drinking distilled spirits was a cause of mental illness.

Did Rush's writing, as probably the most illustrious physician in terms of patriotism and in the practice of medicine, result in the newly founded nation swearing off distilled spirits and, therefore, enjoying a burst of better health? Oh, if it were that easy! No, but his writings were widely distributed, read by many, and influenced generations of public-health-minded individuals. His writings also were instrumental in the founding the first organization with a constitution and bylaws for the specific purpose of advocating abstinence both for themselves and for others to emulate. This first society was organized, in 1808, by Dr. Billy J. Clark of the small town of Moreau in Saratoga County, NY.[1]

The common knowledge that habitual drinking of distilled spirits seemingly caused a great deal of misery gave credence to those advocating temperance. Temperance movements eventually morphed into prohibition movements. Prohibition movements which began humbly in 1808 grew steadily until 1919. In 1919, the USA enacted legislation outlawing the sale of intoxicating beverages, nationwide. The movement was one of the largest social movements in the history of the USA. It was clearly the first strong social movement in which women had predominant, powerful roles. For those interested in the history of the temperance movement in the USA, I recommend histories by Fleming (1975), Gately (2008) and Mattingly (1998).[8] The temperance movement led to the Prohibition of the sale of alcoholic beverages in some states and eventually in the entire USA.

One impetus for prohibition was a cultural institution of the times, the saloon. The saloon prior to Prohibition was virtually a man's drinking club and often served as a community center supporting activities such as postings for jobs. The saloon featured heavy drinking, opportunities to gamble and often prostitution. The activities of the saloon had a number of dire consequences. As mentioned, the spending on the beverages and the related activities of gambling and prostitution was at the expense of the women and children of the family. Another unfortunate circumstance was that wives could become infected with syphilis, a common venereal disease. Prior to the availability of penicillin, syphilis was extraordinarily difficult to treat and the infection often led to debility and death. One of the most effective organizations lobbying for the prohibition of the sale of alcoholic beverages was the Anti-Saloon League (ASL).

There is little benefit to us in our relating, in detail, the story of the rise and fall of Prohibition. It has been done thoroughly and recently in a book by Daniel Okrent (2010). Cooperating with Okrent, Ken Burns, our masterful chronicler of the American experience along with his collaborator, Lynn Novick, have produced a digital account of Prohibition. Their production was first shown on public TV in October, 2011. These productions provide a better history of national Prohibition than we can. In brief, the impetus for Prohibition was the high prevalence of alcoholism and its attendant problems. In the righteous attempt to correct the problems, Prohibition emerged from a long history of political activity that finally culminated in the 18th Amendment to the Constitution of the USA. The combination of events such as WW I, greater prosperity associated with advances in technology and industrialization, women's suffrage and the reactions to Prohibition combined to produce dramatic changes in American culture. Relevant to our topic, these impactful events changed how we drank alcoholic beverages and it changed *who* drank them.

During Prohibition, authorizes destroying confiscated alcoholic beverage. This picture was taken from Wikipedia and is considered to be in the public domain. c1923. Source unknown.

Prior to the 1920s, most women abstained or were either temperate drinkers. There were considerable social constraints on women's drinking that made it uncomfortable for women to drink in excess. Post WW I and during the roaring '20s, it became more socially acceptable for women to drink more and in more situations than previously and they did drink more than previously. This may seem surprising since large numbers of women were the nearly constant crusaders for national Prohibition and it was a time of national Prohibition.

The noble experiment of outlawing the production and sale of alcoholic beverages began January 16, 1920, a year after the enactment of the 18th Amendment to the US Constitution. It ended, with the repeal of the 18th Amendment, December, 5, 1933 (the 21th Amendment). Relevant to the general temperance movement that led to Prohibition, the 19th Amendment insured women the right to vote nation-wide.

Because taxes on alcoholic beverages were a major source of Federal revenue, it was necessary for the passage of Prohibition to establish new ways of collecting taxes. As a step toward Prohibition, the amendment for taxation of income was passed. To refresh your knowledge, please note again the content of the four amendments relevant to these social movements.

The 16th Amendment states (enacted in 1913):

The Congress shall have power to lay and collect taxes on incomes, from whatever source derived, without apportionment among the several States, and without regard to any census or enumeration.

The 18th Amendment states (enacted in 1919):

1. After one year from the ratification of this article the manufacture, sale, or transportation of intoxicating liquors within, the importation thereof into, or the exportation thereof from the United States and all territory subject to jurisdiction thereof for beverage purposes is hereby prohibited.

2. The Congress and the several States shall have concurrent power to enforce this article by appropriate legislation.

3. This article shall be inoperative unless it shall have been ratified as an amendment to the Constitution by the legislatures of the several States, as provided in the Constitution within seven years from the date of the submission hereof to the States by the Congress.

The 19th Amendment states (enacted in 1920):

The right of citizens of the United States to vote shall not be denied or abridged by the United States or by any state on account of sex. Congress shall have the power to enforce this article by appropriate legislation.

The 21st Amendment states (enacted in 1933):

1. The eighteenth article of amendment to the Constitution of the United States is hereby repealed.

2. The transportation or importation into any State, territory, or procession of the United States for delivery or use therein of intoxicating liquors in violation of the laws thereof, is hereby prohibited.

3. The article shall be inoperative unless it shall have been ratified as an amendment to the Constitution by conventions in the several States as provided in the Constitution within seven years from the date of the submission hereof to the States by the Congress.

In terms of eliminating the consumption of alcoholic beverages, the "noble experiment" of prohibition by amendment of the United States Constitution was, by nearly all accounts, a colossal failure. Among the many reasons for its failure was that the enforcement of the amendment was poorly organized, poorly financed and hence poorly done. Drinking was popular and many otherwise law-biding citizens chose to drink rather than obey the law or support the enforcement of the law. Criminal organizations prospered because they now had a profitable and nearly safe way of "doing business."

The 18th Amendment did not provide the specific means of instituting national Prohibition. The law that specified the means to achieve the goal was the Volstead act. The Volstead act was riddled with exceptions to the ban on production of alcoholic beverages. One of them was that alcohol could be prescribed as a medicine. Another was that wine could be produced for common religious rites. Yet, another was that wine could be produced in the home, in limited amounts, for family consumption. And still another, it was legal to use ethanol in the manufacture of a number of products. All of these exceptions surely seemed reasonable to enough law makers and regulators; they curtailed the existence of saloons of the day and their associated problems, yet left intact some other more cherished institutions. These exceptions, however, quickly led to "legal" ways to provide the market with alcoholic beverages for recreational purposes.

In addition to the legal exceptions to the use of alcoholic beverages, illegal means of producing and selling alcoholic beverages developed very rapidly. This included the trafficking in alcoholic beverages from places where it was legal to produce it for the US market (or from places where it may have been illegal to sell it but not really illegal to produce it). Given that alcoholic beverages are relatively easy to make, a goodly number of citizens started making and selling the beverage despite it being illegal to do so. Unskilled producers of distilled products often produced poor quality spirits including those with toxic contaminants.

In a number of big cities, the illegal trafficking in alcoholic beverages came under the control of criminal gangs. A cultural shift emerged from this mix of legal and illegal marketing of alcoholic beverages sustained by well-developed appetites for the beverages. The distinction between criminal activity and legal marketing became blurred. Criminality became more acceptable. The legal saloon was indeed destroyed, but replaced by other institutions. For example, the cocktail party in the home became more common. A host could provide guests with a product they desired and which signified the host's ability to provision a high quality beverage that might not otherwise be available.

Prohibition had consequences its proponents never desired. One of those unintended consequences was that it took women's drinking, which was rare but surely not absent, into the open and made it considerably more respectable. As mentioned, cocktail parties where women were guests as well as hosts became a feature of home entertaining.

The following is a quote from Al Capone, the leader of a criminal organization that prospered selling illegal alcoholic beverages: "I make my money by supplying a public demand. If I break the law, my customers, who number hundreds of the best people in Chicago, are as guilty as I am. The only difference between us is that I sell and they buy. Everybody calls me a racketeer. I call myself a business man. When I sell liquor it's bootlegging. When my patrons serve it on a silver tray on Lake Shore Drive it's hospitality (Gately, 2008, p 384)."[9] Capone was not, however, merely a business man, he also used violence, even murder, to protect and enhance his businesses. His wealth derived from his illegal businesses protected all of his illegal activities for a considerable period, by way of bribes and other means of buying undue influence. Capone is probably the most notorious of the criminals selling illegal alcoholic beverages in the USA during prohibition, but he surely was not the only one so engaged. Except for their trafficking in illegal alcoholic beverages, many law-abiding citizens participated.

A mug shot of Al Capone taken June 17th, 1931. This photograph was found on Wikipedia and is in the public domain.

Another product of Prohibition was the development of illegal places to drink, the speakeasies. Many, but not all, speakeasies were different than the notorious saloons whose activities were the very reasons for Prohibition. These drinking establishments had characteristics more like a private club than a public saloon. Many were fronted as restaurants that provided entertainment. Tables and chairs replaced the bars of the saloon. The restaurant-like speakeasy became common in big cities, but not so common in rural America. The speakeasy presented an opportunity to drink in public, but did have the stigma of being illegal, a bit dangerous (a speakeasy could be raided by the police and some owners arrested but usually not the patrons). Many of the speakeasies of the day catered to the upper classes and were expensive. They presented a more respectable atmosphere and often provided entertainment including jazz.

Their respectability provided respectable women the opportunity to drink in public, a rare feature during the days before Prohibition. The speakeasy was open to women, provided, almost always, if they were accompanied by a man.

Women were enjoying new found freedoms by virtue of the lifting of oppressive legislation surely propelled by the fact that they could vote. The economy was strong and people, particularly the upper classes, had considerable money to spend on recreation. These confluences gave rise to a cardinal feature of the roaring twenties. Women could now drink in public, albeit at an illegal speakeasy that featured jazz. They dressed in more alluring costumes than anything common during the earlier days of the Republic. They danced the Charleston under the influence of illegal booze to their and men's delight. Many women who did not fully engage the prototypical dress-styles of the times or the dancing in illegal night clubs watched glamorous people do so in the movies.

The hypocrisy of (a) doctors writing prescriptions for distilled spirits to cure myriad diseases many caused by whiskey and the like, (b) the religious folks making and distributing more wine than any religious rite could justify (except those of Dionysus), (c) the grape growers who prospered by selling grapes for home fermentation of wine in greater amounts than any family could drink, all weighed heavily on the sensibilities of rational folks. The police were corrupted by way of bribes fueled by the profits from illegal trade in alcoholic beverages. Gangsters were attracted to the illegal trafficking in alcoholic beverages that, by virtue of their extant criminal proclivities, were not committed to following all of the other laws of the land. For many reasons, national Prohibition became unpopular and unwieldy. Consequently, it was abandoned and the regulation of the sale of alcohol relegated to the States.

The general consensus is that national prohibition will not be tried again. Yet, as will be detailed in the next chapters, the magnitude of the problems associated with the drinking of alcoholic beverages is so problematic as to demand attention. Attempts to mitigate the harmful effects of wide spread use of alcoholic beverages continued after the end of national Prohibition and continue to this day.

After Prohibition

The adoption of the 21st Amendment did not eliminate prohibition across the land. Eighteen states continued it. It was not until 1966 that all states abandoned state-wide prohibition. Furthermore with the end of national prohibition, almost two-thirds of the states adopted some form of local option, i.e., local governments could establish prohibition or not. Many localities opted to continue the prohibition of the sale of alcoholic beverages. As a consequence about 38% of the population still lived in places where the sale of alcoholic beverages remained illegal. As manifest by the retention of laws prohibiting the sale of alcohol during the early years of post-Prohibition, it is estimated that a full third of the citizens of the USA still supported prohibition.[12] Circumstances changed and by 1946, those favoring Prohibition was 19% and has steadily decreased subsequently.

Men and women drinking beer at a bar in Raceland Louisiana, September 1939. Pre-Prohibition salons were mostly male establishments. Post-prohibition bars catered to both men and women. This picture was taken from Wikipedia and is in the public domain. Source unknown.

With the end of Prohibition, there was the continuance of the great economic depression which, as we all know, began in 1929. The depression, to say the least, reduced the available money to spend on discretionary activities such as partying and reduced the exuberance of the roaring 20s. And then, there was World War II. The period between the end of national Prohibition and the end of WW II was a period of relatively low intake of alcoholic beverages compared to the period before Prohibition and after the war. Raw materials were scarce and expensive, discretionary money was scarce and Americans were focused on war. Also, the temperance movement was not without success; it did change attitudes toward drinking. The amount of alcohol consumed steadily decreased as the movement progressed.

During the first years of national Prohibition, average consumption dropped rather dramatically, but began to increase during the later years of Prohibition. With the end of national Prohibition, there was *not* a dramatic increase in average consumption. The separate states of the Union which allowed the sale of alcohol introduced stringent laws restricting the sale of alcoholic beverages. Under the new set of rules, drinking levels did not spiral upward.

After World War II

Beginning during the late '40s, there had been a dramatic decline in the support for prohibition and strict regulation. Throughout the decades following the end of Prohibition, the restrictive laws were gradually weakened or were abolished. Local options supporting prohibition were gradually reduced one by one until there were only a few localities banning the sale of alcohol. There are vestiges of the restrictive laws enacted post Prohibition. For example, California's laws allow all kinds of alcoholic beverages to be sold in stores selling food whereas New York's more restrictive laws only allow beer and low alcohol-content "wines" to be sold in supermarkets. Other alcoholic beverages are sold in stores specifically for that purpose and, in theory, under strict control by the State government.

With a return to prosperity of the late 1940s and early 1950s, alcoholic beverages were cheap and people had money to spend. Consequently, drinking alcoholic beverages became more common. Big Booze was advertising their products to not only increase sales but to distance their products from their bad reputation of the days of the saloon.[10] The concept of "Demon Rum" was to be transformed by clever (even scientifically honed) advertising into a mark of sophistication. The sophisticated drank "heritage" cocktails such as the martini, the old fashion, the Manhattan, the whiskey sour, or the delicious brandy Alexander, each containing a goodly amount of distilled spirits. There were those in the know who had the money to drink 12 year old Scotch neat (only over ice). Wine was marketed as a sophisticated accompaniment of meals. Beer was marketed as the wholesome drink of moderation.

The rationale of the temperance movement that led to Prohibition is based in some rather stark facts. Drinking alcoholic beverages can lead to some very harsh consequences (some of which are detailed in the next chapters). From the perspective of promoting public health and general well-being, it is rational to limit the adverse effects associated with alcoholic beverages by restricting their use. Consequently, there emerged a new temperance movement in the late 1940s and 1950s. This new movement was in response to a marked increment in the amount of beverages being drunk, hence increments in dire consequences of drinking. The advocates of the new temperance movement were painfully aware of the failure of national Prohibition. They were also vaguely disturbed by the consumer culture that emerged post WW II which was fueled by manipulative advertising leading people to buy products regardless of their utility. The new temperance movement focused on restricting the advertisement and promotion of the sale of alcoholic beverages, particularly on the then new, popular medium of television. The movement, for example, did sustain the ban on advertising distilled spirits on TV by putting pressure on the TV networks.

In response to the increased drinking in the late '40s and '50s and the consequences of such, there was considerable public support for further restrictions on Big Booze. Such public support were instrumental in moving, from 1947 to 1958, the US Congress to hold nine hearings relevant to issues such as warning labels and restrictions on advertising. In response to the pressure, members of Big Booze agreed to police themselves more. They did publish and abide by a code of conduct that limited the advertisements that might encourage underage drinking and drinking by women.

The temperance movements of the 1950s were not markedly successful, despite the attention given by Congressional hearings. The supporters of temperance legislation of the 1950s were inclined to provide rationale for their cause based on the idea that drinking was immoral. Although a case can surely be made that there are moral issues associated with drinking, such arguments did not have the same public support as they did during earlier temperance movements. Later supporters of restrictive legislation supporting the cause of temperance were more successful and their rationale was based in a public health perspective and reliable data that had became available. Subsequent attempts to encourage temperance by way of changing the law and restricting the open encouragement of drinking via advertising were more successful. Among the successes was the establishment of warning labels on containers of alcoholic beverages associated with drinking while pregnant.

This is the label that followed the Anti-Drug Abuse Act of 1988 which was enacted in November of 1988:

GOVERNMENT WARNING:

(1) According to the Surgeon General, women should not drink alcoholic beverages during pregnancy because of the risk of birth defects.

(2) Consumption of alcoholic beverages impairs your ability to drive a car or operate machinery, and may cause health problems.

On May 3, 1980, 13 year old Cari Lightner was killed by a drunken driver at Sunset and New York Avenues in Fair Oaks, CA. The driver left her at the scene of the "accident." The driver had recently been arrested for another hit-and-run incident when his out of control driving killed Cari. Cari's mother, Candice Lightner, organized and became the founding president of Mothers Against Drunk Driving (MADD).[11] Her considerable zeal in organizing MADD stemmed from her outrage at the leniency of the penalty for driving while intoxicated that was instrumental in her daughter's death. MADD became a powerful lobbying group for more restrictive laws regarding driving while intoxicated with a mission "... to stop drunk driving, support the victims of this violent crime and prevent underage drinking." MADD was instrumental in getting laws enacted nation-wide that established the standard blood alcohol level for driving illegally to 0.08% and greater.

In 1984, President Reagan signed into law an act that eventually led to the establishment of the legal age to purchase and publically possess alcoholic beverages as 21 years of age. MADD was influential in the legislation. The law only prohibits the purchase and public possession of alcoholic beverages by minors and the various states have variants to the basic restrictions, for example, concerning whether it is illegal for those under 21 to drink in a private residence.

The laws that demand warning labels and a uniform national "drinking age" were strongly opposed by Big Booze. The International Center for Alcohol Policies (ICAP) has used the Ms Lightner's unhappiness with the organization she founded as a talking point for a curb on restrictive legislation.[12] She maintained that MADD had become a neo-prohibitionist organization. She related that she was primarily interested in dealing with the issue of drunk driving, not to deal with the public health issues surrounding alcoholic beverages. ICAP clearly says it is against drunk driving, but also clearly states that some legislation that might curb the consumption of alcoholic beverages overreaches and cites Ms Lightner's sentiments to bolster their arguments.

Magazines such as *Playboy* emerged on the national scene with sections devoted to educating the young man aspiring to a life-style of sophisticated pleasures associated with sexual liberation and consumption of distilled spirits as well as other alcoholic beverages. *Playboy*, and other popular magizines, thrived by advertisements paid for by Big Booze.

An accomplishment of the modern temperance movement was to increase the legal drinking age to 21 throughout the nation. During the '70s, some states lowered the legal age to purchase alcohol to 18. During the '80s, social movements such as Mothers Against Drunk Driving (MADD) were successful in getting legislators to establish 21 as the legal age to buy alcohol in all states of the Union. In many college towns, however, the enforced age for drinking is the age at which one enters college.

The advertisements of the times (post WW II until now) were and are designed to attract new customers, justify the alcoholic's habit, and to make drinking of alcoholic beverages a mark of sophistication. Big Booze worked toward making it socially acceptable to market to women, a source of many potential new customers. Big Booze would have you believe that only the prudish, the stuffy, the up-tight, the intolerant and the like were for prohibition or anything like it. Life according to Big Booze's ads is to be lived large with a bottle of beer, a glass of wine, or a cocktail.

Although not part of a chronicle of use of alcoholic beverages there are some topics that need to be briefly discussed to make other topics easier to talk about. They are: (a) some features of the modern alcohol beverages industries, (b) how do you measure people's drinking? and, (c) the ingredients in alcoholic beverages.

Big Booze Just Keeps Getting Bigger

Across recent years, the products of brewers Anheuser-Busch, Adolph Coors, Miller and Modelo (Makers of Bud, Miller and Coors Light & Corona Extra) have dominated the market for beer in the USA having among them about two thirds of that market. In many countries without strong religious prohibition, there are often one or a few dominant brewers and some smaller ones similar to the current scene in USA. Beers, ales and similar drinks come in a wide variety, but all seem to have somewhat similar tastes (it's about the ethanol, malt and hops). One of the consequences of the basic similarities of modern beers is that competition among the various brands is in terms of the how they promote (advertise) their products. They compete with one another, but they collectively are interested in increasing the sale of beer. It is one thing to have a slightly more or less sized slice of a small pie and a different thing to have a slightly more of less sized slice of a large pie. The new owners of Budweiser want both, a bigger share of the beer market and an enlarged market (i.e., more people drinking beer).

Anheuser-Busch, the makers of Budweiser has nearly half of the beer-market in the USA. Recently, Anheuser-Busch merged with InBev, a giant brewer that can trace its history to a brewery that flourished in the late 1300s. InBev has acquired or merged with brewers in China, Brazil and Canada as well as Anheuser-Busch. InBev also owns shares in other brewer's companies. As a consequence InBev (current corporate name) has enormous influence over the sale of beer world-wide. The merged company employs over 114,000 people and has profit of over 4 billion dollars (2010 data) (about 3 times the profits of Bank of America or Coca-Cola). Its headquarters are in Leuven, Belgium. Some of the profit is from the sale of soft drinks.

The beer industries compete with the wine producers and the producers of distilled beverages. During the past few decades, wine consumption in America has increased considerably. Despite competition among the beer, wine and liquor companies, they realize that what they have in common is that they sell ethanol and that ethanol can be an addictive agent. Increases in sales of beer, for example, are apt to be translated eventually into sales of other alcoholic beverages. They have a common goal of masking the dire consequences of selling an agent with addictive properties.

The distinction between the major components of Big Booze is apt to fade. For example, the E. & J. Gallo Winery company, a major marketer of a variety of major brands of wines, has an aggressive campaign to market New Amsterdam Gin and Vodka, a highly flavored product-line. Their ads feature slogans such as "Going out is YOUR civic duty," "Practice the Right to Assemble" and "A Model Citizen" all featuring young women and their hard liquor. Their videos show plenty folks partying with shots of gin and vodka. It all looks fun and sexy with youthful exuberance.

Particularly across the most recent decades, there has been considerable consolidation of the distilled spirits companies. For example, Diageo owns brands such as Smirnoff (world largest seller of vodka), Johnnie Walker (a popular brand of Scotch), Bailey (best-selling brand of liqueur) plus a number of others.

The wine industry is also experiencing considerable consolidation; for example, Constellation Brands is the world's leading producer of wine with large sales in the USA, UK, Australia, New Zealand, and Canada. Such consolidation produces considerable resources in the hands of these transnational corporations. As consequence of such consolidation, multinationals can direct a lot of resources to thwart activities showing signs of gaining support for restrictive regulations. A question of some interest is whether such transnational companies are loyal to any particular nation. A citizen of the USA might ask whether any of these transnational companies are particularly interested in the health and well-being of the USA, and whether they pay their fair share of taxes. There is a group with the explicit goal of being "The Industry Watchdog" and promoting policies that would restrict Big Booze's goal of increasing the sale of alcoholic beverages. That group is now titled *Alcohol Justice*.

It was formally called the *Marin Institute*, in recognition of the area of California that was of interest to its major donor, Beryl H. Buck legacy trust. It is interesting to compare the Web sites of *Alcohol Justice* and *International Center for Alcohol Policies*.

Measuring People's Drinking

There are a number a ways of trying to measure how much and when individuals drink alcoholic beverages. Such data are needed to make rational decisions about drinking. For example, data are needed on the effects of various regulations on health and well-being. Big Booze also finds such data useful.

One index of drinking is the tax revenue collected by the various governments. This information can be turned into clearer indices such as the gallons of ethanol consumed per person during a year. Such an index can provide trends in overall consumption, but does not reveal which individuals are drinking. Also, such data does not account for the untaxed wine and beer produced by individuals in their homes and by illegal production distilled spirits.

The best data would be a measure of the amount of ethanol in the blood from the time of starting to drink until there is no ethanol in the blood. Unfortunately, one cannot ask individuals to plot their blood ethanol level as a function of time during their Saturday night parties. Another way of measuring drinking is by asking people how many drinks were consume and when were they consumed. This, in turn, brings us to what is a minor controversial issue: the standard drink.

A Standard Alcoholic Drink

Big Booze and government agencies in the USA define a standard drink as one that contains 0.6 ounces of alcohol (14 grams). This definition is convenient when asking people how much they drink. The 0.6 ounces specifies the amount of ethanol in (a) a usual 12 ounce bottle of beer containing 5% ethanol, (b) 5 ounces of wine (at 12% ethanol by volume), a usual glass served in restaurants and (c) roughly one cocktail using 1.5 ounces of 80 proof liquor (or one shot). Proof is a label for alcohol content that is twice the percent of alcohol measured as volume, e.g., 80 proof vodka is 40% ethanol by volume.

A person being interviewed might consider a double martini or a 16 ounce can of a high ethanol-content brand of beer as one "drink." A single serving of 16 oz Old English 800 (8% ethanol by volume) beer is clearly more than one "standard drink." Many wines have concentrations of ethanol closer to 14% than 12%. Many cocktails contain more than one shot of liquor.

The *San Francisco Chronicle's* expert at making cocktails (their mixologist) recently featured a cocktail with 4 ounces of 80 proof liquor. One of these is sufficient to get a small woman sufficiently drunk to be over the legal limit for driving for hours. Two of them are sufficient to get that same small woman too drunk for most anything productive and is surely not healthy (see Chapter 4).

The translation of one standard drink to an amount of ethanol that might be toxic is very rough indeed. There are a lot of variables that affect the amount of ethanol in blood, hence in brain, that are not captured by asking a person how many drinks did you have last week. One variable that makes a significant difference is the weight of the drinker. A cocktail served to a 120 pound woman will produce considerably more toxicity than that same cocktail to a 200 pound man. Further that cocktail might contain a shot of rum (an ounce or more) and a shot of another alcoholic beverage along with sweeteners and other ingredients to mask the harsh taste of ethanol. When asked "how much did you drink last week," both a big man and a small woman might report one drink.

Given the propensity of individuals to report that they drank less than they actually drank (indexed by independent observers) and given the propensity for drinks to contain more ethanol than the standard amount, the usual estimate of amount drunk is a conservative one.

Added Ingredients in Alcoholic Beverages

In the USA, The Food and Drug Administration (FDA) is charged with the responsibility to ensure that the food sold is safe and that the marketing of food, in general, involves informative information. The FDA is a subdivision of the Department of Health & Human Services. In contrast, products of Big Booze are regulated by the Bureau of Alcohol, Tobacco, Firearms and Explosives (BAT), a subdivision of the Department of Justice. Consequently, the labeling practices of the FDA with respect to food do not automatically apply to the drinks accompanying many people's meals. Recently, the regulation of the sale of tobacco products has been transferred to the FDA where they are working out the details of how this will change things.

Can a consumer easily know what is in their alcohol drinks? The answer is: Yea, sort of, but precisely, no. We know that a can of beer will be mostly beer, a bottle of wine will be mostly wine, and a bottle of rum will be mostly rum, but we do not know what has been added to the beer, wine, or distilled spirits. We do know each will be some amount of water and ethanol. In the USA, the labels on containers of alcoholic beverages are required to have a statement of the concentration of ethanol as well as a number of other bits of information. We know, for example, that most wines sold in the USA have sulfites added to them, but we do not know if they have sweeteners or dyes added to them. There is no requirement for a complete list of ingredients such as required on soft drinks. In terms of carbohydrate and calorie listings, there are regulations about claiming a product is a low carbohydrate ("low-carb") product (cannot be more that 7 grams of carbohydrate per standard drink). Governments require considerable information on a label of a loaf of bread, but do not require similar information on a can of beer. There are citizens who are pushing for more complete labeling for alcoholic beverages.

After fermentation, both wine and beer require further processing, processes known as clarification and stabilization. With respect to wine, one needs to remove the grape peels, seeds, and vines and other solids as well as dead yeast cells and bacteria. Often this is accomplished by merely letting these solids drift to the bottom of a container; a process to be truly successful might take a long time. After the solids have sunk, the clarified wine is siphoned from the top of the container.

Letting solids settle usually is not sufficient to produce a clear product. A process called fining is employed to achieve further refinement. Fining is achieved by adding products to the unfinished alcoholic beverage that bonds with the suspended products, thereby making it more likely for the combined substances to settle or making the suspended products large so that they can be filtered out of the liquid. Fining agents include substances such as egg whites, milk products, bentonite ciay, and a substance obtained from dried swim bladders of fish (isinglass).

Australia and New Zealand have regulations that require the label to specify fining agents that might be allergenic which includes egg and milk products. The wine producers in the USA have resisted such requirements as being unnecessary and burdensome.

Big Booze Has Some New Flavors

In an effort to attract new customers, Big Booze has flavored their products primarily with sweeteners. The result is that some beverages taste more like soft drinks than the usual beer, wine or even mixed drinks served in bars and taverns.

If a producer of alcoholic beverages knew of an ingredient that would make an alcoholic beverage more addictive, other than sweeteners, they could put it into the beverages and increase sales. Further, they would not have to reveal that they spiked the beverage. Actually, I (Larry) know of an ingredient that is potent enough to affect the appetite for the beverage but in such small amounts to not be easily detected by taste or ordinary chemical analyses. Given such, it would be of interest to the public to have a complete list of the chemicals added to their products' containers.

Two of the major transnational marketers of vodka have recently decided to market flavored vodkas that taste like desserts. Both marketers sell vodka, for example, that tastes like whipped cream or marshmallows. Perhaps, the first to sell whipped cream flavored vodkas was White Rock distillers.

White Rock was, at one time, a small distiller located in Maine. However, they changed to a bottling, branding and distribution company. They bought highly refined ethanol from France. They then produced flavored vodka, specializing in dessert-flavored vodkas within the general brand of Pinnacle. The general marketing strategy was to use the Internet and other outlets to promote cocktails made with their flavored vodkas. Past President of White Rock, Mr. Coulombe, made it clear that his target market was 21 to 25 year old women "who gravitate to flavors."

In 2008, Pinnacle Vodka sold fewer than 300,000 cases; in 2010, they sold 1,400,000 cases; and in 2011, they sold 2,700,000 cases. The surge in recent sales was driven by Pinnacle Whipped (whipped cream flavored vodka) and similar brands such as Cherry Whipped. The success led White Rock to be sold to a company held by Beam Suntory, a large Japanese holding company.

Flavoring alcoholic drinks with sugar and other ingredients is a well-established practice. The new age of flavored alcohol is made possible by advances in the chemistry of flavors. Sophisticated chemistry can reproduce the molecules that characterize the flavors of most berries, many products such as chocolate and even apple pie. These flavor-molecules can be added to vodka and other alcoholic beverages. Because Big Booze is not regulated by the FDA they would not automatically have to list the chemicals producing the flavors. Long lists of chemicals on a label might discourage buyers; consequently you can expect Big Booze to resist such labels.

Given that flavored alcoholic beverages were developed particularly for marketing to young women, we return to this topic in subsequent chapters.

Summary

Throughout history, alcoholic beverages and the consequences of their use have been issues of considerable controversy. Alcoholic beverages are no ordinary commodities. Today, they are marketed by large corporations (Big Booze) who make large profits from the sale of a wide variety of beverages containing ethanol. The marketing of Big Booze is highly sophisticated and is highly successful. One consequence of that successful marketing is alcoholism. Another consequence is that the frequency of alcoholism among women has grown to be very similar to that of men. Later we make the case that the frequency will be greater among women than men.

Chapter 3. Marketing Alcoholic Beverages

Historian Pamela Pennock has written a delightful book dealing with the issues surrounding the marketing of tobacco and alcoholic products, particularly in the USA.[1] In Professor Allen Brandt's comprehensive history detailing how tobacco has been integral to America, he relates the struggles associated with the marketing and regulation of tobacco products.[2] Both historians detail how Big Tobacco and Big Booze use similar tactics to protect themselves from regulations that might reduce their sales. Big Booze has been more successful than the tobacco interests, but in many ways both industries have remained extraordinarily successful. Both historians, but particularly Pennock, pointed out that the regulation of marketing of potentially dangerous but popular products such as tobacco and alcoholic beverages pit two perspectives that are reoccurring themes in modern capitalist societies. Pennock sums the situation thusly: "The marketing control debates tapped into tensions between the strong traditions of restraint, virtue, and health and the equally powerful ideals of individualism, liberty, and economic gain (Pennock, 2007, p 222)."[1]

The '40s and '50s temperance movement's initial efforts were attempts to counter the successful marketing of Big Booze. This temperance movement pits a public health perspective against the interests of Big Booze's goals to increase sales and profits. Both the public health perspective and the industries' perspective focus on public relations and advertising to achieve their differing goals. The industries' perspective is fueled by the knowledge that to increase, and even to maintain sales of alcoholic beverages, it must spend heavily on public relations and advertising. The public health perspective fosters the goal that is contrary to industries' goal, i.e., reduced sales. Public health advocates advertise the dire consequences of using alcoholic beverages and hope to curtail the marketing of the beverages by way of political activity.

There were and are constraints on the marketing of alcoholic beverages in the USA. Recently, for example, there was a limit on advertising of distilled spirits on TV (of the major networks which had a monopoly on content of TV until the rise of cable TV and the Internet). Currently, there have been a few ads for distilled spirits on programs of the major networks.   There are some warning labels on alcoholic products. In many locales, there are strict restrictions concerning where and when alcoholic beverages are sold.   It is illegal to sell alcoholic beverages to persons under the age of 21.   Alcoholic beverages have an excise tax beyond the ordinary sales tax.   Constraints can be and have been increased and decreased.

Some propose even more restrictions and argue that it is in the public interest to curb sales of alcoholic beverages. They cite the high costs to personal and societal well-being associated with drinking. They further argue that it is a responsibility of government, even a moral obligation of government, to do what it can to protect the public interests and the individual from the problems inherent to wide-spread use of alcoholic beverages (potentially toxic beverages).

There are those who argue that there are too many restrictions on the marketing of alcohol.[3] The essence of their position is: Although alcoholism and alcoholics pose problems, most people drink responsibly and should not be restricted from the pleasures of drinking just because some people cannot drink responsibly. They further adhere to the idea that alcoholism is a disease affecting only a few and, therefore, they should not be subject to curbs on advertising. They ask, for example, would you resist the marketing of sugar just because some people are diabetic and expect the answer: No. Then, by analogy, they say that the marketing of alcoholic beverages should not be so limited. They further invoke the idea that marketing is the essence of a capitalistic society which, in turn, creates wealth and prosperity and, hence, should not be interfered with. They further rely on the

First Amendment rights of free speech to protect their advertising and public relations campaigns.

Many of the beliefs sustaining the arguments of those advocating more restrictions of the marketing of alcoholic beverages are very similar to those leading to national Prohibition. Those arguing *against* more restrictions agree that the rationale is similar to the temperance movement. They, then, point out that Prohibition was a failure and that giving in to the idea of more regulation is a slippery slope leading to the evils of Prohibition (e.g., the rise of criminality). They might argue, for example, that a higher tax on alcoholic beverages merely leads to bootlegging (crime) and the marketing of less safe beverages.

There is a consensus among the World's economists, and perhaps virtually everyone, that regulated capitalism is the system most amenable to democracy and the development of wealth, prosperity and well-being. The results of the grand experiments of communism carried out in a number of nations, notably the Soviet Union and China, in contrast to various forms of capitalism provide considerable support for the conclusion that capitalism has numerous virtues. The modern issue is how much governmental regulation is optimal: Too much is acknowledged to be problematic as well as too little. Since the beginning of the American democracy and particularly germane to alcoholic beverages, the issues of government regulation have been and are very contentious. The consequences associated with national Prohibition support the idea that total prohibition is not a solution to the alcohol-problems in America.

Overcoming the Image of Demon Rum

Subsequent to the abolition of the 18th Amendment, the sale and use of alcoholic beverages was still not thought of, by many, as a respectable enterprise (the temperance-prohibition movement did change many attitudes). As Pennock pointed out, for example, in 1938, many newspapers would not advertise alcoholic beverages. One supposes that they refused to advertise on the grounds that it was not proper to encourage alcohol consumption. In 1951, there were many newspapers that would not advertise, but as many as 20% fewer than previously. Now, some American newspapers actually solicit such advertisement, but not all college newspapers.

From 1948 to 1955, there was 118% increment in money spent on yearly advertising in newspapers and a 33% rise in ads in magazines promoting the sale of alcohol. In 1957, two of the most popular magazines of the times, *Look* and *Life,* derived 10% of their revenue from ads for alcoholic beverages. In 1958, the *Saturday Evening Post*, a very popular magazine, finally accepted ads for the beverages. *Look, Life* and the *Saturday Evening Po*st were stocked in many schools' libraries. During subsequent years, the amounts spent on advertising continued to increase except the ad money was going to new outlets such as radio and TV.

Big Booze Worries

Professor Mike Daube, a researcher at a large university in Western Australia, claims to have discovered many of Big Booze's worst fears.[4] He and his colleagues have searched the vast, supposedly confidential material made public as a result of litigation in USA against the tobacco industry (circa 1990). Some tobacco companies also owned beverage companies; hence there were communications about both tobacco and alcohol by the executives of these companies as they planned their public relations campaigns. According to Professor Daube, the alcohol industries fear that alcohol issues will become an important part of the public health agenda and that Big Booze will gain the same status as Big Tobacco (as if you don't know, big tobacco companies do not have a wholesome image, they sell an addictive agent known to induce cancer). The industry fears tax increases and restrictions on their advertising.

International Center for Alcohol Policies

Professor Daube could have found support for his conclusions by consulting the current public statements of the industry that are on the Internet. For example, one can read the material of the International Center for Alcohol Policies (ICAP), a not-for-profit organization sponsored by the major producers of beverage alcohol; material easily accessed by using a modern search engine.[5] The Center makes best use of the old adage that the best way to lie is to tell the truth about nearly everything except what it is in your interest to lie about. The Center indicates that they provide "Analysis, Balance, Partnership." They relate many of the problems with excessive intake of alcoholic beverages. They then state that policies that are known, from extensive research, to reduce the incidence of consumption and, thereby reduce the dire consequences of excessive intake *do not* reduce consumption or dire consequences. The following are known to lead to less adverse effects: increased taxation, reduced numbers of outlets, and strict enforcement of drinking laws (especially with regard to underage drinkers). There is an abundance of evidence to indicate, for example, that substantial increases in taxes do reduce consumption and dire consequences of drinking.[6] Big Booze's advocates just say that there is no such evidence and put forth some counter claims. They lie (they are surely not ignorant of the available literature), because it is in their interests.

The strongest counter argument to strict governmental restrictions on marketing alcoholic beverages is industries' promise to regulate itself. The current principles of self-regulation are available at ICAP's Web-site. For the most part, they sound good. They say, for two examples, marketing communication (any form of communication produced by the marketers) should be "... legal, decent, honest and truthful..." and "should not present alcohol beverages as a means of removing social or sexual inhibitions, achieving sexual success, or making an individual more sexually attractive." Question: Is jumping up and down in exuberance at a party a removal of social inhibitions? Or, depicting a woman being waited on by a number of nearly naked handsome men (as in an ad by Pinnacle vodka directed toward a female market) a subtle message that if you drink our product you might achieve some measure of sexual success?[7] We don't know the answers to these questions, but we imagine the ad agency that put the ads together probably knows the answer.

Big Booze is for maintaining the current situation (they are highly profitable institutions and those that manage them are more than well-compensated). They promote the general idea that government regulation is intrusive and foster the general idea that their taxes are excessive. This general support for less regulation and no new taxes fits their specific agenda of less regulation on the sale of beverage alcohol and no new alcohol-taxes.

Big Booze maintains that they should have a "seat at any table that might discuss regulation of their industries' practices." This concept is captured in ICAP's headline banner on its Web site: "Analysis, Balance, [and] Partnership." They wish to partner with those promoting public health. Partnership is a nice sounding idea. What they are interested in is preventing sound public health policy and protecting the size of their profits. Do citizens who are concerned with advertising dessert-flavored vodka directed at girls really want to be partners with spokespersons for Big Booze? Maybe, but how would that partnership work? Their goal is to sell more alcoholic beverages which is at odds with the public health goal of fewer sales. The industry will steadfastly not agree to policies that will reduce sales. Big Booze has learned lessons from Big Tobacco: Appear cooperative while protecting profits. They blame the dire consequences on the use of their products on "bad genes," "irresponsible people," (their best customers), "a lack of understanding of the proper role of government" and "a lack of understanding of all of the benefits of drinking." They deny that alcohol is addictive (except for a few who unfortunately have a disease, a handicap, a disorder or are weak-willed). Their goal is to induce habitual drinking, while publically denying what they surely know: habitual drinking will almost always shorten years of healthy, happy life. As will be discussed subsequently, the strong possibility that habitual drinking will reduce years of healthy, happy life is particularly relevant to women.

The industry promotes the idea that alcohol-use is not a general problem. Any problems that might emerge, according to Big Booze, are caused by relatively few people. As one example, they promote the idea that automobile accidents associated with drinking and driving are primarily the result of repeat offenders with extraordinarily high blood alcohol levels.   Rather often that is the case, but their message hardly takes into account the number of young men and women who are not old enough to be repeat offenders who are permanently disabled or die as a result of driving while drunk. And, of course, they take no responsibility for inducing alcoholism.

Marketing Directed at Girls and Women

Although an unintended consequence of Prohibition was the cultural shift that made it more acceptable for women to drink in public, to be a party to a drinking party in the home, to have a glass of wine with dinner, and to drink at celebrations, there remained in the decades post WW II considerable restrictive social norms that limited drinking by women.   The mores and norms of these decades made it socially unacceptable for a woman by herself to walk into a bar and set about drinking.   It was legal to do so, but that experience would have been unpleasant.   She most likely would be pressed to have sex by drunken men and be generally regarded as someone who might be O.K. to have sex with, but not be someone a man might want to marry and be the mother of his children.   A drunken woman was thought to be more disgraceful than a drunken man.

There were enforced restrictions that limited women's opportunities to drink. For example, during the 1950s, at many colleges in the USA, the rule was that the women on campus must be in their dormitory by 9:00 pm during week days and somewhat later on the weekends, a curfew that restricted   their   drinking   but   not   men's.   The   adults supervising these dormitories (yes, there were house mothers who served as guardians of young women away from home) were not pleased if a young woman came in drunk.

From the '50s onward, there have been increasingly strong social pressures for women to be fully liberated. Women could rightfully ask why they were restricted when men were not and they did ask. They not only asked, but demanded equal treatment in all spheres of the culture. This change opened new markets for Big Booze, i.e., they could more assuredly market their products to women. Since women of those decades were generally not avid consumers of alcohol, they represented many potential new customers for Big Booze.

Because the social constraints on women's drinking curtailed their drinking until recently, alcoholism was still considered a man's problem. Based on incidence rates (circa 1980s), it was estimated that men were five times more likely to succumb to alcoholism than women. Until recently, in many places in the USA, there were even no facilities for the treatment of women alcoholics. As will be detailed subsequently, we now have about as many alcoholic women as men and as many alcoholic girls as boys.

How did we go from the prudent norms of temperance (some would say the prudish norms) for women to the current state?[8] It was part of broad social and cultural changes in the United States. The increment in women's drinking, hence drunkenness, can hardly be attributed to a single cause. However, a powerful factor inducing women to drink were the billions of dollars spent on advertising and public relation campaigns by the alcohol producing industries. Their campaigns were and are relentless and persuasive. They emphasize the pleasure of drinking and mask the adverse effects.

As mentioned, Big Booze has advocated for self-regulation and has been remarkably successful in achieving that goal. They have published codes to guide their advertising and, generally speaking, have abided by them. They surely do not try to get the girl scouts to engage drinking games such as beer pong. The self-regulation is designed to counter government regulation in response to what the general public deems is unacceptable. Post WW II, the prevailing attitude, the social norms and mores held it to be wrong (or at least unseemly) to encourage women to become drinkers in the way men had become drinkers.

It was not until 1958, that Big Booze lifted their own ban on portraying women in ads. Their code did, however, prescribe that the women in the ads be tastefully dressed and not actually drinking a beverage. Throughout the '50s, the industries continued public relations campaigns that involved attractive women holding classes on how to mix drinks and how to pour beer. In 1963, their self-regulatory code was further relaxed allowing a woman to hold a beverage and even be shown consuming it. By the mid '60s, women appearing in ads started to exude sexual appeal. In response to advisors trained in Freudian personality theory, there was a time when ads contained a number of symbols representing supposedly sexual symbols thought to arouse unconscious desires which were to be paired with alcoholic beverages. Throughout the advertising and public relations campaigns designed to encourage drinking by women, a goal is to mask the deleterious effects of habitual drinking of alcohol.

In addition to the direct advertising that may be "more friendly" to women, the industry is engaging in a number of public relations campaigns designed to pair drinking with the ideas of sophistication and fun. This includes product placements and placing informational items in the media that clearly promote the ideas the industry believe will benefit their sales.

In some instances, the public relations and advertising machinery of Big Booze have clearly co-opted some of the most popular women's magazines. The approach is not only direct advertising, but the "advertising" of the kind that made diamonds a girl's best friend (see below). The approach is to pair the idea of fun and romantic sex with drinking. Because these same magazines have Web-based content, the potential influence of their content is spread far beyond those who subscribe to the magazine.

Here are only a few of the titles of articles that appeared in *Cosmopolitan*,[9] a magazine catering to young women:

"The 20 sexiest cocktails to sip on,"

"6 Sexy Retro Cocktails,"

"Booze-infused cupcakes,"

"Cosmo Cocktails."

The alcohol beverage industry might pledge to not put ads in magazines for teens, but a goodly number of teens probably read *Cosmopolitan*. And, therefore, teens are being exposed to articles whose titles clearly convey the message that drinking is sexy and sophisticated. The typical "Cosmo Woman" is being courted to become a habitual drinker.

In a pre-Christmas issue of *Cosmopolitan*, an ad extolling the virtues of Macallen's 18 year old scotch had the following tag line: "He will love this gift … and you." The fifth of scotch was priced at $137.99. If a young woman buys this gift for a young man, she should probably leave the price tag on the bottle to ensure that he sees the expense. Because, unless he is a very experienced drinker of scotch, it is unlikely that he will know that the bottle was expensive by virtue of taste and unlikely to know that he was expected to exude love. If he is so into scotch that he can really appreciate any subtle differences between expensive 18 year old scotch and cheaper ones (beyond a placebo-effect due to price), he is probably not apt to be a fit long-time lover. This kind of sophistication indicates considerable experience with drinking and men who drink a lot of liquor are apt to develop alcoholism. On the other hand, a 6-pack of Bud is not a very glamorous gift.

In the magazine and in their Web-based contents, there were articles clearly advocating moderation (not really temperance). One article detailed some of the dangers when a woman engages in drinking games. It was clearly pointed out that women get drunker on the same amount of beverage than men. It was also pointed out that drinking clearly toxic doses of alcoholic beverage was indeed toxic with respect to things like walking, nausea (vomiting in a bar or at a party is so not sexy). It was also pointed out that being drunk made it more difficult to control sexual encounters.

A *Cosmopolitan* article titled "Don't be dumb about drinking" strongly advised moderation with a long list of the dire consequences of drinking excessively. The article, however, also said "But as we all know, cutting yourself off after one or two drinks every time you imbibe is a pretty unrealistic goal." Yes, alcoholic beverages do have that tendency to reinforce the act of drinking, thereby, increasing the likelihood of one drink leading to the next, the next to the next, etc. That is why it is an addictive agent. To acknowledge the experience of that (the second drink clearly leading to the next few), indicates that the writer is likely to have fallen in love with booze and that is not apt to be an uplifting romance.

Cocktail recipes featuring Pinnacle's dessert flavored vodkas have been promoted widely on the Web, for example, on the web site for *Cosmopolitan,* and they generally call for more ethanol than that of a standard drink. Often the cocktails are similar to milk products spiked with vodka. On other sites, there are promotions for milk shakes and root beer floats that are spiked with vodka. There is also, currently on the market, vodka infused whipped cream and ice cream. These flavored alcoholic products are specifically marketed toward women and girls.

An associate editor of *Woman's Day*, Alexandra Gekas, posts a comment (on the Web) that encourages drinking wine by saying, among other things: "I am a big fan of wines, and I've definitely noticed that family and friends who never drank before have started educating themselves and enjoying an occasional bottle" (2011).[10] Notice how the editor justifies her drinking by saying, in effect, "everybody is doing it," so it must be O.K. We suspect that she is having more than an occasional bottle, she is a big fan. Notice also that it is part of a modern life-style to be an "educated," sophisticate with respect to wine. The public relations campaign of the wine producing industry is having considerable success. They are not merely selling a couple more bottles of wine; they are promoting a life-style that makes it almost a necessity to be knowledgeable about wine. How can you be really educated and sophisticated without indulgence? ✩

Advertising Is Successful Because ...

Professor Buonomano, in his recent book, pointed out that our ability to associate features of the environment with one another makes us particularly susceptible to being manipulated by advertising.[11] Not only did humans evolve with the capacity to associate features of the environment with danger and where to find nutrients but also capacities to be very successful social animals (e.g., being good at imitation of apparently successful activities of our kin). These abilities also, accordingly, make us particularly susceptible to public relations campaigns and advertising. Further, he used the example of the marketing of diamonds "as a girl's best friend" and "a diamond is forever" to show how advertising and public relations campaigns can easily manipulate behavior.

Diamonds Are a Girl's Best Friend

During the late 1930s, the company with a near monopoly on diamond mining and trading, DeBeers, was having trouble selling diamonds. Consequently, in 1938, they hired the N.W. Ayer advertising company to promote the sale of diamond jewelry. The Ayer's campaign did not promote sales by running ads touting "a sale on diamond rings," but rather by promoting the idea that diamond rings and love go together. The campaign involved inserting the giving of diamonds in romantic scenes in movies, by having celebrities tout their rings as something special, and in advertisements that paired diamonds with romance, signs of wealth and sophistication. Advertising a price-reduction on diamond rings (a typical advertising ploy) was not this kind of advertising. In fact, keeping prices high for diamond rings associated them with wealth and prestige. According to Professor Buonomano, we easily, by way of our very make-up, relate to signs of prestige. We attempt to imitate the behaviors of the successful.

The Ayer's campaign was a success; by 1941, sales of diamond rings had increased 55%. Across the next 20 years, diamond rings had gone from being just another kind of ring to a necessary sanctification of an engagement. This kind of promotion continues with respect to diamonds. A striking modern advertising campaign promoting the sale of diamonds is the one featured on TV by the retailer Kay. These ads picture a gorgeous woman gleefully kissing the man who just gave her diamond jewelry with a singing tag line "every kiss begins with Kay." This ad campaign is evidently working because they continually use it. The ad evidently works despite the fact that it kind of puts women in the role of being bought for sexual pleasures; or the other way around, puts a man in the position of having to buy sexual favors.

It is a mistake to assume that advertisements for a specific alcoholic beverage (say a brand of beer) are designed to merely sell a few more bottles of that kind of beverage. The outstanding success of marketing diamonds was and is surely imitated by Big Booze's public relations and advertising campaigns. They were and are designed to make the drinking of alcoholic beverages not only acceptable, but drinking to be perceived as an integral part of life well-lived. The industry has a product that can be addictive which makes selling it easy. Their products also cause great misery, a fact that needs to be masked by public relations. No ad for a Budweiser beer will ever feature a skid-row drunk sleeping on the sidewalk and awakening to beg for money to buy a beer, despite the fact that it shows that beer is highly desired. Drinking alcoholic beverages are paired in advertisements with signs of youth, health, sexuality, wealth, successful aging, and joyful celebration. Advertisements paid for by Big Booze are clearly not truthful perspectives on the habitual use of their products.

If It's Expensive, It Has to be Good

Professor Buonomano pointed out that there are a number of studies showing that price and quality of wine are hardly related. He then summarized a study by Plassmann and colleagues: subjects were presented with five samples of wine, with labels indicating they cost 5, 10, 35, 45, or 90 dollars a bottle.[12] However, the subjects were given only three different kinds of wine. The $5, $35, and $90 labels did reflect the actual purchase price of the wines. The wines with the labels of $10 and $45 wines were the $90 and $5 wines, respectively. Professor Buonomano (p 189) summarized the results: "Subjects rated the same wine significantly higher when they were told it was $45 than when they were told it was $5, and again when they believed it was $90 compared to $10. Additionally, in a blind taste test that does not bode well for our gustatory sophistication, or for the wine industry, there was no significant preference for the more expensive wines. In fact, there was actually a slight preference for the cheaper wine."

In an 2011-article appearing in the *San Francisco Chronicle*, the wine critic Jon Bonne had a piece called "Great Wines at any price: 20 new world-class picks, all for $20 or less." For each wine, the critic gave its name, its retail price and a paragraph-sized vignette relating something about the wine and its maker. After giving the actual price, he said that the wine tasted like a wine priced at a higher value. For example, the critic stated that a Louis M. Martini Sonoma County Cabernet Sauvignon which sold for $13 tasted like a $26 bottle of wine. The critic provided precise dollar figures for each of the 20 wines in the "tastes like" description. In accordance with the idea that these wines retailed for less than $20, they were a great bargain, because he claimed that each tasted like a wine at a higher price. By such apparent precision in measuring taste and value, the critic promoted the idea that the price of wine was nearly linearly related to the quality of its taste as judged by self-designated experts. Such precision is almost impossible to believe based on blind taste tests such as the one described above. Wine tasters and wine critics have been hesitant to engage blind tastings ever since blind taste tasting by French critics indicated that California's wines were better than French wines much to the surprise of the world who just knew, as the experts knew, that French wine was better.

Wine critics are well-practiced at wine-tasting and are experts at distinguishing tastes of wines. A consumer's tastes and preferences, however, are apt to be very different than those of the critic merely because she has not had the extra ordinary practice of tasting wines and then not drinking them, a characteristic of a wine-tasting professional. The assignment of relatively arbitrary values allows for price manipulation that has little to do with quality. Some wines taste better than others. Nearly all of us dislike wine that has become vinegar-like. Within the scope of the wines being sold, consumers' preferences for a kind of wine differ widely. Further preferences can be manipulated by marketing. It appears that connoisseurs of wine have a great opportunity to manipulate price by their pronouncements and we suspect that they do and favor companies that favor them.

The whole scheme of wine-tasting, price setting, magazines and books describing the varieties of wine and their value, the assured statements that wine X is the best wine for food M are all powerful marketing tools. It separates the cheap wines favored by the drunk from those sophisticated wines favored by privileged folks in the know. It separates, by advertising based in classical Pavlovian conditioning, the drunk who uses "bad cheap wines" from the sophisticate who uses a "good aperitif" before dinner, a "good expensive wine" with dinner and a "good dessert wine" after dinner.

Another example, related by Munching in his book *Beer Blast*, is the following.[13] Sales of the scotch branded as Chivas Regal's were increased considerably, not by changing the quality of the scotch, but by merely increasing the price. As the marketing of diamonds shows, we are susceptible to public relations that establish a link between a product and prestige. Munching also pointed out that so-called premium beers are really little different than ordinary ones, but maintain their sales by advertising and by their higher price which makes them seem premium.

Non Paid Advertisers

Big Booze has many converts to their cause who can shape public opinions. Authors known to be habitual drinkers, often wax elegantly about the virtues of consumption of alcohol (think, for examples, Fitzgerald, Hemingway, London, Waugh, Twain, Menken). There are those who manifest a near worship of their god Bacchus and as religious zealots seek converts to their cause. One can learn to love drinking and write about that love with the passion of a teenaged boy's love for his first close girlfriend. These love affairs with alcohol are the essence of a problem.

A recent book relates women's "love affairs" with their favorite alcoholic beverages.[14] They speak about alcoholic beverages in ways that brings to mind some women's recollections about the first boy that they loved, their good times in bad marriages and their divorces. It is clear from their accounts that women too can fall in love with alcoholic beverages and can wax elegantly about the joys of drinking. Modern women authors can also become zealots in the service of Bacchus.

Politicians and regulators can also fall in love with their favorite alcoholic beverage and can also come to be dependent upon Big Booze for campaign money. The industries have many tools available to them to increase sales, despite a public health perspective.

Big Booze's Best Customers

Consider the following. About 5% of American drinkers consume about 40% of the alcoholic beverages sold (i.e., they drink 3,015,210,400 gallons of beer, wine and spirits yearly, based on 2006 data).[15] Those heavy drinking consumers account for about a quarter of the gross income of the industry. About 10% of drinkers consume about 55 to 60% of the beverages sold and account for about a third of the industries' income. Although we do not define alcoholism in terms of amount drunk (but amount of adversity associated with large amounts drunk), it is reasonable to expect that the 5 to 10% who drink the majority of sold alcoholic beverages are those at serious risk for adverse events. In other words, Big Booze's best customers are habitual drinkers of large amounts of alcohol, i.e., alcoholics. The public relations arm of the industry does not want that observation to be associated with their product. So, the producers structure their ads to console their best customers by putting distinguished looking older guys and successful, retired athletes in their ads.

There is interesting implication of the fact that a small proportion of the drinkers account for a large proportion of the alcohol sold. It is not in the best interests of the industry to have successful treatments for alcoholism. Such would reduce the numbers of their best customers.

Often the perspectives of the alcohol beverage industry and perspectives associated with public health agree with one another. They agree that the most efficient way to create lifelong customers is to have adolescents begin drinking. Both animal research and survey data indicate that the habit of drinking alcohol beverages is easy to instill in adolescents and once established, difficult to undo. Big Booze has been accused of marketing directed toward children and adolescents. Spokespersons for Big Booze deny that they direct advertising toward those under the age of 21.

Big Booze's New Best Customers: Young Women

Currently, advertisements generated by Big Booze are using new strategies such as those made possible by the Internet, cell phones and viral marketing. Viral marketing is the hope that advertising messages are forwarded to others who in turn forward the message. Big Booze's message is that romance and drinking go together and being a "party girl" is a mark of sophistication. An indicator of the success of the public relations campaign is that almost all 14 to 17 year olds in the USA are aware of the advertising and many of them recognize the brands being sold, consider the ads to be funny, attractive and fun to watch.

Professor David Jernigan is Director of the Center on Alcohol Marketing and Youth (Johns Hopkins U.). Here are some of his thoughts on the marketing opportunities presented by mobile computing and social networks (as reported by Johston, 2003).[16] These new marketing opportunities are being used by Big Booze. Such marketing "… is the ultimate extension of lifestyle advertising. The brand is now a human being. It's interacting with you in real time. It's talking to you on Facebook. These are worlds that are being created by the brand in conjunction with, in cooperation and collaboration with, their user base. It is a marvelous innovation in marketing and it is a disaster for us." When Prof. Jernigan says it is a disaster for "us," we suppose he means all of us. It is particularly a disaster for girls and young women. It just seems that adults ought not to take advantage of girls just because they can.

We mentioned earlier that alcoholics were Big Booze's best costumers. Those best customers were, for the most part, middle-aged men. The fastest growing brands within Big Booze's product line are highly flavored alcoholic beverages that mask the taste of ethanol. These products were developed specifically to aid the sale of alcoholic beverages to young women. The insiders of Big Booze call these products: chick beer, starter drinks, drinks of initiation, and cocktails with training wheels.[16] In a later chapter, we provide evidence that women are particularly vulnerable to becoming alcoholics (a sort-of-novel idea). Girls and young women are susceptible to highly sophisticated advertising and public relations (not differently than boys and young men) and Big Booze is using every opportunity to provide "girl friendly" messages directed toward media outlets used by young women. We contend that these marketing ploys will dramatically increase drinking among women. If the trends currently underway continue, a reasonable prediction is that mothers and grandmothers will be Big Booze's new best customers. The topic of next chapter is alcoholism.

Chapter 4: Alcohol Abuse and Alcoholism (AAA)

Some people drink alcoholic beverages too often; and when they drink, they drink too much. Exactly, what is too often and too much? For believers in some major religions, drinking any alcoholic beverage is too often. In cultures that condone and even promote drinking alcohol, there are times when one drink is too many (e.g., when a woman is pregnant). At other times, drinking alcoholic beverages is not only sanctioned by the prevailing social norms, it is even encouraged (e.g., drinking a celebratory toast).

In most countries, there are large industries that manufacture and distribute alcoholic beverages and they strive to increase drinking (Chapter 3). There are also organizations that spend millions of dollars (or euros, pesos, rubles, etc.) trying to get people to stop drinking. Some nations allow advertising campaigns designed to increase consumption of alcoholic beverages while concurrently sponsoring advertising with the opposite goal. Big Booze sponsors extensive public relations campaigns masking the dire consequences of drinking. Many nations' educational programs teach their youth about the same dire consequences. Many nations have bars and taverns devoted to drinking and clinics and hospitals devoted to getting people to stop drinking.

When it comes to alcoholic beverages, it may seem that many nations have a confusing set of norms. They do, yet, there are social norms with which nearly everyone can agree. We doubt if any rational person wants drunken people (other than themselves) to drive on their roads, near their home, or near their children. We surely do not condone the domestic violence seemingly abetted by alcohol. We surely do not condone people drinking so much that it interferes with their roles as student, worker or parent (particularly when the worker is your surgeon or airline pilot). Most Western societies condone drinking, but do not condone drinking that seems to be out of control and causes mayhem. Most Americans, as well as citizens of many other nations, think moderate drinking *among adults* is O.K.

The definition of moderate drinking is, however, an issue. For the owner of a tavern, the customer that stops by the tavern and has two or three drinks after work is a moderate drinker and a valued customer. If, however, that same person while driving home should fail to stop soon enough to prevent hitting a pedestrian in a crosswalk and kills her, then the drinking is not moderate. Furthermore, the driver in such a situation will probably be in serious legal and financial trouble.

It was Jack Mendelson who quipped "Society tends to define alcohol abuse in rather personal terms, e.g., anyone who drinks more than I do (Mendelson & Mello, 1985, p 269)."[1]

Definitions of AAA

AAA is defined in terms of the problems that come from drinking too much, too often. Generally, AAA is not defined in terms of the amount drunk, although there is a strong relationship between amount drunk and the probability of having problems.

Those who study psychology of abnormal behavior professionally (namely, some psychologists, psychiatrists, psychiatric nurses, and some social workers) have agreed to (with considerable controversy) a set of definitions for mental disorders. These specifications are useful in helping make many decisions such as (a) are the presenting problems of sufficient intensity to warrant treatment by a professional health care provider, (b) should insurance plans pay for the treatment, and (c) aiding research designed to improve prevention and treatment.

The book defining mental disorders most used in the USA is the *Diagnostic and Statistical Manual of Mental*

Disorders, published by the American Psychiatric Association. The Manual (DSM) has been updated rather frequently and the 5th edition (DSM-5) has been agreed upon and published in its final form May 2013. The disorder associated with the compulsion to drink too much too often is called *alcohol use disorder*. Alcohol use disorder, with the specification of severe, is to be the "official label" for what nearly everyone else calls alcoholism. The following, with some comments was proposed as the "official diagnosis" for AAA in DSM-5 (taken from the Web using the search term dsm v., circa 2012).

Alcohol use disorder is defined as maladaptive use of alcoholic beverages leading to significant impairment or distress that has lasted for a year or more. Impairment or distress is signified by having at least two of the following.

1. The use of alcoholic beverages has resulted in a failure to meet obligations at home (e.g., neglect of children), at school (e.g., repeated absences, failures in making progress toward educational goals, expulsions), or at work (e.g., not doing work adequately, being late for work and being absent often).

2. Drinking alcoholic beverages in circumstances that are physically hazardous (e.g., repeatedly driving an automobile when intoxicated).

3. Habitual drinking that is causing interpersonal problems (e.g., arguments with spouse or other family members about drinking, alcohol-abetted family violence).

4. The emergence of the apparent need to drink more to get the same effect as previously (or to drink more to prevent withdrawal symptoms, see item 5).

5. The appearance of marked withdrawal symptoms when alcoholic beverages are not taken regularly.

6. The tendency to drink more than was planned (e.g., when going out to have a couple of beers, the result is often eight or more; when the plan is to have only a glass of wine with dinner but usually drinking a bottle of wine with dinner).

7. There is a persistent desire to cut-down on the amount of alcoholic beverage used.

8. A great deal of time is spent in alcohol-related activities (e.g., spending large amounts of time in taverns and bars, drinking when engaging in nearly every recreational activity such as ball games, family outings, etc.; in other words, the person's life seems to be characterized by habitual drinking).

9. Related to item 8, important occupational and recreational activities are given up in order to drink alcoholic beverages.

10. Drinking continues even in the face of mounting alcohol-induced health problems.

11. There is strong craving for alcoholic beverages when there is a period without them.

If an individual manifests two or three of these circumstances, the diagnosis is Alcohol Use Disorder, Moderate Severity. If an individual manifests four or more of the list, the diagnosis is *alcohol use disorder, severe*. The diagnosis should also specify whether withdrawal symptoms are apt to occur with the beginning of abstinence.

Notice, in some ways, this standard is lenient; for example, the problems should last a year. A semester of heavy drinking does not get you the diagnosis. Drinking that apparently does not interfere with usual on-going activities but may be slowly producing problems may not be diagnosed (e.g., a women who drinks regularly what might be considered moderate amounts but is incurring liver disease; in other words, item 10 may be difficult to recognize).

Some have complained that the new standards for alcoholism (i.e., DSM-5, alcohol use disorder) have been broadened unnecessarily (e.g., including craving as a critical sign). Being diagnosed as having a disorder as defined by DSM-5 indicates that insurance companies and government programs should pay for treatments; consequently, a broadened diagnosis could be costly. Others claim that if treatment for alcoholism is begun earlier than previously that it is more likely to succeed and stop the progression to serious illnesses, hence be less costly.

Binge Drinking or Hazardous Drinking

Ethanol's adverse effects are clearly dose-related: The greater the drinking, the greater the risk of adversity; and, this generalization holds across all circumstances of drinking. A large number of variables affect the toxicity of an alcoholic beverage, for examples, age, sex, bodyweight, what is taken with alcohol and history of drinking. All of the mentioned variables modify the amount of ethanol getting to the brain. Nevertheless, when large amounts are drunk during a few hours, everyone shows signs of intoxication. Furthermore, repeatedly taking toxic doses of alcohol induces organ damage; the more drinking, the more damage.

As mentioned, providing a precise definition of what constitutes "a drink of alcoholic beverage" is a bit of a problem. Nevertheless, given the usual circumstances, we can use the concept of a single drink as a measure, not a precise measure, but nevertheless a useful one. A given number of drinks will induce intoxication regardless of variables such as height, weight, gender, amount of food eaten, etc. Consequently, there has been a consensus among relevant professionals of what constitutes hazardous drinking. Binge drinking (or hazardous drinking) is defined as 5 or more ordinary drinks on occasion of drinking for men and 4 or more ordinary drinks for women. This definition is useful because it indexes the amount of drinking that will almost assuredly induce intoxication as indexed by the performance on measures of coordination and cognitive ability. We discuss why there is a different standard for men and women in a later chapter.

The consensus: binge drinking, i.e., hazardous, drinking, is 5 or more drinks on an occasion (usually a matter of hours) for men and 4 or more for women. Big Booze does not want hazardous drinking to be so defined, because their best customers drink more than that.

Duration of Alcohol's Toxic Effects

About 95% of the alcohol a person drinks is broken down by enzymes collectively called alcohol dehydrogenase. The other 5% is excreted unchanged (as in urine or as alcoholic breath). The amount of alcohol in breath is closely related to the amount of ethanol in the blood which, in turn, is closely related to the amount of alcohol in the brain next to neurons. The close relationship of the amount of alcohol in breath to the amount in the blood is the basis for the breathalyzer test as a measure of degree of intoxication.

Most of the ethanol is processed (metabolized) into potentially useful products (e.g., those that provide energy). Complete metabolism (breakdown) of ethanol involves a number of steps. The first step involves alcohol dehydrogenase. A small proportion of the ethanol consumed (about 15% in men, less in women) is processed by the alcohol dehydrogenase in the lining of the stomach. The balance is processed in the liver.

In the liver, ethanol is transformed into acetaldehyde. There is a necessary coenzyme in the liver called nicotinamide adenine dinucleotide (NAD). NAD and alcohol dehydrogenase are both necessary to effect the change from ethanol to acetaldehyde. The amount of NAD is limited. Consequently, only a limited amount of ethanol can be processed (metabolized) at a time. If a person drinks a lot often, the amount of NAD produced will be increased somewhat. Nevertheless, the amount of NAD remains limited. Given that NAD is limited, only so much ethanol can be processed regardless of amount being drunk. The situation is similar to a bucket with a hole in it. As water is put into the bucket, some leaks out. If the amount of water being put into the bucket is greater than the amount leaking out, water accumulates in the bucket.

The enzymatic system associated with the breakdown of acetaldehyde involves aldehyde dehydrogenase. Aldehyde dehydrogenase metabolizes acetaldehyde to other compounds. When aldehyde dehydrogenase is in short supply, acetaldehyde can accumulate. Acetaldehyde is a toxin at modest concentrations. More will be said about this subsequently.

Toxic doses are a function of amount drunk during a period of time. Episodes of hazardous drinking (large amounts in a short time usually a matter of hours) are associated with most of the asocial behavior occurring during such episodes. Alcohol-use is associated with more than a half of all murders, more than a third of all rapes and sexual assaults, and about two-thirds of all cases of domestic violence (USA data). The dose-related effects of ethanol on the functioning of the brain set the stage for considerable behavior that would be unlikely in a sober state.[2]

Labels Are Both Useful and Sometimes Prejudicial.

When a person drinks too much, too often, the person may be labeled an alcoholic. In colloquial terms, the person might be labeled a drunkard (or other unflattering labels). When a person has drunk too much and shows behavioral signs of ethanol's toxicity, we say that the person is drunk (is intoxicated).

Although the effects of a single episode of drinking can lead to extraordinary mayhem (e.g., accidents), such toxicity is not alcoholism. It is a case of acute alcohol-poisoning, but not alcoholism. AAA are characterized by a *habit of drinking* which usually involves an escalation of amount drunk during an episode of drinking and usually rather mild toxic effects which accumulate over time to become serious problems. When a habitual drinker gets intoxicated, she risks making bad judgments by the mere fact that ethanol reduces the capability to reason clearly. When individuals are in a state contrary to sound reasoning, it just follows that they are apt to make poorer judgments than otherwise.

Because the toxic effects on organ systems of single episodes of drinking are usually small, they tend to go unappreciated until the many small effects have combined to produce so much damage that obvious problems emerge. Further, if there is abstinence from drinking, the toxic effects of drinking are often reversible with the mere passage of time. When, however, habitual drinking continues, damaging effects accumulate. With more damage, longer periods of abstinence are necessary for recovery. Because the toxic effects of single episodes of drinking are seemingly mild, it is easy to come to the conclusion that habitual drinking is O.K., and that is a characteristic of AAA.

The labels of alcoholic, alcoholism and alcohol use disorder should refer to temporary propensities and circumstances and not an enduring characteristic of the person. *Alcoholic* refers to the observation that the person in question frequently drinks too much presently. The issue of whether that propensity endures is an open question. When the individual stops drinking, she is no longer an alcoholic. The propensity to drink too often, too much is alcoholism. At various times, an individual can be afflicted with alcoholism or not.

Although there are blood tests indicative of a state of advanced toxicity due to habitual drinking, there are some rather simple questions that when answered truthfully provide a reliable measure of advancing toxicity. One of those questionnaires is called the CAGE test and is named after a concept of each of its four questions.[3] The questions are:

1. Have you ever felt you needed to **C**ut down on your drinking?

2. Have people **A**nnoyed you by criticizing your drinking?

3. Have you ever felt **G**uilty about drinking?

4. Have you ever felt you needed a drink first thing in the morning (**E**ye-opener) to steady your nerves or to get rid of a hangover?

The CAGE questionnaire is, perhaps surprisingly, very effective in detecting alcohol-related problems. Two or more "yes" responses indicate a high probability that the respondent is having trouble with drinking or will soon have trouble due to drinking.

A recent book by Maria Gifford titled *Alcoholism* provides a list of short tests similar to the CAGE; some modified for particular populations, for example, teenagers.[4] They are similar to one another and are useful in diagnosing AAA. Rather than using the CAGE questionnaire, one can use the conditions of alcohol use disorder listed in DSM-5 as a check list to diagnose alcoholism. Appendix 1 provides another simple test, i.e., The Alcohol Use Disorders Identification Test (AUDIT) developed by the World Health Organization.

Persons Are More Than Their Drinking-Habits.

It is a good idea to make a distinction between the behaviors associated with excessive drinking (being drunk often or having AAA) and the general characteristics of the person. A person can be a respected member of the community but exhibit problematic, asocial behavior when drunk. Persons can be typically smart; but when drunk, behave stupidly. A person can produce extraordinary work, but drink too much, too often to sustain good health. The label alcoholic can tag the whole person. The label can then be a problem, because it fails to isolate the behaviors that need to be changed. The habit of drinking excessively can be changed and the problems incurred while drinking can often (but not always) be remedied. It is impossible to remedy all the problems incurred by alcohol-related murder or "accidental" death as well as a number of other dire consequences; nevertheless such alcohol-related consequences have to be managed. The fact that some problems associated with drinking are not amenable to resolution makes prevention of AAA a reasonable step toward creating a happier society.

When a woman drinks too much, too often and when she is drunk engages in asocial behavior, it is convenient to tell a colleague that she is a drunkard. Labels tend to stick. A person that has stopped habitual drinking and, therefore, does not engage in problematic behaviors, no longer deserves to be labeled a drunkard (or even a recovering alcoholic except by the person in question).

Withholding judgments about a person until you have considerable information and then to only hold tentative opinions is the essence of tolerance and non-prejudicial thinking. We should not *pre*judge people. That indicative, however, does not mean we can or should suspend judgments. In the spirit of attempting to end racial prejudice and similar injustices, social commentators have urged people to not make judgments about other people, to be open to the potential goodness in all of us. That is sound advice. We should not judge a person based on skin color, ethic identification, gender or merely because they appear different than some ideal of normal because the data indicates that false conclusions are rampant when that is done.

Tolerance, however, should not be extended to the point of condoning what many judge as bad behavior. For example, a man who gets drunk and beats his wife should not necessarily be judged a bad person. However, without hesitation, we can and do judge wife-beating as an asocial behavior, a shameful act. A man who in a drunken moment does violence to a family member and who upon reflection does not feel shame has committed a second wrong. One can hate wife-beating without hating the man who has beaten his wife (perhaps a very difficult chore, but nevertheless one worthy of attempting). A wife-beater need not be hated to make the judgment that he has to be responsible for his asocial behavior; that is: he needs to do penance, make amends, and reform and, thereby, again become a respected member of the community. There are clearly incidences of domestic violence calling for agents of the broader society to intervene and such intervention may involve reducing the civil liberties of the perpetrator.

A feminist agenda calls for non-prejudicial thinking. A woman should not be judged unfit to wield power merely because she is a woman. On the other hand, a woman who gets drunk and beats her child, should not be excused from the responsibility for her acts merely because she was drunk, is a woman, or because motherhood confers special privileges.

Snap, even prejudicial, judgments are often useful. When a drunken man appears belligerent, it is probably smart to conclude that he is possibly mean when drunk. He is not the person to engage in conversation about the latest football game, politics or religion or to be overly friendly with his female friend. This is prejudicial thinking (he is being pre judged before relevant facts are known); a judgment is being made with very little information (a snippet of belligerence) about a man who had been apparently drinking alcohol. Knowledge, however, that violence is often associated with intake of alcoholic beverages and the observation of some belligerence is sufficient to make a snap judgment, a judgment different from the kind of prejudice that we abhor. It is prudent to use small amounts of information to come to a conclusion in cases where violence might emerge and to act on that information by avoiding the circumstances of violence. These kinds of judgments are different from detrimental generalizations about a person (harmful prejudice), because they should be very temporary, tentative assessments. Even though tentative, they are nevertheless well-founded enough to be acted upon.

When a drunken man makes unwanted sexual advances, it is prudent to come to the conclusion to not be alone with that man. Even if, he appears to be a nice, reasonable man when sober. Drunken men are known to rape.

The message is simple. Drunkenness is a toxic state and with some regularity produces asocial behavior.

Alcoholism as a Disease

There has been enough written surrounding the issue of whether alcoholism is a disease or a moral problem to fill a large city's public library. It is both. It is neither. The issue is moot. The current consensus is that it is better to define alcoholism as a disease than otherwise because of the following practicality. We have mechanisms in our society for funding research on diseases and funding for treatment of diseases that are not as easily marshaled for resolving people's moral problems. The criminal justice system deals with crime and many moral failures. The health care system and social services are, accordingly, a better place to deal with alcoholism and its attendant problems. Of course, when a person commits murder under the influence of alcohol, the person is dealt with in the criminal justice system where being drunk is not a defense.

Professors Jack Mendelson and Nancy Mello, prominent researchers on alcoholism, stated that the solid evidence for "the transformation of alcoholism from depravity to disease" (1985, p 265) was the findings that clearly established that excessive, sustained intake of alcoholic beverage leads to observable withdrawal signs and symptoms (findings documented in 1950s and beyond).[1] Withdrawal symptoms are clearly disease-like, something that could be studied objectively, thereby lifting the study of alcoholism from "a quagmire of moral turpitude" (p 265).

Mendelson and Mello summarized the characteristic physiological events that support the idea that alcoholism is best considered a disease thusly: "Within six to eight hours after their last drink, alcoholics develop a series of signs (observable by others) and symptoms (reported by the patient), which usually become most severe within twenty-four hours, then gradually diminish over the next forty-eight to seventy-two hours. The major signs include tremor of the arms and hands, and sometimes the tongue and torso, sweating, a flushed face, a mild increase in heart rate (tachycardia), rapid involuntary movements of the eye (nystagmus), hyperactive reflexes, nausea and vomiting. Patients often report some disorientation, nervousness, insomnia, nightmares and occasionally hallucinations" (1985, p 265)[1].

They go on (p 265-6) to discuss two features of withdrawal that can have fatal consequences: (a) grand mal seizures (sometimes referred to as rum fits) and (b) delirium tremens. "Delirium tremens develops in about 5 percent of alcoholics in withdrawal and in about 30 percent of those with 'Rum fits.' … Delirium tremens usually develops … within three to five days after drinking has stopped. It is characterized by profound confusion and disorientation, vivid hallucinations, and fever as well as tremor, agitation, sweating and tachycardia."[1]

There is no doubt that withdrawal can be manifest in observable physiological events that appear disease-like. Further, there is every reason to believe that the cause of the withdrawal signs and symptoms is the sustained presence of ethanol affecting the central nervous system in such a way that when ethanol is not present for a period that there are the reactions known as withdrawal signs and symptoms. Withdrawal signs are not due to other factors such as malnutrition and other adversities. Factors such as poor nutrition are obviously not helpful in reducing the complications of withdrawal sickness, but a well-nourished individual with a long history of intake of alcoholic beverages will experience withdrawal when ethanol-intake is stopped. Alcoholics also show signs of tolerance (it takes a lot of ethanol to prevent withdrawal symptoms). The presence of tolerance and the likelihood of withdrawal signs and symptoms are the cardinal symptoms of what has been described as alcohol dependence, a disease.

The following is relevant to this discussion and the discussion on depression. Drugs that are used to treat depression such as SSRIs (selective serotonin reuptake inhibitors) produce dependence, i.e., withdrawal symptoms and signs. Does taking SSRIs produce a disease called SSRIism? To be consistent with the criterion (i.e., withdrawal signs and symptoms) used to define alcoholism as a disease, it makes sense to call the prescription of SSRIs a risk factor for the disease of SSRIism.

A beneficial consequence of defining alcoholism as a disease is related to the discussion in a preceding section. The definition tends to separate the acts of drunkenness from the broader characteristics of the person; it separates the generally honest, gentle man from the same man's acts of hostility when drunk. Of course, that can be done regardless of whether AAA are defined as diseases.

There are some problems associated with adopting the idea that alcoholism is a disease as demonstrated by withdrawal signs and symptoms. First, withdrawal distress is usually over in a matter of weeks, but the tendency to drink, to crave a drink usually remains. Further, many of the problems associated with AAA occur among individuals who do not experience marked withdrawal signs. To handle these inconvenient truths, some theorists postulated a state called psychological dependence. Psychological dependence is marked by excessive drinking and its attendant problems when marked withdrawal symptoms are not part of the picture. The concept can and often has become merely a circular definition; it explains excessive drinking by defining excessive drinking as psychological dependence and psychological dependence is defined as propensity to drink excessively.

Inherent to having two definitions for the disease of AAA, one physical and one psychological, is that such glosses over a salient fact: all that is physical is potentially psychological and all that is psychological is physical. The distinction, therefore, distorts reality and thereby impedes rational theory that can lead to practical solutions.

When alcoholism is defined as a combination of physical and psychological dependence, the definition takes into account that alcoholism is more than withdrawal distress, but it does more than that. It makes desires and wants diseases. It makes life-styles diseases. The idea of disease seems to lose its specificity and becomes, therefore, sort of useless. Such thinking seems to pathologize all emotions, all behaviors, all cravings, etc. There are other reasons for questioning whether we should define alcoholism as a disease.

When alcoholism is defined as a disease, it puts the treatment and prevention of alcoholism into the hands of the medical profession, and, in turn, into the hands of the healthcare insurance companies. Until recently, the insurers were unwilling to pay for the extended care necessary for optimal treatment of alcoholism. New legislation may lead to modification of that practice. Further, physicians usually do not have the luxury of spending considerable time with each patient, a necessary condition for optimal treatment.

Another problem with defining alcoholism as a disease is that the burden for getting well falls to the person treating the disease. The problem for the alcoholic goes from reform to recover (one recovers from an infection without much of a life-style change in the patient). A life-style change is usually necessary for alcoholism to remit. Physicians clearly understand that life-style reform is the best "medicine" for a host of "diseases," but arranging for life-style changes is difficult, if not impossible, within the context of a modern medical practice as developed in the USA.

Another reason for not calling alcoholism a disease is that it absolves the alcohol beverage industry from responsibility for alcoholism's mayhem. The industry readily indorses the idea that alcoholism is a disease, even a hereditary disease. Advocates for the industry can claim that they are not responsible for causing alcoholism; it is in the genes of an unfortunate few.

Morality involves choices. Albert Camus commented "Life is the sum of all of your choices." J.K. Rowling had the Hogwarts' headmaster Albus Dumbledore of Harry Porter fame counsel "It is our choices that show what we truly are, far more than our abilities."[5] Starting to drink alcoholic beverages and continuing to drink in the face of emerging problems associated with drinking are choices. As Mendleson and Mello pointed out, alcoholics do not stay drunk. They tend periodically to go three or more days without a drink, even suffering some withdrawal signs, then return to more regular drinking. Further, many regular drinkers have had rather prolonged periods of abstinence in their history. To sort of steer clear of the complication that alcohol-intake is a choice, many experts claim that the alcoholic is "out of control," a defining condition of alcoholism, i.e., have no choice. Alcoholic Anonymous also states, as a cardinal concept, that the alcoholic is out of control and must rely on a higher power to save her. Yet, whatever else treatment must do, it ultimately must instill better choices (do not drink tonight, go home, take the money and buy the baby shoes). When we speak of right choices we are talking about taking responsibility for one's acts; doing good, not bad.

A problem with defining alcoholism as a moral problem is that it often refers the problem to religious authorities who claim some special privileges in the realm of morality. Unfortunately, modern religions in societies that separate church and state have few, if any, resources to bring to the problem of alcoholism other than preaching, which has been shown to be ineffective. Morality, however, transcends any given religion despite officials of a particular religion denying such.

Any complex society must have most adults, if not nearly all adults, behave in moral ways for it to function in a way that provides adequate means to pursue happiness. It is good for an individuals' word to be as good as the individuals' bond. It is good for individuals to respect authorities such as parents, teachers, police and judges. It is good to not have corrupt public servants. It is good for people to work toward the common good. It is good for businesses to have high moral standards; do good and, thereby, profit. It is nice for people to have manners, to respect one another, etc., etc. To be a moral person is to have the behaviors that are conducive to a well-functioning society in which citizens can live happily. It is bad for people to lie, steal, murder, and to engage behaviors that are harmful to others. We used to call these bad behaviors sin. To label these previously labeled sinful behaviors as diseases is inefficient. The problem is that the current criminal justice system and the medical profession which are in charge of crime and disease, respectively, are ill-equipped, by themselves, to prevent and remedy some of the most prevalent "sins" of our times.

Professor Steven Pinker discusses the value of a moral sense with respect to the broad issues of peace and the contrary, violence. He stated "... most applications of the moral sense are not particularly moral but rather tribal, authoritarian, or puritanical ..." (2011, p 669).[6] It is these associations with morality that many find distasteful if not downright obnoxious. There is, however, as Pinker and others have pointed out, a reasoned morality based on personal and public health considerations as well as considerations such as the greatest happiness for the most people that is by its very nature more reasonable. Reasonableness, according to Pinker demands a degree of ability to think, reason abstractly which, in turn, takes education to perfect. However, this ability to think in nuanced ways often gets in the way of drawing the conclusion that some behaviors are bad and others good. There are moral choices; choices that lead to dire consequences and choices that lead to happy circumstances. There are bad habits and there are good habits. Bad habits develop by making unfortunate choices; good habits develop by making fortunate choices.

The foregoing does not diminish our profound respect for those of religious faith who have devoted themselves to the care of the unfortunate and, in particular, alcoholics. Usually they have limited resources with which to work and yet valiantly carry on.

So, where does that leave us? It leaves us with problems needing resolution. Alcoholism is probably defined best by a very old definition. Alcoholism is a bad habit, a habit that is very difficult to change once established. The habit can be so instilled that often help is needed to modify or stop the execution of the bad habit. It is a *bad* habit because of the dire consequences inherent to engaging the habit.[7] Also, germane, to the issues, we all prefer to not suffer the dire consequences. The ideas expressed in this paragraph are elaborated throughout the balance of the book.

Traits of the Alcoholic

There are some correlations between characteristics such as traits and personality variables and likelihood of developing alcoholism.[8] None of the variables that will be discussed are powerful determinants of alcoholism. Furthermore, only some of the traits are particularly problematic in the absence of excessive intake of alcoholic beverages. A person can be nice or not so nice as well as a nice alcoholic and a not so nice alcoholic. What is problematic is "not so nice," regardless of whether one is a drinker or not. A generally happy individual can drink little or nothing as well as drink too much, too often. Of course, happy individuals who drink excessively incur problems that may erode their disposition to be happy. The one clear variable associated with alcoholism is the propensity to drink too much, too often.

An important variable associated with the degree of damage related to excessive drinking is the status of an individual's health. Unhealthy people suffer more alcohol-induced problems.

Alcoholism tends to run in natural families. An individual whose natural father and mother have a life-style that includes excessive drinking is at risk for developing a similar life-style. If an identical twin becomes an alcoholic, it is likely (but not assuredly) that the other twin will also. This is true even if the twins are reared apart. If a fraternal twin becomes an alcoholic, the other twin has about the same likelihood of developing alcoholism as other siblings of similar parents. These kinds of observations lead to the concept that there is a genetic basis for alcoholism, i.e., the idea that certain genetic characteristics are causally related to the likelihood of alcoholism.

For a genetic predisposition to be related to the life-style that leads to alcoholism, ethanol must affect some people differently than others. For some, for example, ethanol-intake might make them nauseated and, therefore, drinking alcoholic beverages is not pleasant; hence drinking alcoholic beverages is done very little, and no alcoholism. For others, ethanol might produce drowsiness and sleepiness without much of anything else. These individuals do not see much sense in drinking and drink sparingly and, therefore, do not become alcoholic. For others, drinking alcoholic beverages usually produces a pleasant feeling and, additionally, for some of them drinking might not lead to a bad hangover. For these people, the likelihood of developing a life-style that leads to alcoholism with all of its harsh consequences is more likely. It is straight forward: the extent of liking the effects of alcohol is a determinant of the risk of alcoholism.

How could one's genetic makeup affect how much one might like alcohol's effects? The following is one example. Among those whose ancestors lived for an extensive period in East Asia (e.g., Chinese and Japanese), intake of ethanol produces a tendency for nausea and a tendency for the face to flush red. These effects are due to a slightly different way their bodies metabolize ethanol compared to others and that is related to a genetic variable (i.e., genes that produce different amount of enzymes associated with the full metabolism of ethanol).

Ethanol is first broken down by enzymes in the stomach and then mainly in the liver. These enzymes modify ethanol by turning it into constituent parts (a few details of this were given above). One of those parts is acetaldehyde. In many individuals, the enzymes for converting acetaldehyde to its products are sufficient to almost never have significant amounts of acetaldehyde in circulation. In some persons of Asian extraction, these enzymes are less abundant than those of others. Acetaldehyde is, therefore, eliminated slowly and acetaldehyde can accumulate when there is considerable ethanol in blood. Acetaldehyde produces a variety of effects (e.g., red spots on cheek, slight to harsh nausea, and drowsiness) which are judged to be unpleasant. Persons with this reaction seldom develop alcoholism (although strong social norms encouraging drinking can override the negative feeling resulting in drinking that is less than pleasant).

Antabuse is a drug that interferes with the metabolism of acetaldehyde and is used to treat alcoholism. The individual who drinks while under the influence of Antabuse becomes ill. Supposedly, this teaches the alcoholic not to drink. Put another way, it changes the person of European extraction by having a characteristic common among persons of East Asian extraction. It is not a permanent change. Consequently, as soon as Antabuse is no longer taken by an alcoholic, the intake of alcoholic beverage again produces its ordinary effects, not nausea. A drink or two re-establishes the habits of drinking very quickly post use of Antabuse. Although Antabuse is often prescribed as a medicine to curb alcoholism, controlled studies show that it is at best only marginally effective in inducing long term abstinence or near abstinence among alcoholics. Also, Antabuse has other effects than interfering with acetaldehyde metabolism that are potentially problematic (and, high levels of acetaldehyde are potentially carcinogenic). The risks compared to benefits make the prescribing of Antabuse an ineffective approach to treating alcoholism. While not directly related to a discussion of why some like to drink while others do not, I note that punishment for drunkenness is a notoriously ineffective way of curbing a well-established habit of drinking (been tried often and failed nearly as often).

Given that alcoholism seems to run in natural families and given that people seem to marry and have children with persons similar to them, it follows that alcoholism would be more prevalent among some groups than others. When we tabulate incidents of alcoholism and classify people into groups, some relationships emerge. For example, some tribes of American Indians have a very high rate of AAA. Generally speaking, women of African ancestry living in the USA drink less than others.

There are correlations between problem drinking among under-aged drinkers and some variables. Teen-age drinkers often skip school, engage in asocial behavior, have committed petty crimes, and are prone to use illegal recreational drugs (particularly marijuana). These variables seem to go together. The correlations are small, but perhaps have meaning in alerting a counselor to ask about potentially related problems when addressing a presenting problem. These data do not rule out the possibility that the well-behaved teenager is currently drinking sufficient alcoholic beverage to put her at risk for developing serious problems.

The modern way of discussing the issues of what kind of person is apt to become or has become an alcoholic is to speak of risk factors. This has a number of advantages. An advantage is that it allows a reasonable discussion of how to combine circumstances which are only marginally related to developing alcoholism into a meaningful statement. The tabulation of risk factors has been used extensively to try to predict which youngsters will develop AAA and illegal drug-abuse.

As mentioned a risk factor associated with the development of alcoholism is having parents and close relatives who exhibit alcoholism. Another risk factor is doing poorly in school. Students who have friends who use "forbidden substances" (alcohol, cigarettes, marijuana) are also at risk for using those forbidden substances. A general rebelliousness, particularly when manifest as asocial behaviors such as fighting, vandalism, and stealing, is a risk factor. Knowing interesting adults who drink a lot is a risk factor. Although not tabulated in the surveys, it is clear that being exposed to constant advertising extolling the virtues of drinking (and perhaps featuring a bit of rebelliousness) and masking the dire consequences of such is a risk factor. Being in a community that seemingly condones drinking at a young age contributes to the likelihood that youngsters will indulge. As the separate risk factors accumulate, the greater the risk that the individual will exhibit hazardous drinking at a young age. When youngsters develop a habit of drinking alcoholic beverages at a young age, it is highly likely that they will continue the habit into adulthood and are at risk for alcoholism. Furthermore, when the habit of drinking alcoholic beverages is established at a young age, the habit of drinking is considerably more difficult to modify for the better.

The risk factors are based on correlations. Correlations are not causes. Perhaps, for example, the rebelliousness and use of forbidden substances could be related to some variable not tabulated such as perceived unfairness in the culture. Or, perhaps, the alcohol-use is a major contributor to the development of the other factors that supposedly predicts alcohol-use. Given the multiple factors that have some small correlation with developing AAA, it is unlikely that focusing on just one of them will be successful at reducing the incidence of AAA.

Summary

We concur with those who suggest that alcohol-related problems vary along a continuum. Alcoholics suffer inordinately while others suffer less.   The one problem that seemingly accounts for much of the disease and mayhem associated AAA is the fact that alcoholics drink often and, when they do drink, they drink intoxicating amounts of alcohol. Some of the toxic effects of drinking too much, too often are presented in the next chapter.

Chapter 5. Consequences of Alcoholism

We begin a discussion of alcohol's toxic effects by relating the gruesome fact that drinking too much, too often increases the risk of dying prematurely (prematurely meaning before retirement, e.g., 65 or before the expected age of death based on mortality tables). Excessive drinking seemingly causes an average of 79,000 American deaths yearly.[1] It is estimated (circa 2008 data) that 1,700 college students between the ages of 18 and 24 die yearly from alcohol-related unintentional injuries, including motor vehicle crashes.[2] About half of them are under the age of 21. A summary of high quality research on the relationship between alcohol intake and death from a motor vehicle accident indicates: all levels of consumption increase the odds of dying in an accident. At the legal limit for driving, the odds of a fatal accident are 13 times higher than when there has been no drinking.[3]

The same survey that tabulated alcohol-related deaths among college students provided some other statistics.[2] It was estimated that 599,000 students between the ages of 18 and 24 are unintentionally injured under the influence of alcohol each year. Further estimates for a year: more than 696,000 students between the ages of 18 and 24 are assaulted by another student who had been drinking; 97,000 students between the ages of 18 and 24 are victims of alcohol-related sexual assault or date-rape. The drinking culture prevailing on and about many college campuses apparently sets the circumstances for considerable unnecessary mayhem.

A study of Swedish women provides some relevant data on how alcoholism might shorten a women's life.[4] The women studied were those who came for treatment of alcohol-related problems for the first time. During this first contact, they were functioning relatively well, but clearly had problems. They were followed for 25 years. For comparison, another group of women of the same age and comparable circumstances were followed. The women who were identified as having alcohol-related problems had a 2.4 times greater risk of dying during the 25-year follow-up period than their counterparts. The greatest risk was during the first five years of the study (when women were younger, obviously) and the most frequent causes of death involved accidents.

Alcohol-use is a Risk Factor for Major Diseases

Why do those who drink excessively die younger than temperate drinkers? The usual account of alcohol's toxicity is given by a long list of enhanced risks of getting many diseases. The list includes nearly all of the ailments that a reasonably informed citizen is apt to know about. In addition, drinking alcoholic beverages contributes to accidents. Here, we are merely going to discuss a few of the risks.

Aging, of course, is a significant risk factor for early death and death in general. The major proximal causes of death in the USA are cardiovascular diseases (diseases of heart and brain, i.e., heart attacks and strokes) and cancer. A life-style characterized by AAA increases risk of cardiovascular diseases and cancer in comparison to merely aging. Said in a different way, cancer and heart diseases occur at younger ages among those who habitually use alcoholic beverages.

Heart Disease and Stroke

There has been a great deal of interest in the relationship between heart disease and alcohol intake. Heart disease is the leading cause of death among people of prosperous nations and many people of those nations drink alcoholic beverages. Drinking is related to other adverse events (e.g., advanced liver disease, breast cancer), so the question arises about the relationship between drinking and heart disease.

There have been a number of studies following large groups of Americans for years with some knowledge of their drinking habits. A controversial conclusion that has been drawn from some of those studies is that light to moderate drinking may increase years of life a bit. The beneficial effects of light drinking seem to be related to some decrease in heart disease. On the other hand, drinking larger amounts is related to increases in heart disease.

A recent book by Dr. Amitava Dasgupta, a professor of pathology and toxicology, provides a comprehensive account of the studies indicating that moderate rates of drinking alcoholic beverages is a healthy practice.[5] There are a goodly number of such studies typically involving large numbers of people. If one carefully reads these large scale studies, as Professor Dasgupta has surely done, it is reasonable to conclude that modest drinking is a healthy practice but that drinking more than a modest amount is unhealthy. The primary basis for such a conclusion is that those who claim to drink none during a previous time-period (e.g., a month, a year or even a life-time) die somewhat earlier than those who drink no more than one or two drinks a day. All of these large studies indicate that morbidity and mortality increase as drinking increases beyond an average of more than three drinks a day for men and an average of over two drinks a day for women. Further, the health problems leading to early death are dose-related; the more one drinks beyond a modest level, the more the problems.

A recent article, by commentator Tanya Chikritzhs and her colleagues of the National Drug Research Institute of Australia in the journal *Drug and Alcohol Review,* was titled: "A healthy dose of skepticism: Four good reasons to think again about protective effects of alcohol on coronary heart disease."[6] At issue was the general conclusion that moderate intake of alcoholic beverages, in some way, reduces the risk of heart attacks. This supposedly beneficial effect is touted widely by Big Booze to mask the well-known facts that greater than moderate drinking is toxic. One of the ways that the results may not reflect a beneficial effect is that most of the studies of the relationship probably includes the very ill, who are not drinking which, in turn, makes it appear that those who drink moderately live longer than those who are not drinking. A problem may be that the data are almost always associated with verbal reports of drinking history (e.g., respondents reporting their moderate drinking may say that they have a drink with dinner, but in fact do that only when they engage rather formal dinners).

We believe the issue is sort of confusing with respect to males; they may or may not get a benefit from light drinking. Given ethanol's heightened toxicity among women, drinking one drink a day may be more risky than justified by the conclusion that "moderate drinking may be beneficial with respect to cardiovascular disease." It may be that the only beneficial effect of drinking alcoholic beverages among women is the pleasure achieved with the initial effects of alcohol. Drinking *may be* fun for women across a number of circumstances and even across a number of years, but drinking for the fun of it can clearly be risky in terms number of happy years lived (A later chapter provides more on women's issues).

For vascular diseases of the heart and brain, there may not be a significant increased risk until intake of alcoholic beverages is greater than, on average, two drinks a day. Women who drink moderately may be at greater risk than men who limit their drinking.

Perhaps the most complete analysis of the association between diseases of the heart and drinking alcoholic beverages studied the results from 81 previous studies of the relationship.[7] The number of adults for whom the researchers had data on both heart disease of various kinds and drinking rates was well over a 1,000,000. They looked at the data from the previous studies and submitted that data to further statistical analyses. The results of this comprehensive review of the available research confirm the general conclusion reached by many of the individual studies. An average drinking of one or two drinks a day reduces the risk of death from diseases of the heart and the incidents of non fatal coronary events. Drinking one or somewhat less than one drink a day (2.5 to 14.9 grams a day) was associated with a 14 to 25% reduction in cardiovascular disease.

Another group of researchers studied the issue of the relationship between drinking and diseases of the heart from a different perspective.[8] They claim their methods provide a better index of level of drinking with respect to causing or preventing cardiovascular diseases. They had data on whether a specific genetic variation (the label of the variation is ADH1B rs 1229984) was present in a large number of people of European ancestry (261,991 individuals) and data on cardiovascular disease (e.g., 20,259 individuals had incidents of heart disease). This genetic variation is associated with the metabolism of ethanol and was known to be associated with less drinking than those without this specific genetic variant. The genetic variant is associated with a flush response (reddening of the cheeks, blushing) with alcohol-consumption.

Those with the genetic variant took 17% less alcohol as indexed by drinks per week. There were fewer of them in the top third of the distribution of drinkers, they reported less binge drinking and more of them abstained from drinking. Those with the genetic variant had lower systolic blood pressure, weighed less, had smaller waist sizes, showed fewer signs of inflammation (i.e., stress), and somewhat, surely not considerably, better profile of blood levels of cholesterol. These modest drinkers had fewer incidents of heart disease and fewer risk factors for heart disease even though some of them drank considerable amounts of alcohol.

There are many traits among the variant group which could have led to their reduced risk of heart disease. The group's combined factors of lower body weight, reduced stress, and reduced drinking could all contribute to a reduced risk of heart disease. If you are concerned about heart disease, it is advisable to be more active, find healthy ways to cope with stress, and to limit and even reduce your drinking.

Figure 5.1 provides an average risk of stroke for persons who drink different amounts of alcoholic beverage. There is considerable variability around the average risk values, e.g., in any given large sample one can expect those who have drunk more than 60 grams daily to have risk ratios from 1.30 to 14.4.

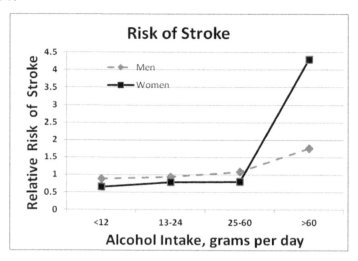

Figure 5.1. The figure shows the average relative risk of stroke as related to average daily intake of alcohol compared to the risk of those who are abstinent (whose risk is 1.0). A value less than one indicates a reduced risk and a value above one an increased risk. A value of 2 indicates twice the risk. Data taken from Reynolds, K., Lewis, B., Nolen, J.D.L., Kinney, G.L., Sathya, B. & He, J.(2003). Alcohol consumption and risk of stroke. *JAMA* 289, 579-88.[7,8]

The data are an example of the type of results that indicate that that modest consumption of alcohol can reduce risk of vascular disease. A 12 gram amount of alcohol is about the amount in one drink. The data indicate that those who drink moderately do have a slightly reduced risk of stroke compared to those who habitually drink hazardous amounts. The data also are an example of how alcohol is more toxic to women than men at anything more than modest drinking.

Cancer

It is well-known that the habit of drinking large amounts of alcoholic beverages contributes to the risk of cancer, in particular cancer of the gut and liver. A 2012 issue of the medical journal *Annuals of Oncology* reported the results of an analysis of all well-done studies concerning the possible relationship between *light drinking* of alcoholic beverages and the incidences of cancer.[9] Light drinking was defined as one drink a day or somewhat less. In contrast to those whose drinking was light, a comparison-group drank seldom if at all. There were a surprisingly large number of well-done studies (i.e., 222) that reported on the relationship between light drinking and the incidence of cancer. A tabulation of all persons (cases) involved in the separate studies was very large (light drinkers: 60,371; control cases, non-drinkers: 92,230).

In the study of the relationship between light drinking and incidence of cancer, there was no statistically significant relationship between light drinking and incidences of some kinds of cancer. For example, even though there is a strong relationship between heavy drinking and liver cancer, there was no significant relationship between light drinking and liver cancer. Light drinking does increase the risk of cancer of the oral cavity, pharynx, and esophagus, that is, areas of the body that come into direct contact with alcohol. The increment in risk of cancer is not large, but sufficiently large to detract from the conclusion that light drinking is healthy.

Light drinking also increased the risk of breast cancer. There is more discussion of AAA and breast cancer in a later chapter.

Alcohol-related Diseases of the Liver

Habitual drinking often leads to damage to the liver. Livers are vital; hence extreme liver-toxicity is fatal. Ethanol's insult to the liver is an example of how the accumulated effects of mild toxicity can become a fatal malady.

The liver performs two related vital functions. It transforms the parts of food that get into the blood into useable compounds for the production of energy and for the maintaining the body's structure. It also transforms poisons into products that can be eliminated.

In the liver, ethanol is metabolized into products used as energy (calories) and waste-products. When the amount of ethanol circulating in the blood is greater than the ability of the liver to process it in a timely manner, the liver can become diseased. There are three recognized liver diseases induced by excessive ethanol: (a) fatty liver, (b) alcoholic hepatitis, and (c) alcoholic cirrhosis.

Fatty liver is characterized, as the name implies, by a buildup of extra fat in cells of the liver. It is a precursor of more serious complications. Usually, there are no symptoms; and if one stops drinking, fatty liver goes away. Continuance of heavy drinking may lead to alcoholic hepatitis characterized by swelling of the liver and damage to some liver cells. These events may be manifest as nausea, abdominal pain and jaundice (a symptom is yellowing of the skin and eyes). Reduction in functioning of the liver can cause a number of problems including reduced ability of the liver to metabolize poisons and drugs. Even though they may not exhibit inordinate drunkenness, from 10 to 35% of those who drink regularly develop alcoholic hepatitis.

Cirrhosis of the liver occurs in about 10 to 15% of those who drink habitually. It is a very serious disease. One has to drink a lot for a long time to develop cirrhosis. Cirrhosis develops quicker, of course, in malnourished or otherwise unhealthy people. Excessive alcohol-intake is often accompanied by malnutrition. Cirrhosis is a disease in which hard scar tissue gradually replaces the healthy soft tissue and eventually completely destroys the vital functions of the organ. A treatment for cirrhosis is a liver transplant.

As the liver becomes progressively diseased, it loses its capacity to clean the blood of substances that might damage the brain. Although there is a mechanism in the blood vessels of the brain that guards the brain from toxins (the blood-brain-barrier), it is not a perfect shield. Consequently, neurotoxins (e.g., ammonia and manganese) are apt to reach the brain when there are alcohol-induced diseases of the liver. Tests show that cognitive abilities are considerably reduced in patients with early signs of cirrhosis.

Well before advanced cirrhosis is produced, the liver does not function as usual. For example, ethanol toxicity affects the amount of circulating testosterone, in part, because the liver is not functioning as usual. The consequence is less testosterone in circulation. Testosterone is the male sex hormone and in adult men sustains some of the secondary sex characteristics such as heavy muscles and a deep voice. Testosterone is usually important for sustaining an interest in sexual activity in both males and females. It follows that the alcoholic man is often less interested in sexual activity than he appears to be. He may even blame some feature of his wife for his lack of interest rather than his life-style involving drinking too much, too often. As you might quickly discern, this is not a condition for a happy marriage.

Alcoholic Beverages in Combination with Drugs

Individuals who drink alcoholic beverages daily come to believe that such is normal. When they take medicines or recreational drugs, habitual drinkers often fail to realize that they are different, in terms of pharmacology and toxicology, than those who do not drink. Further, there is a marked tendency to believe that warning labels stating that a drug should not be taken when using alcoholic beverages only applies to those who take large amounts. Habitual drinkers often think they are not large consumers of alcohol. When taking drugs, drinkers' sort-of-unconsciously held biases modify their decision-making. They fail to realize that there are serious toxic effects of being drunk (intoxicated) and concurrently taking drugs. Sometimes, the consequence is death. In fact, alcohol-in-combination is a leading cause of death among adolescents, that is, accounts for about 20% of all adolescent deaths (USA data). Alcohol-in-combination is one of the leading causes of death among all persons.[10]

Alcohol-in-combination is a classification indicating just what the label indicates. When data are collected concerning the number of individuals who are so sick they wind up in an emergency room and it is determined that the sickness is induced by the combination of alcohol and use of a drug, it is classed as an incidence of alcohol-in-combination. There, of course, can be subclasses; for example, alcohol-in-combination with oxycodone. Based on data collected for the years 2004 to 2010 there was about 166 yearly incidents per 100,000 population of alcohol-in-combination admittances into hospital emergency rooms (USA data).[11]

In 1994, as a result of some tabulations allowing for rather definitive conclusions, the medical community and the general population became aware that the fourth leading cause of death in the USA was adverse reactions to drugs; not illegal drugs but drugs obtained from the hospital pharmacy or from the local drug store.[12] Illegal drugs can also cause adverse drug effects, particularly when they are combined with legal drugs and the intake of alcoholic beverages. A conservative estimate is: over 100,000 deaths are incurred yearly in the USA which are attributable to lethal drug-effects (in some tabulations, these effects are classed as accidental deaths). Death, obviously, is the most serious manifestation of adverse effects of drugs. There are many more instances of drug-induced problems, including drugs inducing serious organ damage.

The risk of an adverse drug reaction is increased as the number of drugs taken by an individual increases; the more the drugs, the more the adversity. The USA constitutes about 5% of the World's population but consumes about half of the drugs sold. In brief, Americans take a lot of drugs. Many citizens of the USA drink alcoholic beverages frequently. It just follows; alcohol-intake and drug-intake are likely to occur together.

There have been steps taken to control the instances of adverse drug effects; but the incidence of sickness and death from adverse effects remains a serious problem. One preventive step, for example, is the demand that physicians have their computers print the name of the drug and the doses to be used by the patient, contrary to merely scribbling the instructions on a prescription pad. More health care professionals are being more systematic in asking about the drugs patients are taking. They should and do ask about all drugs taken including nutritional supplements which can also induce adverse effects.

The chance of an adverse drug reaction increases with the number of drugs taken and that includes drinking alcoholic beverages. In Amitava Dasgupta's, *The Science of Drinking*, there is a long list of drugs and how they interact with alcohol.[4] We are not going to repeat the list. We are, however, going to point out some of the more serious alcohol and drug interactions in the hope of preventing some of the problems. One can prevent all of the alcohol-in-combination adverse effects, of course, if one does not drink alcoholic beverages when taking drugs (as is often advised in warning labels and dosing instructions).

The drugs you pick up from the supermarket or drug store shelves and take or dispense yourself (e.g., to your children) are called over-the-counter drugs. Many over-the-counter drugs interact unfavorably with alcohol. This includes many cold and allergy medications. The active ingredients in these drugs tend to produce sedation. Alcohol also reduces alertness. When cold and allergy medicines and alcoholic beverages are used at roughly the same time, the results make it difficult to stay alert enough to safely drive a car or use heavy machinery.

Acetaminophen, at recommended doses, is effective in controlling pain and fever. Acetaminophen is the active ingredient in a number of over-the-counter drugs, such as medicines with the brand names of Tylenol and Datril (as well as other brands). Many medications sold over-the-counter contain acetaminophen. Recently, acetaminophen was recorded as the 10th leading cause of visits to hospital emergency rooms. Alcohol-in-combination with acetamino-phen is very toxic to the liver and is also a leading cause of visits to emergency rooms.

As an example let us inspect a product marketed as *Tylenol for arthritis pain*. It is an extended release product. This means that the acetaminophen in a single caplet (pill) circulates longer in the blood than it would if not so formulated. If taken as directed by a habitual drinker, there will be hours when both acetaminophen and ethanol will be transiting the liver. This dose-relatedly causes liver disease. If the situation presents daily, the amount of damage can lead to a fatal condition. The warning labels on the bottle indicate that acetaminophen when taken at more than the recommended dose is very hazardous. The warning about alcoholic beverages on the label states, "if one consumes 3 or more alcoholic drinks every day, ask your doctor whether you should use acetaminophen or other pain relievers or fever reducers. Acetaminophen may cause liver damage." Notice the warning states "...3 or more drinks every day... ." The usual conclusion is that drinking more than an average of 3 drinks a day, not 3 drinks *every* day increases morbidity and mortality. The marketers are counting on the drinker to recall that she does not drink every day and to not ask their doctor about the potential hazards of taking acetaminophen while drinking 3 or more drinks on any day. If she would ask, the doctor most assuredly would indicate that three drinks a day combined with acetaminophen can surely be problematic and suggest a less dangerous drug (and counsel to reduce drinking). The marketers may meet some minimal standard for a warning label but, at best, a minimal standard. The National Institute for AAA define low risk drinking as no more than 14 drinks a week for men and no more than 7 drinks during a week for women.[13] Imagine a young woman weighing only 110 pounds who takes this extended release preparation and drinks only a couple of glasses of wine with her evening meals. She is at near toxic doses of both agents individually and in combination she is at clearly damaging doses.

The warning label on the bottle of *Tylenol, Arthritis Pain*, is deceptive. The marketers know that potential customers in a drug-store with arthritis-like pain are not going to call for an appointment with their doctor to ask whether they should take the pills, while revealing that they drink often, before buying the product. The consumer is looking for some relief. They buy the product based on the bold statement for "Arthritis Pain" and once purchased take some of it. Most of us trust a company like Johnson & Johnson (the marketers of this product via a subsidiary) to not tempt us with dangerous drugs. We trust that the FDA is looking out for us. Yet, by barely meeting regulations, the marketers willingly attempt to sell a product that is likely to be used in a dangerous way. Further, the warning label on the bottle is so small that is barely readable (particularly by the elderly). Although the marketers are barely meeting government regulations, they are not meeting a reasonable standard of morality. They are choosing to encourage people to do something that they know will make some people sick while also knowing that there are better alternatives for the treatment of arthritis pain. In a previous time, we might call their behavior sinful, now we call it "good business."

Acetaminophen is an active ingredient in some prescription medicines, particularly opioid preparations for chronic pain. Opioid pain medications include morphine, codeine, and oxycodone. Oxycodone was introduced by Purdue Pharma in 1996 (no relationship to Purdue U.) for the management of pain. The new formulation lasts longer and supposedly induces fewer incidences of nausea than morphine. Morphine may cause itching and oxycodone supposedly produces less itching. Oxycodone and other similar opioids were marketed in combination with acetaminophen and sold under the brand names of Percocet, Tylox, Roxicet, Vicodin ect. Soon after these drugs were introduced, they were widely prescribed and yielded drug companies more than a billion dollars in 2003.

Oxycodone is a highly addictive drug. It has much the same properties as heroin. Oxycodone became a popular recreational drug. Opioid analgesics are dangerous when not used under professional guidance. Data from the national tabulation of drug-related deaths from a sample of medical emergencies (DAWN-data) indicated that prescription opioids were the leading cause of drug-related deaths during recent years. Alcohol-in-combination was also a leading cause of death. The prescribed, "legal" drugs killed more people than illegally used drugs such as heroin and cocaine.

I (Larry) tested theories about how the effects of drugs such as morphine, (i.e., opioids) might be related to AAA. Our tests, all involving rats, indicated that methadone, morphine and related opioids enhanced rats' intake of alcoholic beverages. In other words, the data supported the idea that opioids in general might enhance appetite for alcoholic beverages (more to say about this later). An implication of that conclusion is that people who took prescription pain-killers with active ingredients such as oxycodone and acetaminophen would be prone to drink more alcoholic beverages than otherwise. Ethanol in combination with acetaminophen is toxic to livers.

Researcher Laura M. Garnier of the Center for Substance Abuse Research, University of Maryland, with her colleagues surveyed three groups of students:[14]

Concurrent users of opioids and alcohol,

Users of both kinds of agents, but currently not doing opioids (previous users) and

No use of opioids, alcohol users only.

They asked the students how much they drank. The prediction from the studies with rats is that those who were taking both opioids (primarily prescription pain-killers) would drink more than the other two groups.

Here are their tabulations for number of drinks on a drinking day:

Concurrent users = 7.5

Previous users of opioids = 5.8

Alcohol users only = 5.2.

Here are tabulations for number of drinks in the previous six months before the survey:

Concurrent users = 588

Previous users of opioids = 265

Alcohol users only = 191.

The statistics indicate that none of the differences among the groups can be accounted for by chance. These data support the conclusion that taking opioids enhances an appetite for alcoholic beverages.

The shocking part of this study was not tabulated by the investigators. If the students were taking prescription pain-killers that were a combination of opioid and acetaminophen (and they probably were), the students who were taking both were probably incurring liver damage.

Imagine a worker who has wrenched her back and is in pain. She is a habitual drinker, usually stopping off after work to have a few cocktails with her buddies. She goes to the doctor and complains about her sore back and states she needs to get back to work. The doctor prescribes one of the pain-killers that have both oxycodone and acetaminophen. The drugs reduce the pain. She resumes her work and her usual routine of drinking after work. She, however, drinks more than usual. The combined toxicity of ethanol and acetaminophen is causing liver damage. The poor woman does not know what is hitting her.

Yet another Reason Not to Drink

Based on previous research using lab animals, an experiment involving only a few adults (11 men and 14 women plus controls) provides some novel and disturbing results. The experimenters tested the idea that a single binge drinking episode reduced the effectiveness of the gut to keep bacteria in the gut.[15] Social drinkers took enough ethanol (vodka in fruit juice) to produce sufficient blood alcohol concentration (BAC) to be just greater than the legal limit to drive in the USA at a half hour to two hours after their drinking. As expected, although the adults weighted nearly the same and drank the same amounts, the BAC of the women was greater than the men. They measured indices of bacteria in the adults' blood periodically after drinking the alcoholic beverage. They found statistically significant increases in numbers of bacteria just after drinking (1 to 4 hours after) and even 24 hours afterwards. As expected given an increase in circulating bacteria, they found increases in immune responses as well to counter the increase in bacteria. Stated another way, ethanol reduced the ability of the drinkers' guts to keep gut-bacteria from getting into the blood. The adverse effect was greater in women than men.

The novel results showing that binge-like drinking increased circulating bacteria in humans has a number of limitations (e.g., small number of subjects, limitations of the measures to truly count the numbers of circulating bacteria), but nevertheless has potentially important implications. We knew before these results that habitual binge drinking was clearly associated with a wide array of signs of poor health (e.g., increases in liver disease and, of course, decreased ability to cope with the daily demands of living). Consider this: If a young woman has developed a life-style of partying on the weekends and binge drinking she may *in effect* regularly (or even every so often) inject bacteria into her blood stream. Her immune system reacts and keeps her from being immediately sick, but a hyperactive immune system is known to be unhealthy, that is, produces a stress reaction. In brief, we knew before this study that binge drinkers had increased signs of stress (as indexed by measures of stress hormones). A gut that leaks bacteria could be a source of stress. Chronic stress, in turn, is known to be associated with a wide variety of ill effects including generally not feeling well and, when extreme, damage to the brain.

We have for a long time known that regularly getting intoxicated (drunk, wasted, high) was problematic. This new study may indicate that drinking may increase the number of toxins that a body has to contend with. Also, there is a chance that bacteria in food that is usually controlled in the gut may not be easily controlled in the blood (e.g., some bacteria in the gut control other bacteria in the gut). Notice how becoming sick due to increased bacteria in the blood is never associated with the drinking during last Friday's party (why should you, the study showing the effect was just published). Our thinking may attribute the sickness to bad luck, not washing hands sufficiently or catching our co-workers' sickness. O.K., O.K., it is just one more reason not to develop the habit of binge drinking. And, potentially, just one more reason young women shouldn't regularly drink alcoholic beverages.

The Alcoholic Is Often Malnourished.

The calories in alcoholic beverages often provide a signal that enough has been eaten; hence healthful food is not eaten in sufficient amounts. Also, the general life-style of the typical alcoholic is not conducive to maintaining good nutrition.

In addition to generally unhealthy eating habits of alcoholics, there is a specific problem. Alcohol impairs absorption of thiamin (vitamin B_1) and hastens its excretion. Thiamin deficiency leads to diseases such as beriberi/Wernicke's encephalopathy. Wernicke's enceph-alopathy is manifest by confusion, ataxia, and visual problems.[16] The treatment of Wernicke's encephalopathy is large doses of thiamin. If, however, Wernicke's encephalopathy is left untreated, it can result in death; and if not death, then Wernicke-Korsakoff syndrome in 85% of survivors. Wernicke-Korsakoff syndrome is manifest as memory loss, both memories of the past as well as ability to remember new information. Most individuals are so handicapped that they cannot care for themselves and need to be institutionalized. Although there is minor recovery of memory in some individuals with the passage of time, once memory is lost it usually does not return. The memory loss follows from nearly the complete destruction of areas of the subcortical forebrain that are critical to memory, for example, the mammillary bodies.

Wernicke's encephalopathy and Wernicke-Korsakoff syndrome are the extreme manifestations of general malnutrition and specifically thiamine deficiency. It has become increasing clear that thiamine deficiency is considerably more common among drinkers who do not yet meet the formal diagnosis of AAA. Mild thiamine deficiency can lead to mild cognitive dysfunction.

Sleep

Ethanol, barbiturates and benzodiazepines all interfere with a satisfactory period of sleep. Ironically, ethanol, barbiturates and benzodiazepines have each, at one time, been touted as a treatment for insomnia. Currently, barbiturates are seldom used as sleeping aids. Benzodiazepines are a class of drugs that enhance the effects of the brain's major inhibitory neurotransmitter. Valium and Librium are both benzodiazepines. Currently, some of the widely advertised drugs for insomnia are also benzodiazepines or work at the same receptors in the brain as benzodiazepines. How can it be that drugs for insomnia are also drugs that interfere with a good night's sleep?

Until the 1950s, there had been very little scientific study of sleep. There was, of course, a considerable amount written about sleep and dreams. The ability to record the electrical signals of the brain from electrodes placed on the scalp (electroencephalography, i.e., EEG) provided a way of studying some features of brain activity. EEGs were first recorded in 1924 and were refined subsequently until they became a widely used tool for noninvasively studying some features of brain activity. Distinct patterns of activity made manifest by EEG recordings are associated, respectively, with being awake, doing concentrated mental activity (such as arithmetic), and sleep, as well as seizures, coma, brain-trauma, and death (no EEG activity).

In the study of sleep, a major breakthrough was achieved with the publication of a seminal article in *Science*, 1953.[17] The scientist who made the discovery was Eugene Aserinsky who used his son Armond as the subject. Aserinsky was working in the laboratory of Nathaniel Kleitman, a scientist recognized as the father of sleep research. Aserinsky recorded the EEGs of his son periodically throughout the night. He noticed that there were periods during the night when the EEGs of his son were similar to the EEGs of being awake, yet his son was observably still asleep. Because of the apparent contradiction between what the EEG indicated and his son's apparent deep sleep, the phenomenon has been called paradoxical sleep. Other things were also noticed: (a) when the EEGs indicated wakefulness during apparent sleep there was also rapid eye movements (REM), and (b) when individuals were awakened while showing paradoxical sleep, they indicated that they were dreaming.

Further study by the discoverers of paradoxical sleep, as well as others, has led to the conclusion that sleep has two phases: rapid eye movement sleep (REM sleep) and non REM sleep. REM sleep is associated with dreaming; non REM sleep is not. It was discovered that REM sleep occurred periodically throughout the night, every night. We are typically not consciously aware of the dreams of REM sleep during a good night's sleep. We only become aware of a dream when we are awakened during a REM episode.

Another surprising, and important, discovery was that REM sleep was essential to ordinary functioning of the brain during wakefulness. When both laboratory animals and humans were deprived of REM sleep, there were serious consequences. Of course, when it became apparent that humans suffered, the experiments ended. Further study with animals has confirmed that REM sleep is necessary for optimal functioning. Reduced REM sleep has been associated with cognitive decline, depression, and signs of serious stress. Deprivation of all sleep is clearly detrimental. Before modern research, the idea that REM sleep was essential for brain-health was not recognized.

The topic of sleep deprivation usually brings to the fore: How much sleep is optimal? It depends on a number of variables, such as whether the sleep time is at night or during the day. The easiest answer, however, is straightforward. If one awakens, feels refreshed and apparently ready to start the day, then the appropriate amount and quality of sleep has been achieved regardless of the hours of sleep which can be somewhat short (as little as 5 hours) or longer (say 9 or somewhat more hours).

When there is sleep deprivation, including REM sleep deprivation, there is marked sleepiness and a tendency once asleep for REM sleep to be pronounced. As probably everyone has experienced, prolonged sleep deprivation produces a powerful urge to sleep and, perhaps, not as apparent, to dream.

Ethanol, barbiturates and benzodiazepines all suppress REM sleep. The combination of drinking alcoholic beverages before starting to sleep and having only a brief period of sleep produces deprivation of REM sleep. Reduced REM of a single night induces sleepiness throughout the day, feeling tired and cognitive slowness. Some modern sleep aids that act as benzodiazepines are metabolized rather quickly so that they are not in the system throughout an eight hour period of sleep. Consequently, they allow dreaming toward the late part of the sleep period. People whose work demands interruption of sleep and who drink before sleeping or use sleeping pills may awaken with little or no REM sleep and not be in the best condition to carry out demanding work (think doctors and emergency workers).

It is clear: a restful night's sleep is a good circumstance. Drinking alcoholic beverages is often antithetical to a restful night's sleep despite the fact that drinking often induces a tendency to want to start sleeping.

This brief discussion of sleep and dreams is background for adding to the topic of alcoholic beverages in combination with drugs. Antidepressant drugs are known to affect sleep.[18] Many of the drugs prescribed as medicines for insomnia can reduce REM sleep. Selective serotonin reuptake inhibitors, the most commonly prescribed antidepressants, tend to reduce REM sleep.

We guess it goes without saying, but we must: sleep deprived, dream deprived, drunken people are accident prone.

Depression[19]

Depression and alcoholism often occur together. While trying to cope with the ordinary chores of daily living, a woman can be anxious, depressed and alcoholic all at the same time. As easily inferred, this presents problems that are difficult, but surely not impossible, to solve. About half of the time depression occurs before alcoholism and about half of the time alcoholism occurs before depression.[20]

Generally speaking, depression is sort-of-the opposite of happiness. When things are generally going well, happiness (being satisfied with how things are going) is the normal emotional tone of everyday living.[21] Depression, however, is a deviation from the ordinary and is surely not a preferred state.[22]

Depression is characterized as a reduced capacity to experience pleasure.[22] This diminished capacity is accompanied by a number of other characteristics such as being sad, lethargic, pessimistic and often irritable. A deeply depressed person is very sad, views the world with negativity, is pessimistic and views nearly all decisions as being a choice between awful and terrible.

A major textbook on psychiatry included in its description of depression the following: "A majority of patients with major depression look lifeless, boring, or dull, rather than sad and crying" (Maxmen & Ward, 1995, p 207).[23] Other common symptoms include difficulty concentrating and excessive fatigue. The depressed person seems to have considerable loss of cognitive ability; however, cognitive ability is restored with the lifting of depression.

The deeply depressed person might be diagnosed as having a major depressive disorder (MDD). In prosperous nations, MDD is a common disorder. In the USA, it is estimated that about 7% of the adult and near adult population meets the criteria for MDD at any one time.

Women represent about 70% of those diagnosed with MDD.[24] Suicide and suicide attempts are serious, but rare, manifestations of MDD.[24]

For decades, the standard treatment for depression was the prescription of an antidepressant drug, e.g., Prozac or Zoloft. There are many antidepressants sold in prosperous nations. Despite the popularity of this treatment, it is only marginally effective.[25] Nearly all antidepressants get about the same "cure-rate" (indexed by a temporary lifting of depression).[25,26] Because episodes of MDD have a tendency to get better with the passage of time regardless of whether treated or not, it is difficult to tell if an antidepressant induced the better mood or the patient enlisted whatever reserves they had to change for the better. Antidepressants have different side-effect profiles.[26] Consequently, if anti-depressants are prescribed, it is prudent to prescribe with side-effects in mind. For example, some antidepressants diminish interest in sexuality whereas others increase risk of weight gain and diabetes. Obviously, patients reporting that their worry and depression is related to diminished sexuality, some antidepressants might make the patients' problems worse.

Interestingly, beginning an exercise program seems to be a reasonable treatment for depressed persons, particularly for those who have not developed a habit of regular exercise.[27] In general, it seems that when harsh life events (e.g., being unemployed) and harsh living conditions (e.g., loneliness) change for the better, many episodes of depression change for the better.[28] Both alcoholism and depression dampen one's ability to cope and work toward reducing the some of the harshness that might have been instrumental in inducing depression.

Although drinking alcoholic beverages might occasionally relieve depression for a brief period, it is clear that a habit of hazardous drinking is not a remedy for depression (actually, will likely make things worse).[29] Taking antidepressant-drugs, does not usually reduce the instances of hazardous drinking.[30] When alcoholism and depression occur together, it makes sense to focus on treating alcoholism. When hazardous drinking is suspended, livers and brains begin to heal and that healing may also be a setting condition for engaging in coping behaviors which, in turn, will lift how one feels about life in general.[31]

Cognitive behavioral therapy, when done in ways shown to be effective, are helpful with both alcoholism and depression (more on that later).[32]

AAA and Cognition

The most problematic toxic event associated with drinking alcoholic beverage is ethanol's effects on the brain. The effects are manifest by reduced ability to think well and that makes it difficult to handle all sorts of challenges. As doses increase during a single session of drinking, the toxicity to brain is manifest as muddled thinking, inability to talk well, walk well, and eventually to think at all (coma) and even to breathe. The toxic effects of a single session of drinking are often problematic, for example, accidents of all kinds (car accidents, boating accidents, falling asleep with a burning cigarette and causing a fire, falling down stairs, etc.).

The first sign of toxicity associated with drinking is the interference with ability to engage abstract thinking involved with planning. A manifestation of reduction in planning is that the intoxicated individual tends to be living in the moment which, in turn, makes her particularly susceptible to the events of the moment. Unfortunately, the reduced ability to think well is usually not apparent to the drinker, particularly when the dose of ethanol is relatively small. The signs that are least likely to be affected by mild toxicity are engrained habits such as walking without staggering. If one staggers while walking due to recent intake of alcohol, almost assuredly that person will not be capable of well-reasoned, abstract thinking.

In discussions of theories of alcoholism (a later topic), we address why a known toxin is taken repeatedly. In brief, ethanol produces multiple effects in the brain, some of which are related to its toxic effects and some of which produce rewarding effects (i.e., pleasant effects). The toxic effects are a side-effect. The rewarding effects are the desired effects. To avoid this kind of thinking to be more than a statement of the obvious (people do not drink for the bad things, but drink for the good things), it is necessary to provide some specificity: for example, specifying how ethanol's effects can be rewarding.

The value of any theory specifying how ethanol's effects reinforce ethanol's intake is assessed by it functionality. A valuable theory provides knowledge of how to improve the prevention and treatment of AAA. Before further discussion of theories of AAA and their practicalities, let us consider the possibility that the habit of drinking can lead to enduring cognitive decline. If cognitive decline is a common characteristic of the habit of drinking to intoxication, then perhaps that should be taken into account as theories of AAA are developed.

It is obvious that a small woman who has just had three martinis (probably 3 or more ounces of ethanol) during the previous two hours will show signs of intoxication that includes slurred speech and a reduction in ability to walk or to drive a car. In this section, the topic is not acute toxicity, but chronic effects. Does getting drunk regularly induce permanent brain damage? The answer is surely *yes*, for example, when it contributes to a thiamine-deficiency (see above). The interest here, however, is with the possibility of brain damage long before the most obvious brain damage that is characteristic of the aged, skid-row alcoholic who has trouble remembering when he had his last job.

Measuring cognitive ability began in earnest with the development of the classic intelligence tests (circa 1916). Since the first tests, psychologists have continually refined their measurements of cognitive ability and currently there are well-designed tests for measuring a number of facets of cognition. An interesting innovation of recent years is the development of safe ways of scanning the brain to get pictures of the detailed anatomy and functioning of the brain while people do various things. The modern brain scanning technology is even able to discern which areas of the brain are more active than other areas when people are doing various cognitive tasks. Current psychological tests of cognitive ability and the analysis of the brain scans are congruent with one another; for example, when the tests show a deficit in ability to plan ahead (an executive function) there are signs of malfunctioning in the part of the brain that has been found to be involved in ability to plan (e.g., frontal cortex).

Among those patients who have been diagnosed with alcohol use disorder (i.e., having problems associated with drinking) over half of them show signs of reduced cognitive ability compared to others that are similar to them except they drink little or none. Also, there are longitudinal studies in which the same persons' cognitive ability has been measured before the development of a habit of drinking and shortly after they stopped drinking and a long time after they have stopped drinking. From these kinds of studies, evidence converges to support the conclusion that regularly drinking alcoholic beverages is a risk factor for reduced cognitive ability that is manifest weeks, months or even years after the last drink.

We have said two things that may appear to be contradictory. We said alcohol-induced cognitive decline is often subtle and yet can be dramatic. The decline can be subtle in the sense that it is not obvious when merely chatting with an alcoholic when she is sober. The milder forms of cognitive decline do not affect such things as a reduction in vocabulary or the carrying out of routine activities. Further, the decline in ability accumulates slowly and is easily attributable to merely getting older or merely having a bad day. Differences in cognitive ability become apparent when those with a history of alcoholism are asked to solve problems, whether they are problems presented on psychological tests or problems faced with everyday living.

The late Professor Oscar A. Parsons working at the Oklahoma Center for Alcohol and Drug-related Studies spent decades studying the possibility of neurocognitive deficits in sober alcoholics (no longer drinking). Here is a summary of his findings: "both male and female adult alcoholics-- compared with peer nonalcoholic controls--have deficits on tests of learning, memory, abstracting, problem-solving, perceptual analysis and synthesis, speed of information processing, and efficiency. The deficits are equivalent to those found in patients with known brain dysfunction of a mild to moderate nature. Attempts to identify factors other than alcoholism to account for these differences have been unsuccessful. The deficits appear to remit slowly over 4 to 5 years. ... Results of recent studies support the hypothesis of a continuum of neurocognitive deficits ranging from the severe deficits found in Korsakoff patients to moderate deficits found in alcoholics and moderate to mild deficits in heavy social drinkers (more than 21 drinks/week)" (Parsons, 1998, p 954).[34]

A recent study of the effects of alcohol in those being treated for alcoholism indicates that the greater the damage to the structure and function of the brain, the greater tendency to relapse back into drinking. The authors concluded "...relapsers displayed increased brain atrophy in brain areas associated with error monitoring and behavioral control;" namely, in the "...bilateral orbitofrontal cortex and in the right medial prefrontal and anterior cingulate cortex, compared with healthy controls and patients who remained abstinent" (Beck et al., 2012, p 842).[35]

As mentioned during the brief discussions of ethanol's effects in terms of diseases of the liver and malnutrition, liver-malfunction and malnutrition have effects that can do serious harm to brain functioning that can be manifest in great loss of cognitive ability. There is a good chance that mild brain damage occurs with levels of intake that are considered safe but may induce mild problems such as malnutrition. It follows that a well-planned therapy centered about treating AAA should take into account how to prevent further brain damage and when damage has occurred how to restore brain functioning. Topics explored subsequently.

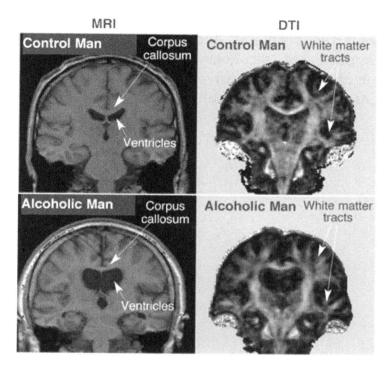

Figure. 5.2. Pictures of the brain via brain scans of a 61-year-old healthy man (upper images) and a 60-year-old alcoholic man (lower images). The high-resolution MRI slices (left column of picture) provide a faithful representation of the anatomy of the brain. The right column involves a procedure that highlights the white matter of brain. Note on the MRI the thinner corpus callosum displaced upward by enlarged ventricles and, on right column, less well delineated white matter tracts in the alcoholic man compared with the healthy man. Source: Rosenbloom, M., Sullivan, E.V. & Pfefferbaum, A. Using magnetic resonance imaging and diffusion tensor imaging to assess brain damage in alcoholics. *Alcohol Research & Health* 27(2):146–152, 2003.

Summary of the Problem

Alcoholic beverages are no ordinary commodity. They are toxic when taken in large amounts or taken often. They have the capability of inducing a powerful habit of drinking and the tendency, across a history of drinking, to drink more and more. The habit of drinking toxic amounts of alcoholic beverages is related to a wide variety of health problems and considerable asocial behavior. These basics

113

have been known for thousands of years. The issue is how to prevent the problems and when the habit of drinking toxic amounts of alcoholic beverages has become so powerful that it is clearly harmful, how to treat the emergent state called alcoholism. These are the next topics.

Chapter 6: Treatment and Prevention of AAA

We have just devoted a considerable number of pages to describing the dire consequences of drinking too much, too often. The contents could have been expanded considerably. Without that further expansion, we hope that it has become clearer that (a) ethanol, the active ingredient in alcoholic beverages, is dose-relatedly a toxic substance and (b) hence, alcoholic beverages are not ordinary commodities. We have not devoted much content to discussing why alcoholic beverages are widely used by many people despite the fact that their use is associated with a wide variety of really horrible consequences (think, again, cirrhosis of the liver, Korsakoff syndrome, murder, mayhem, mental retardation, etc.).

Given that AAA are prevalent and often have dire consequences, it just makes sense to prevent and treat AAA. The bad news: Because the problems are extensive and reoccurring, it is apparent that on both a personal a societal level, the prevention and treatment of alcoholism is not being done well. Surely, the treatment and prevention of AAA is not being done well enough and there is plenty room for improvement. The good news: new knowledge, if applied, can improve the treatment of alcoholism.

If first attempts to treat any problem do not succeed, then it makes sense to get more detailed knowledge about the problem (do research, the more systematic the better). One might study those who have become alcoholic in reference to those who have not. One might get some solid knowledge of how often and when potential treatments fail. Theories might be developed to explain the failures and limited successes. One might address the problem, by trying various treatments on a small scale, particularly if the problem is extensive (i.e., by doing experiments, by making models). This common sense approach to problem solving was made more detailed and explicit during the Age of Enlightenment with the development of modern scientific research. This straight forward approach to solving difficult problems can be applied to solving the issues of AAA and it has been.

Treating Alcoholism; Less than Satisfactory Approaches

We surmise that the first attempts at treating alcoholism were merely to tell the alcoholic to stop drinking to intoxication. When mere advice didn't work (and often it didn't and does not), other steps were taken. Social norms were established that threatened reprisals or direct punishment if caught being drunk. If mild punishments didn't work, often the harshness of the punishments was increased. History has taught that preaching, teaching about the bad consequences of the habit of drinking, social ostracism, and often harsh punishment are at best marginally effective. For example, jailing the alcoholic for being drunk and creating mayhem, of course, did stop drinking while in jail; but shortly after being released, drinking often resumed at the same pace as before being jailed with similar consequences. Also, it became apparent that some punishments had undesirable consequences. For example, jailing the major wage earner of a family for being drunk and causing trouble surely punished the drinker, but also might have propelled the drinker's family into poverty.

In a society in which drinking is common, AAA frequently emerges. Various practices are established to blunt the harsh consequences. Some practices are codified in Law. Some laws and their enforcement produce some beneficial effects whereas others seem to make the problems worse. Unfortunately, often both kinds remain on the books hence producing their own kind of confusion and mayhem.[1]

Recall Prohibition in the United States Failed.

When many attempts at resolving the problem fail or the attempts have undesirable consequences, the conclusion is often derived to prohibit the production and sale of alcoholic beverages. There are societies that have been rather successful in establishing prohibition and there are societies that have not been successful. The following sections mention some treatments that have been tried post WWII that have not been successful (our society induces alcoholism, but is only marginally able to successfully treat it).

Harm Reduction Strategies

From time to time, the idea arose that it was nearly impossible to get large numbers of alcoholics to become abstinent; consequently, another approach might be successful. The idea was to teach the alcoholic or at least the heavy social drinker to drink at low risk levels, say no more than 3 drinks on a day of drinking (2 drinks for women) and not drinking every day. The idea was that we should try to reduce the harm rather than being rigid about striving for abstinence which may be particularly difficult in a culture that promotes drinking.[2] There are surely people that have had an early episode of hazardous drinking that have stopped hazardous drinking, but have sustained a habit of daily drinking in small amounts without marked, if any, difficulty.[3]

Treatments attempting to get alcoholics to modify their drinking to nonhazardous levels have occasionally been shown to be helpful; however, when applied on a larger scale they almost always are not. Because drinking alcohol seems to reinstate much of the habit of drinking too much, too often, teaching moderation for those with strong habits of excessive drinking only sets the stage for being highly tempted to drink "more than a few." There is, of course, no problem with teaching the virtues of temperance and no problem with reducing harm. Nevertheless, for an individual alcoholic, the goal of temperance may be more difficult to achieve than total abstinence.

Punishment by Drugs

Disulfiram (brand name: Antabuse) produces illness when alcoholic beverages are ingested. Antabuse and similar "punishing" drugs have been used as treatment.[4] The idea was that bringing punishment close to the act of drinking

117

would discourage drinking. It does as long as the conditions for punishment are in place, i.e., when the alcoholic has taken the drug. These drugs are not effective medicines for treating relapse. Typically, alcoholics just stop taking the drugs and return to drinking. Also, these drugs have some serious side-effects.

Prolonged Inpatient Treatment

If one holds that alcoholism is a disease and that the disease is manifest by withdrawal signs and symptoms, it just makes sense to conclude that controlling withdrawal would go a long way toward curing AAA. Given this kind of thinking, the most prevalent treatment program post WW II was a 28-day stay in a clinic in which the alcoholic was withdrawn from alcohol, and provided rest and good nutrition.[5] After the most serious withdrawal symptoms, group therapy was often programmed. During the group sessions, personal problems were discussed and patients were cajoled into realizing that their drinking was clearly problematic. Patients usually promised, in front of others, to reform, to stay sober. Usually, patients were urged to join Alcoholics Anonymous (AA), a social support group, subsequent to their 28-day period of institutional care.

AA's web-site describes AA as a "… fellowship of men and women who share their experience, strength and hope with each other that they may solve their common problem and help others to recover from alcoholism. The only requirement for membership is a desire to stop drinking. There are no dues or fees for AA membership; we are self-supporting through our own contributions. AA is not allied with any sect, denomination, politics, organization or institution; does not wish to engage in any controversy, neither endorses nor opposes any causes." AA's main purpose is for its participants "to stay sober and help other alcoholics to achieve sobriety (quotations from the Web site: www.aa.org)." A feature of AA is frequent meetings during which individuals support each other in their quest to sustain sobriety and share their experiences.

We urge anyone who wishes to know more about AA to go to AA's web site by typing AA into any search engine. The site is professionally well-done and very informative. Alcoholics that recover with the help of AA are strong advocates for AA and its philosophy.

Although AA claims to not to have a fixed theoretical bent, it does have a number of core beliefs. AA clearly subscribes to a disease model of alcoholism. AA clearly subscribes to the idea that it is very difficult for the alcoholic to quit drinking and that an alcoholic needs help in order to remain sober. Participants in AA believe that their social group provides substantive help and they also believe that a spiritual conversion is very helpful.

The approach just outlined was and is still common. Its underlying rationale focuses on the idea that the behaviors of drinking provide some sort of relief, most notably relief from discomforts of withdrawal and relief from stress.

Alcohol as a Medicine for Anxiety

During the decades following WW II, the prevalent idea was that alcohol-intake provided relief: relief from withdrawal sickness and relief from anxiety, depression and stress.[6] Onset of relief is the circumstance for negative reinforcement (negative reinforcement is not the same as punishment). Negative reinforcement increases the probability of the behavior associated with *relief*. The theory was that drinking provided relief from prevailing negative emotions such as anxiety, guilt and fear. The relief reinforced the act of drinking. There was also the idea that certain persons had a deficiency of some sort (perhaps, a chemical imbalance) for which alcohol's effects provided some remediation and such relief reinforced the act of drinking.

If a woman regularly reduced her prevailing anxiety by taking alcohol and thereby reinforced the act of drinking, it follows, according to some theorizing, that if the source of her anxiety was treated that she would not be motivated to drink. Valium and Librium were highly popular treatments for anxiety from 1969 to 1982 during which time they were called minor tranquillizers (later labeled anxiolytic agents or antianxiety drugs). They were and are prescribed drugs. They were prescribed to persons drinking too much, too often with the idea that their anxiety was a cause of their drinking.

Despite the fact that Valium and Librium were sold to many, many people to treat their anxiety and made drug companies billions, Valium, Librium and similar drugs are not very good antianxiety medicines. Their use did dampen anxiety in the short-term, but people did not learn to cope with their prevailing anxiety while receiving the drugs.[7] Further, the drugs have considerable addictive potential. Even further, they have a poor side-effect profile, including hindering processes associated with forming memories.

In accordance with the idea that anxiety might be the reason people drank extensively, Valium and Librium were given to individuals as medicines for alcoholism. Unfortunately, the results were that individuals developed the habit of taking the drugs as well as sustaining their drinking.

Research showed that Valium and similar drugs (benzodiazepines) actually mimic the effects of ethanol.[8] To put it into the bluntest terms: taking Valium is nearly the equivalent of taking ethanol nearly constantly (kind-a-like a Martini drip). Both act at receptors in the brain that induce inhibition in neurons leading to behavioral inhibition and a reduced responsiveness to usually stimulating events. Because ethanol and Valium both act at similar receptors, Valium is a medicine to blunt the effects of withdrawal from alcohol. Because both Valium-like drugs and ethanol (in an alcoholic's desired doses) increase inhibitory tone of many neurons, they both disrupt coordination and, when used together, further hinder the ability to drive a car (or a truck, a train, an airplane, a crane, a motorcycle, a bicycle, etc.).

Many of the advertisements designed to get doctors to prescribe Valium-like drugs to treat anxiety featured women. They often dismissed women's complaints with the indication that a little minor tranquillizer would calm "the little women" down. Some dubbed tranquillizers as "mother's little helper." If you wish to outrage a feminist, show her (or him) some older advertisements in medical journals pushing Valium or Librium to control the angst of frustrated housewives. In brief, they are demeaning.

Valium-like drugs surely didn't help individuals remain sober. If an individual did manage a period of sobriety, these drugs may have aided and abetted a return to habitual drinking. A consequence of the failure of Valium-like drugs to help the alcoholic was a distrust of the idea that a drug, any drug, can help an alcoholic remain sober.

Psychotherapies designed to treat a prevailing anxiety, or other supposedly under lying sources of a problem for which ethanol was thought to quell, were also used as treatments for AAA. They did not achieve success in sustaining abstinence.

A Summary of Less-Than-Optimal Treatments

The common practice of providing an extended period to recover from withdrawal, getting counseling in a clinic-like setting and then becoming associated with AA or another social support group just did not and does not deliver a high rate of success. Formal treatments, based on the prevailing theories, were no more successful, on average, than self-treatments.

The following figure is a summary of virtually all treatment programs based in theories of alcoholism that were prominent during the period following World War II until recently. The figure depicts the average outcome.[9]

With the end of treatment, 100% of those treated are abstinent. Within a few months, however, the vast majority of treated alcoholics returned to drinking at pre-treatment levels. The propensity to relapse back into drinking has led to the definition of alcoholism as a chronically relapsing disease. The persons in charge of alcoholism treatment programs were and are well-aware of this circumstance and proclaim that this outcome is similar to treatments for obesity and drug abuse as well as adherence to treatments for other chronic conditions such as hypertension and Type II diabetes. This is true; treatments for these chronic conditions are generally problematic as well.[10]

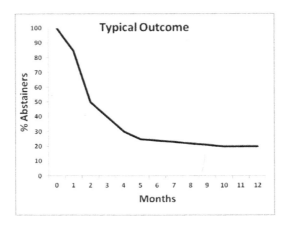

Figure 6.1. The figure depicts a summary of the typical outcome of treatment programs for AAA.[11] At the end of treatment (point zero), one can expect 100% of the individuals to be abstaining from drinking. Within the first few months post-treatment, most individuals will resume drinking at pre-treatment levels. At the end of a year, only about 20% of individuals will be abstaining from drinking.

The data of Figure 6.1 is an average outcome. Some treatment programs got better results; others got worse. What accounts for these differences? First, the following variables did not (and do not) seem to make a difference. It made little difference whether the treatment programs were long or short. It made little difference whether most of the treatment was in special clinics or elsewhere. It made little difference which theory of alcoholism guided a treatment. It made little difference whether the staff was professionally trained or not so well-trained.

What did (and does) make a difference in treatment outcomes? It was (and is) the characteristics of the patients.

When the individuals were (a) being treated for the first time, (b) married or had a significant other being supportive, and (c) were employed, the outcome was often 50% to 60% achieving prolonged abstinence. When the individuals being treated had nearly the opposite characteristics, that is, (a) having had many treatments before the one in question, (b) living alone or having no strong social support, and (c) being frequently unemployed, the rate of achieving abstinence was often about 5% or less. Related to the listed characteristics associated with frequent relapses is the severity of the alcoholism.[12]

There are implications associated with the tabulations of treatment-outcomes. For example, regardless of the type of treatment, it is better to treat sooner rather than later. Relatedly, treatments are more likely to be successful if they intervene while the individual is still generally healthy and functioning reasonably well. Treating those still employed and in a supportive relationship will help about 50% to maintain sobriety for a prolonged period. Withholding treatment (or providing only marginal treatment) until the alcoholic becomes chronically unemployed and has alienated significant others will likely ensure that treatment will be followed by relapse to hazardous drinking.

There is an idea floating around programs that treatments do not work until the individual has "hit bottom" (has become severely debilitated). Holding to that idea is to nearly ensure a program's failure (not an optimistic outlook, yet optimism is probably essential) and may sacrifice the heavy social drinker to considerable misery. Another implication is that our knowledge was, and perhaps still is, not sufficient to guide gradual improvements. Consequently, often treatments continue their standard procedures with the hope that something good will happen while knowing that many of their treated clients will relapse to hazardous levels of drinking.

Toward More Successful Treatments

When research began to tabulate the success rates of the prevailing treatments for alcoholism, it became clear that an alcoholic's history often featured relapse after relapse. The realization that the professional community was nearly incapable of helping prevent relapse should have made prevention a paramount goal. Also, it makes the development of new theories and practices a priority.

Before discussing recent developments, a couple of comments are in order. The idea that Valium and the like are tranquillizers and they act on the same receptors as ethanol led some people to become convinced that ethanol was also a minor tranquillizer. You can often read and hear: alcohol is the oldest and most popular tranquillizer. Neither ethanol nor benzodiazepines are effective tranquillizers. They might quell some anxiety temporarily, but they do not lead to a more contented life-style. Further, aggressive drunks just do not appear tranquil.

Currently, many alcoholics entering treatment are also using other addictive drugs. Drug abuse involving alcoholic beverages is more difficult to treat than alcoholism itself.

Treatment for AAA is a two step process. To begin a life-style of abstinence, the first step, obviously, is to stop drinking. Stopping drinking induces withdrawal signs and symptoms which can be very uncomfortable and even dangerous. Among those with severe alcoholism, withdrawal can even produce fatal conditions. So, the first step toward a life-style without drinking is the management of withdrawal. Those without severe alcoholism often manage withdrawal without professional help. However, those with severe and protracted alcoholism need professional help during the first days of abstinence. After the management of withdrawal conditions, the next step is to help the alcoholic from relapsing back into drinking.

Treatment of Withdrawal

In the past, an alcoholic undergoing withdrawal might go to a refuge such as those maintained by the Salvation Army where he might be treated by a glass of vodka. He might also get some preaching and advice to turn to God and reform. Currently, the alcoholic going into serious withdrawal is apt to wind up in a hospital emergency room, a psychiatric receiving center or a crisis center that specializing in treating alcohol and recreational drug use. When there is a plan to stop drinking, one might go to into one of the special clinics designed to treat alcohol and drug abuse (colloquially, enter "Rehab").

The main treatment for withdrawal from alcohol is apt to be a prescription of a benzodiazepine (e.g., Valium or Librium or a modern version of such) which functions much like a glass of vodka but can be more lasting. Also, under medical management, complications that might arise (e.g., those associated with seizures) can be handled more readily.[13]

Delirium Tremens (DTs) is a serious manifestation of withdrawal from habitual drinking. Prior to medical management, the death rate due to DTs was about 35%; but with medical management, it is currently only about 7 to 3%.[14] An extraordinary advance to help manage DTs is the discovery that results from rather simple blood tests are very good at predicting whose withdrawal might advance to DTs.[15]

During the days of withdrawal, particularly intense withdrawal, the patient is not in a favorable position to profit from educational and psychosocial therapies; cognition is seriously impaired. After the acute effects of withdrawal, some rest and good nutrition, treatment to prevent relapse can begin. Fortunately, given some days of rest and good nutrition (probably should include mega doses of thiamine), cognitive abilities start to return to pre-withdrawal levels. The severity of withdrawal and degree of cognitive decline is dose-related in terms of both duration of drinking and extent of the hazardous drinking. A return to more normal levels of cognitive ability occurs within a week or two; treatment for relapse prevention can then and should begin. Although cognition is more normal within a few weeks of abstinence and is stable enough to begin psychotherapy, it is probably not nearly at an optimal level.

With continued abstinence (we may be talking about years here), there is a good chance of complete recovery of cognitive skills. Among patients that smoke cigarettes, degraded cognition appears to linger and linger even with continued abstinence from alcohol.[16]

Relapse Prevention

If the standard for successful treatment for AAA is abstinence or near abstinence for a period of two years, unfortunately, most treatments prevalent post WW II were unsuccessful (about 20% of treated patients met the criterion and about 20% are successful without treatment)(Figure 6.1). The two-year period is the standard, because after two years, relapse into habitual drinking is highly unlikely.[3] It is unrealistic to expect that 100% of treated individuals will achieve extended abstinence. It is, however, realistic to expect that research and development with the goal of improving treatments should lead to enhanced "cure rates." Because alcoholism is prevalent, a small increment in rate of success will have a marked beneficial effect. If 70% of those being treated for AAA would achieve prolonged abstinence, we would experience an epidemic of health.

To present modern theory of AAA and the theory's practical applications, we need to discuss a number of lines of research. It may seem to the reader that a particular set of experiments is not directly applicable to developing theories of alcoholism. Each set, however, is relevant to the modern theory of addiction, including alcoholism. Further, the modern theory has a number of practical implications that have and will improve the treatment of AAA. Here are some of the topics needing elaboration:

(a) the utility of research with laboratory animals,

(b) modern learning theory,

(c) AAA and addiction to opium,

(d) laboratory animals self-administer addictive drugs,

(e) certain brain stimulation is rewarding,

(f) addictive agents activate the brain's medial forebrain bundle system,

(g) administration of naloxone (a drug that markedly reduces actions of some neurotransmitters) reveals some functions of the endogenous opioids, and

(h) opioid agonists and antagonists and drinking alcoholic beverages among lab-rats.

With this information, we can profitably discuss new theories of AAA and their implications. Usually, it is not a single experiment by a single investigator that provides the knowledge for the development of new theory; it is usually a body of research. Consequently, we are going to summarize the results of sets of experiments.

The utility of research with laboratory animals

I (Larry) spent a goodly amount of my career doing research on alcoholism. My subjects were often domestic white rats. You might well ask, "How can you study alcoholism in humans by studying rats?" Your question makes a lot of sense. No experiment involving rats is directly applicable to human's drinking problems. Even with experiments where it seems that studies with laboratory animals might have direct applicability, such as the study of alcohol-related liver disease, the results are not directly applicable to humans and their problems. Yes, rats and people are different and the contexts of their respective intakes of alcohol are extraordinarily different.

Experiments with rats are used to develop and test theories. *Theories are applicable to humans*. Modern theory of biology provides a context for studying animal subjects. We know (have well-supported theories), for example, that the livers of rats as well as nearly all mammals, including humans, work in nearly the same way. Consequently, when you read a textbook on liver-functioning you are reading the latest theory as formulated by multiple observations and experiments. The experiments providing ideas for how the liver operates sometimes even includes experiments on single cells. It is the developed theory of liver-functioning that is applicable. Developed theories of alcoholism are potentially applicable; if they are not, then further development of theory will lead to practices that have better outcomes (an article of sincere hope of scientists doing research on alcoholism).

If the results of an experiment involving laboratory subjects or humans do not comfortably fit into the prevailing theories, there are a number of possibilities. The experiment may have been done poorly. Another possibility is that the research has observed something of importance that either challenges the truth-value of the prevailing theory or provides new perspectives. The results from experiments with laboratory animals have been used to develop new theories which have a number of implications for preventing and treating alcoholism.

Modern learning theory

Modern learning theory is a well-developed area of academic psychology. Here, we are mentioning a few well-established perspectives that are particularly relevant to AAA and, in general, theories of addictions. Modern learning theory is the study of habit formation. Research has focused on two mechanisms that are critical to establishing habits: (a) positive reinforcement (processes that follow from attainment of a reward) and (b) negative reinforcement, the learning that follows when there is relief from adversity, including the adversity of negative emotions.

A focus of major theories of AAA is that the habit of drinking too much, too often was developed by way of negative reinforcement. The basic idea is that taking ethanol provides relief from adversity. It was suggested that ethanol dampened the emotions of anxiety, frustration, or depression and, therefore, served as an agent that provided a measure of relief from prevailing negativity. The relief nearly automatically strengthened the act of drinking.

Additionally, it is known that regular intake of alcoholic beverages establishes a condition that, in turn, produces withdrawal signs and symptoms. After a period of regularly taking alcoholic beverages and then stopping, there are withdrawal signs and symptoms. Early in the history of drinking, withdrawal signs can be mild but nevertheless unpleasant. A prolonged history of drinking large amounts establishes a condition that produces very unpleasant and even dangerous conditions when the now alcoholic stops taking alcohol. Taking a drink of alcohol is an antidote (a medicine) for withdrawal, hence provides relief. The idea is that drinking itself establishes an unpleasant condition with the stopping of drinking and drinking provides relief from the adversity of withdrawal. What is established is sort-of-a vicious circle: drinking produces adversity for which drinking is a remedy.

Although modern learning theory provides a model of how ethanol might induce sufficient negative reinforcement to account for AAA, it may not be a sufficient explanation to guide the treatment of AAA. There will be other perspectives introduced subsequently that may provide better (or additional) guides toward developing better treatments.

Professor B.F. Skinner was a learning theorist who maintained that it was not particularly useful to speculate about the emotions and mechanisms of positive reinforcement. It was, he contended, practical to study how various known rewards would shape behavior, i.e., how schedules of reward produced different behaviors. He developed a way of studying schedules of reward (i.e., positive reinforcers). Among his favorite subjects were domestic rats. He developed an apparatus for studying what he thought was important. He made a box with a dispenser of small bites of food. In that box, he put a lever, the depression of which activated the dispenser of food. He then put a hungry rat into the box. His first issue was how to train the rat to press the lever for food. He developed a procedure for getting the rat to press for food. After that initial training, he and his colleagues did extensive studies of how behavior changed with different ways of delivering rewards. Skinner's basic approach and his initial findings attracted considerable interest and many scientists studied the applications of what was learned about how reward could shape behavior. His apparatus became known as a Skinner box.

Skinner's findings with rats pressing for food in his apparatus was extended by studying whether the same kind of behaviors were produced when the reward was water to a thirsty rat or whether other animals, e.g., pigeons, would respond similarly to rats working for food. Colleagues also did studies with people and learned that some of the same ideas developed in Skinner boxes could be applied in many circumstances.

A major finding was that a behavior (or a class of behaviors) need not be rewarded every time for a kind behavior to be sustained. Furthermore, the reward need not be large to sustain vigorous behavior. Periodic, even minor reward can sustain vigorous behavior provided there is some reasonable possibility of a reward. For example with some training, a rat will work at lever-pressing to get food that provides less calories than the calories spent working for food. The conclusion is that if an addictive agent induces a positive emotional event that event could sustain considerable behavior even if it did so only sometimes and did so even with small increments in positive emotionality.

It was discovered that habits established by either negative reinforcement (relief from adversity) or by delivery of periodic rewards were difficult to extinguish. With negative reinforcement, if an individual successfully avoided a perceived danger, she may never know that the circumstances of previous danger were no longer dangerous. Results from the laboratory verify what has been commonly observed and experienced; entrenched habits are difficult to change.

Thousands of years ago, it was discovered that the resin of a particular poppy plant had what surely was thought to be magical properties. That resin came to be known as opium. Opium was the first medicine; it was and is useful in treating, for examples, diarrhea and pain. When the smoke of heated opium was inhaled, it produced positive emotions (for many, pleasure, euphoric feelings, and a sense of contentment). During the first years of the 1800s, a young German chemist, Friedrich Serturner, isolated the primary active ingredient in opium: morphine. Morphine is very good at reducing pain, and remains widely prescribed. The isolation of morphine launched a flurry of research that continues to this day. From that research, thousands of compounds were developed, with the hope that they had medicinal value with fewer side-effects. One of those compounds was heroin, a good short acting pain-killer and also, when injected, a pleasure-producing drug. People can become addicted to injecting heroin very quickly.[8]

The research following the isolation of morphine also produced the perfect antidotes for overdoses of morphine. Naloxone was one of them. If naloxone is given just before morphine, morphine has no effect. If naloxone is given after a dose of morphine, all of morphine's effects are reversed. Naloxone also blocks other drugs with morphine-like effects. If a person overdoses on heroin, a dose of naloxone is a potentially lifesaving antidote.[8]

Other drugs can be antidotes to morphine and heroin's effects. The one that plays a role in the development of new theories of alcoholism is naltrexone. Naltrexone does basically the same thing as naloxone, except that its effects are more long lasting. In humans, naltrexone, at moderate doses, can block morphine's effects at usual doses for as long as 24 hr.

Given that naloxone and naltrexone are nearly perfect antidotes to morphine, the idea emerged that there must be specific places where these drugs acted, i.e., there were as yet undiscovered, specific receptors for opioid drugs. Research was done that demonstrated those specific receptors; now called opioid receptors.

If there are specific opioid receptors, they surely did not evolve to interact with a product of a plant. Hence, the idea emerged that it is likely, nearly a surety, that the body must produce a morphine-like agent. A number of laboratories started looking for the native, or endogenous, morphine-like agent for the opioid receptor. Hans Kosterlitz, a retired professor, and a freshly minted Ph.D., John Hughes, isolated compounds from the brains of pigs that were antagonized, or blocked, by naloxone. Others isolated other potential endogenous chemicals whose actions were blocked by naloxone. With time, the term endorphins came to be the name applied to all compounds produced in the body whose effects were blocked by naloxone.

Modern research progresses very fast. We now know that drugs such as morphine mimic the actions of endorphins and that both morphine-like drugs and endogenous opioids act at opioid receptors. We now know which genes produce both the endorphins and the opioid receptors. The body, particularly but not exclusively in the brain, produces its own morphine-like compounds.[17] The morphine-like drugs do not create new neural systems; they act on systems that exist.

Laboratory animals self-administer addictive drugs.

Now to behavioral experiments that involve morphine. Many of them used a variant of the Skinner Box, described above. This time, however, when a rat pressed the lever it received a small dose of morphine rather than food. Before behavioral testing, a rat was fixed with tubes that, when attached to a pump, could deliver to a blood vessel a small dose of morphine. The arrangement allowed the rat to freely move throughout the box. When the lever was depressed, the rat received an injection of morphine. Question: Would the rat avidly press the bar for an injection of a small amount of morphine? The answer is yes. Would rats press for heroin? The answer is yes.[18]

What was revealed with this kind of experimental arrangement is that rats quickly learn to work for doses of morphine without having been previously exposed to morphine. The rats were not working to prevent withdrawal signs because prior to being in the box they had never been exposed to morphine. Rats will also work for other addictive agents. In fact, they will work for doses of virtually every addictive agent that has captured the attention of humans. Additionally, other mammals will self-administer the drugs that interest humans.

It was also shown that rats will drink solutions of morphine if its bitter taste is masked. Rats readily learn to drink alcoholic beverages if the bitter taste of ethanol is masked by a sweetener. Rats readily drink, for example, wine-like beverages and beer without having any chance of developing withdrawal signs. Some rats also learn to drink the functional equivalent of vodka cocktails.[19]

Furthermore, it is difficult to imagine what might motivate the typical lab-rats to self-administer drugs favored by humans, including ethanol, unless they directly liked the effects of the drugs. They do not appear to be anxious, depressed or stressed. Theories of addiction have emphasized the possibility that addictive drugs somehow dampen human's existential angst. But it is difficult to imagine a rat, as it works for an addictive drug, as abating its existential angst. It can be imagined, but the actuality is slim.

Cartoon by Kitty VanderClute

The experiments showing that animals will self-administer addictive drugs with no apparent signs of previous signs of stress provided a new perspective on explanations of why people became addicted. Perhaps when people drink, they get something rather than relief from some adversity. Perhaps, it is more like rats drinking sugar-water when they are surely not hungry. Perhaps, ethanol induces a positive emotional event which in turn tends to reward the act of drinking. Perhaps, some people drink because it induces a positive feeling. Perhaps, for some, drinking enhances other events that produce pleasant feelings such as pleasant social gatherings or delicious food. Or stated differently, perhaps, addictive agents are positive reinforcers.

The idea that an alcoholic beverage induces some positive emotion in some people can easily explain individual differences in propensity to drink: for some drinking is pleasurable and for others drinking may even be aversive. For example, ethanol can cause nausea in some people of East Asian ancestry. Nausea is not pleasant, hence it opposes positive emotionality that might reward drinking, and hence the incidence of alcoholism among this group is small. Perhaps, there are conditions in which ethanol produces an increment in positive emotion and almost no negative effects (no nausea, usually no hangovers, usually no drowsiness) particularly with relatively small doses. Persons experiencing some positivity and little or no negativity would seem to be more likely to develop the habit of drinking. There are data to support this.[20]

The idea that ethanol induces positive emotionality, rather than relieving an adversity, is an interesting idea but has limitations. One limitation is trying to imagine how that might be achieved. Persons who use heroin and cocaine report that they readily experience positive emotionality, particularly with the initiation of their habit. There is, of course, the problem of imagining the mechanism of how heroin and cocaine might produce positive emotionality. The mechanism of positive emotionality is the next topic.

Certain brain stimulation is rewarding.

A Swiss scientist and Nobel Prize winner, Dr. Walter R. Hess, developed procedures for directly stimulating, with a small amount of electric current, the primitive parts of the brain of experimental animals while the animals were awake and free to move about. Some sites of stimulation induced eating even in sated animals. Some sites elicited aggression; some fear. Hess's discoveries took place in the late 1930s and during World War II. A considerable proportion of the scientific community was committed to the war-effort and it was not until the 1950s that other scientists took up the work that Hess began.

A post doctoral student, James Olds, working at McGill University, fixed rats with electrodes for stimulation of the middle parts of their brains using the techniques of Hess. With one of his rats, he observed that brief electrical stimulation of small intensity to a small part of the brain seemed to be rewarding. When the procedures were repeated, Olds became convinced that the electrical stimulation was rewarding (even pleasurable, but surely positively reinforcing, i.e., the stimulation increased the probability that a behavior that proceeded the stimulation was likely to reoccur). He then put rats into a box where they could press a bar and get electrical stimulation to various parts of the brain.

Here is what Dr. Olds observed during his initial experiments: In a Skinner box, rats would vigorously press for the brain stimulation when the stimulation activated only some parts of the brain; rats would not press for stimulation of other parts. The rewarding brain stimulation was brief, small intensities of current at only some parts of the middle of the brain. Rats would successfully run mazes for the opportunity to press for the stimulation of some sites. Olds' claimed that his initial results indicated that something akin to pleasure (at least reward and surely positive reinforcement) could be elicited by direct electrical stimulation of parts of the brain was met with considerable skepticism and critics vigorously claimed that such was not even possible. They, with considerable authority, asked: How could such a gross manipulation of a part of the brain elicit something so subtle, yet complex, as pleasure? Sure, Hess had shown that he could elicit fear-like behavior and even aggressive-like behavior, which had known physiological correlates. But surely, the critics claimed, pleasure was indeed a different kind of experience, more subjective.

The critics were left to explain the basic fact that rats did indeed press bars for direct electrical stimulation of some parts of the brain. They were very creative in coming up with explanations. For example, one idea was that the stimulation induced little seizures making the rat forget it had just pressed a bar and it would then do so again.[21] Some claimed that when they implanted electrodes in cats and tried to train them to press for brain stimulation, they did not press for the stimulation. They concluded that Olds' results were specific to rats and, therefore, somehow peculiar.

I (Larry) fixed cats so that their electrodes stimulated the same (homologous) sites that Olds found reinforced bar pressing among rats and I found that cats pressed eagerly for the stimulation. Among the best sites for self-stimulation was a tract of fibers running along the base of the brain, the medial forebrain bundle (MFB).

I had one big tom cat that I fixed with "pleasure-producing" electrodes. I really liked that cat and often left it out of his cage. He liked to sleep on my desk which was near a radiator. I put him in a Skinner box every day for a couple of weeks at about two in the afternoon for 15 min. During these sessions, he pressed for brain stimulation. Toward the end of the two weeks; he would awaken from his nap on my desk shortly before two and walk across my desk and stare at me. He seemed to be asking for his daily session. He pressed hundreds of times during his 15 min access to a lever which activated the mechanism for stimulation of his MFB.

Subsequent to showing that the big tom would press for brain stimulation regularly during brief daily sessions, I asked what would happen if I left him in the box for 24 hours. I made a better assembly so that he could move more freely in a Skinner box without tangling the wire that delivered the stimulation. I provided food and water in the box.

He began his 24-hour trial as usual: rapidly pressing for the stimulation. This time, however, unlike all others, he could continue pressing and he did. He pressed steadily for about four hours, and then took a break. He ate a little, drank some, groomed some and took a nap. Upon awakening, he set to pressing again. Evidently, he became tired of pressing in the usual way and during one period laid on his back and pulled down to operate the lever. After another bout of hours-long pressing, he again took a break and ate, drank and napped. He continued to press periodically throughout the 24 hours. He eventually accumulated tens of thousands of presses during 24-hour periods with each press yielding a brief electrical stimulation to the MFB.

A notable feature of the experimentation with my favored cat was that although he compulsively pressed for the brain stimulation, he also took care to eat, drink and rest. He appeared quite normal throughout the 24-hour session, except, of course, his perhaps tiring work at pressing for stimulation.

A major textbook on learning written by two distinguished professors at Stanford (Ernest Hilgard and Gordon Bower) amassed a number of reasons, other than the idea that the phenomena was peculiar to rats, why Olds' observations did not induce the equivalent of behavioral reinforcement but some sort of anomaly. Further research[22] carefully examined each criticism, and experiments were devised the results of which supported the idea that Olds and his colleagues had identified a system of the brain whose activity was pleasure, or something very akin to pleasure.

The anatomical system that was identified as the system for positive emotionality was centered about the medial forebrain bundle (MFB).[23] The MFB is a neural circuit that extends from the midbrain to a more frontal area called the accumbens nucleus and to the frontal cortex. The research is still ongoing to determine the exact anatomical and physiological details of the workings of the MFB system, but some things are well-established. What is relevant to our discussion is the realization that brain had a system devoted to positive emotionality. In retrospect, it seems obvious: If we experience pleasure, positivity with meeting our basic needs, and being content, such had to be a product of brain activity. What perhaps was surprising was the knowledge that we could isolate much of that system and it was centered about the MFB.

Addictive agents activate the medial forebrain bundle system.

Those who were studying behavioral reinforcement from direct electrical stimulation of parts of the brain were the first to ask if addictive agents might be activating the MFB system.[18,24] Although it took a while to establish, it is reasonable to conclude that addictive drugs modify the activity of the MFB. For example, addictive agents in doses that are self-administered enhance and sustain pressing for brain stimulation at a small intensity of brain stimulation that would not sustain pressing otherwise. Those same doses that enhanced pressing for brain stimulation were given to rats in one place and not in another. When given a choice, the rats preferred the place where they received the dose that enhanced pressing for MFB stimulation.[25] Collectively these and similar observations support the idea that addictive agents activate a "pleasure system" of the brain, probably the MFB and its immediate connections. These ideas fit nicely with the findings that the brain produced its own morphine-like neurotransmitters, the endorphins.

The next steps toward learning more about how addictive agents work involved a neurotransmitter called dopamine. Dopamine was found to be important to the functioning of the MFB system.[26] Now, the contention is that dopamine, the endorphins, and possibly the endogenous agents associated with marijuana use (called cannabinoids) are critical to the experience of pleasure. Since addictive drugs activate receptors for these neurotransmitters, they produce the same functionality as ordinary pleasurable events. These ideas are the basis of modern theories of addiction.

Opioid agonists & antagonists and consumption of alcoholic beverages

Recall that naloxone is the perfect antagonist at opioid receptors. With that understanding, scientists decided to use naloxone to see how blocking endorphins affected everyday activities of laboratory animals. Experiments showed that doses of naloxone limited the animals' eating and drinking. The next question that was asked was whether naloxone limited the intake of alcoholic beverages. The answer is yes. It limited the intake of alcoholic beverages in monkeys and rats.[27]

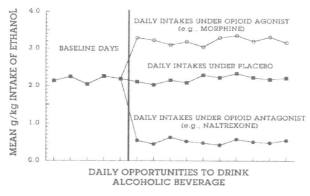

Figure 6.2 This figure depicts a summary of a number of experiments; the data-points are averages across experiments. The data points designated baseline days depicts the stable average intake of groups of rats after about three weeks of opportunity to take a concentrated but palatable alcoholic beverage. After baseline was established, shortly before daily opportunities to drink, subjects are injected with either small doses of morphine, doses of an opioid antagonist, or placebos. Morphine reliably increases intakes. Opioid antagonists reliably decrease ethanol-intake (but do not decrease intakes to zero). Figure taken from Reid (2009).[28]

The conclusion that naltrexone reduced laboratory animals' drinking of alcoholic beverages led to the idea that ethanol modified the actions of the endogenous opioids. That idea was supported by findings that small doses of morphine (doses that mimicked the actions of the endogenous opioids) increased rats' alcohol intake. Figure 6.2 is a summary of those findings.

Another experiment extended the research showing that small doses of morphine increased intakes of alcoholic beverage. The experimental arrangement allowed rats to drink all the palatable alcoholic beverages they wanted during two hours every day. Some rats of this experiment were fixed with small devices that when implanted under their skin delivered a small amount of morphine constantly for up to 28 days. We recorded their intakes from the first opportunity to take a palatable alcoholic beverage for 20 days.

There were other groups as well. One group got a small injection of morphine every day they were given the chance to drink alcohol. Another group received an injection of naloxone every day before the opportunity to drink. Yet another group got only placebo injections daily. Each groups' alcohol intake was tabulated from the very first day they had the opportunity to drink a palatable alcoholic beverage containing 12% ethanol.

The group fitted with the devices for delivery of constant dosing was large enough to be split into two groups. After 8 days of opportunity to drink alcohol, half of the group getting continuous doses of morphine also received a small injection of morphine before given the opportunity to drink for 8 days. The other half of the group received placebos on top of the constant infusion of morphine.

Morphine delivered by way of pumps enhanced intakes much the same way as when small doses of morphine were injected daily. Morphine given by way of the pumps and by way of an injection produced very large intakes of the alcohol. The amount drunk produced clear signs of drunkenness.

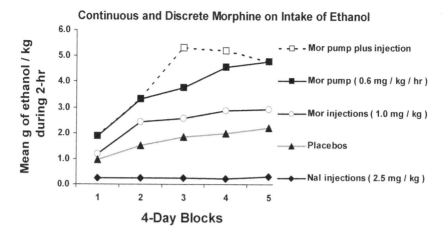

Continuous and Discrete Morphine on Intake of Ethanol

- -□- - Mor pump plus injection
- ■— Mor pump (0.6 mg / kg / hr)
- ○— Mor injections (1.0 mg / kg)
- ▲— Placebos
- ◆— Nal injections (2.5 mg / kg)

(y-axis) Mean g of ethanol / kg during 2-hr

(x-axis) 4-Day Blocks

Figure 6.3. The average intake of ethanol by male rats with a daily regimen of opportunity to take a palatable alcoholic beverage daily, 2 hr a day, for 20 days while various opioidergic manipulations were programmed. The first chance to take beverage was Day 1 of the 20 days. There were two groups fitted with osmotic pumps for the continuous delivery of morphine (Mor pump). They had the same treatment for the first 8 days, and then one group continued to receive the morphine of the pump, but also received a small injection of morphine daily across the next 8 days (open squares).[29]

We believe that the data of Figure 6.3 supports the idea that a continuous high level of activation of an endogenous opioid system is a condition for a high level of intake of alcoholic beverages (the circumstances of the devices producing continuous morphine). Also, a surge in activation of an endogenous opioid system is a circumstance for a high level of intake of alcoholic beverage (the condition of small injections of morphine). Further, a surge in activation is relevant to circumstances where there is a high basal rate of activity (the condition of the continuous morphine) or a low basal level of activity (without devices).

The laboratory of Professor Christina Gianoulakis and colleagues of McGill University collected data that is concordant with the general idea that the level of endogenous opioids might be related to propensity to drink alcoholic beverages. Her findings show that people at risk for AAA due to family history have a low basal level of beta-endorphin, but ethanol produces more release of an endogenous opioid among them in comparison to their low risk counterparts.[30]

The conclusion is both a high basal opioidergic tone and a surge in opioid activity are conditions for extraordinarily large amounts of voluntary intakes of alcoholic beverages. Both conditions can be blocked by a long-acting opioid antagonist, naltrexone.

The evidence supports the idea that (a) morphine in doses that might mimic an increment in activity of the endogenous opioid system increased intakes of alcoholic beverage and (b) the opioid antagonists, naloxone and naltrexone, reduced intakes of alcoholic beverage. Previous research had indicated that the endogenous opioid system was relevant to the intake of palatable food and drink. The idea was that ethanol-intake activated the system that was usually activated by intake of palatable foods and sets into action the motivation for the behavior of taking more of the alcoholic beverage which produced the effect. If this occurred among people, it would be an ideal condition for establishing the habit of regularly drinking alcoholic beverages.

Recall that when we were talking about drug interactions, we related the study by Laura Garnier and her colleagues showing that students that had used prescription opioids during a previous time period drank more alcohol than their counterparts.[31] Their study's data from humans and the laboratory data mentioned above are in accordance with one another. When there is converging evidence from both human and animal data, one has considerably more confidence in the derived conclusions.

Medicines to Treat Relapse

We have discussed a number of issues which we believe would help you to understand that recent research supports new approaches to treating alcoholism. Research supports the idea that the endogenous opioid system plays a role in controlling ingestive behavior. Further, the endogenous opioid system seems to be relevant to the ingestion of alcoholic beverages. An implication of the research: perhaps naltrexone, or another long-acting opioid antagonist, might be useful in the treatment of alcoholism.[28]

Given the findings from the research laboratories, the next logical step was to see if naltrexone would be of benefit in the treatment of persons presenting with alcoholism. Those interested in arranging for a test of naltrexone as a treatment for alcoholism, however, could not initially find the necessary funds. Nevertheless, the idea that naltrexone might be a useful medicine for treating propensity to relapse among alcoholics was compelling enough that the idea was eventually put to the test.

The mounting of a well-controlled, safe clinical trial of any potential medicine is very expensive. There are, in general, two sources of money to conduct trials of potentially new medicines: the government and a pharmaceutical company. Given this circumstance and the knowledge that the DuPont Corporation held the patent on naltrexone, I (Larry) as well as scientists from the University of Pennsylvania (namely Dr. Joseph Volpicelli and Professor Charles O'Brien), approached the professionals at DuPont with summaries of the data from the animal laboratory, as well as additional rationale, and encouraged them to fund a clinical trial of naltrexone. More than one appeal was turned down. Further, initially, there was no indication that government grants to support such research would be forthcoming; in fact, the agency most likely to support the research actually did not even support much of the work done in the animal laboratories.

Despite having no specific funds to do so, Dr. Joseph Volpicelli collaborated with the distinguished psychiatrist Professor Charles O'Brien and two other colleagues, Arthur Alterman and Motoi Hayashida, to run a trial of naltrexone as a medicine for treating alcoholism. Professor O'Brien cobbled together the resources to proceed. Professor O'Brien is the hero in this saga. Those doing animal research had done their jobs, and it was clearly time that someone tried naltrexone in the clinic. O'Brien did what was necessary for a clinical trial.

Volpicelli and colleagues recruited patients who were clearly diagnosed as having problems with alcohol. Subsequent to withdrawal from steady drinking, patients were divided into two groups: one group to receive a 50 mg dose of naltrexone daily and the other a placebo-pill. There were occasional blood tests to ensure that the naltrexone plus any potential intake of alcohol would not injure the liver. Both the group getting naltrexone and placebos were given opportunity for the usual psychosocial treatment in addition to their dosing. Most of the measures were self-reports of drinking. The issue of this first test was to see if naltrexone would prevent the high incidence of relapse back to hazardous drinking.

After one half of the planned number of subjects had finished the trial, the blind (of the double-blind placebo-control procedure) was broken in order to provide a first major report of the study. That report occurred at a symposium associated with the Society of Neuroscience meeting, 1988. Presentations at that symposium featured summaries of the data from both the animal-laboratory and the clinic relevant to naltrexone as a medicine for treating alcoholism and bulimia as well as other presentations. The written reports of that symposium were finished in 1989 and published in 1990 under the title, *Opioids, Bulimia, and Alcohol Abuse & Alcoholism*.[32]

Knowing of the work of O'Brien's group, another study was started at a clinic associated with Yale. The study was directed by Dr. Stephanie O'Malley.[33] She and her colleagues organized a further test of naltrexone's ability to reduce the rate of relapse back into hazardous drinking. The study by O'Malley and colleagues was a placebo-controlled trial of a 50 mg a day dose of naltrexone. It was a test of how naltrexone affected drinking among alcoholics recently treated for withdrawal signs. Of particular interest was whether naltrexone stopped or slowed the rate of relapse. The report of the O'Malley-study[33] was published in its final form at the same time as the completed Volpicelli-study.[34]

The first two trials of naltrexone indicated it did reduce rates of relapse. The alcoholics who received placebos behaved similarly to the average rate of relapse seen with nearly all previous studies of tendency to relapse (see Figure 6.1). Fewer patients under naltrexone relapsed during the 12 weeks of naltrexone administration.

Subsequent to the studies from Penn and Yale, DuPont sponsored the additional research and paperwork necessary to get the FDA to approve naltrexone as a medicine for the treatment of AAA. FDA approval occurred in 1994. Since those first two studies, there has been a steady stream of further assessments of the effects of naltrexone on propensity to relapse. In general, the findings of these studies confirm the results of the first two studies. Fixed oral doses (typically 50 mg tablets, daily) of naltrexone have been shown to reduce the number of drinking days, reduce the number of drinks per drinking episode, reduce the craving for a drink and increase the number of persons not relapsing to hazardous drinking (achieving abstinence or near abstinence) during the time the individual is taking the drug in comparison to those taking placebos. The conclusion from laboratory tests of people's responding after drinking alcoholic beverages indicates that naltrexone reduces the pleasure of drinking and reduces the propensity to continuing drinking once begun.

A summary of all studies of naltrexone available to reviewers during 2009-10 were reviewed to determine if naltrexone had utility in the treatment of alcoholism. There were a total of 50 randomized control trials with 7793 patients. The authors of the review concluded: "Naltrexone appears to be an effective and safe strategy in alcoholism treatment. Even though the sizes of treatment effects might appear moderate in their magnitudes, these should be valued against the background of the relapsing nature of alcoholism and the limited therapeutic options currently available for its treatment" (Rösner et al., 2010).[35] In brief the conclusion is: if treatment programs were to prescribe an oral dose of naltrexone, they could expect a reduction in rates of relapse during the time the patients were taking naltrexone. Days of hazardous drinking would be reduced.

From the initial studies on, it became apparent that not all patients profited from taking naltrexone. Also, a number of patients failed to comply with the advice to take the naltrexone daily. Despite these issues, prescriptions of naltrexone in combination with usual psychosocial therapies remains the only treatment for AAA based in multiple double-blind, placebo-controlled, multi-centered research that has been shown to reduce the rates of hazardous drinking during initial periods of attempted abstinence.

Naltrexone, like all drugs, can produce adverse reactions. During the initial clinical trials, however, naltrexone produced few problematic side-effects. There were instances of nausea with initial dosing. There are indications that doses of 300 mg a day or more can have bad effects on the liver, but doses that high were not administered in the trials involving alcoholics. In fact, because naltrexone reduced hazardous drinking among those taking it, there are indications that liver-health was improved.[32,36]

Recall, naltrexone is an opioid antagonist. For those using alcohol and an opioid such as oxycodone (a prescription pain-killer), the intake of naltrexone will precipitate opioid withdrawal signs including diarrhea, stomach cramps, nausea, as well as other problems such as diffuse pain. Consequently, the advice is to not give naltrexone until someone has been drug-free for at least a week.

An individual addicted to an opioid pain-killer and alcohol and withdrawn from both might profit from a daily regimen of naltrexone. Naltrexone would block all of the opioids' positive effects and blunt alcohol's positive effects and, therefore, help in sustaining abstinence. The issue for an opioid-addicted alcoholic is compliance with the regimen of daily dosing. It is relatively easy to skip a daily dose and use both of the pleasure-inducing agents.

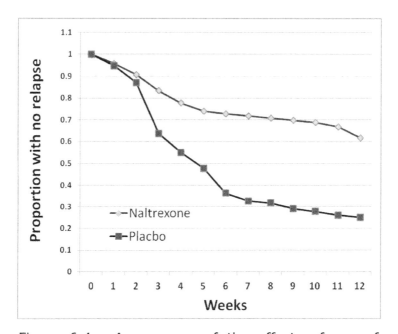

Figure 6.4. A summary of the effects of use of naltrexone in the treatment of AAA. The data are summaries of the first two trials of naltrexone combined with subsequent trials. At the beginning of treatment, all persons are abstinent (the proportion abstinent is 1.0 or 100%). Notice that the placebo-treated group responded as expected from studies of other kinds of treatments; that is, most of them relapsed back into hazardous drinking within the first two months post treatment. On the contrary, fewer of the naltrexone-treated group relapsed back into hazardous drinking.

Many using prescription pain-killers as recreational drugs eventually end up in a court room; usually having been arrested for illegal use of heroin-like drugs. The court could provide an option: arrange to have a regimen of verified intake of naltrexone daily for a year or so, or go to prison as a penalty for illegal drug-use. Such social action would likely provide an opportunity for a life-style change that would be beneficial. In some jurisdictions, this option is available.

It has been known for over a decade that a prescription of naltrexone will improve the treatment of alcoholism, yet it is not widely prescribed. Some groups do not trust naltrexone as a treatment, viewing it as just another pill being used to replace ethanol, like Valium and Librium, which clearly did not work. A frequent criticism of naltrexone as a medicine to reduce relapse is that it is not effective for everyone and that some do not comply with taking the medicine daily (thereby preventing its usual effects). Because of the general safety of naltrexone, however, these are not reasonable criticisms of the general use of naltrexone as an adjunct to usual treatments for alcoholism. Also, as we shall see, there are a number of procedures that might enhance naltrexone's effects.

A problem associated with the administration of naltrexone is that many patients do not comply with the advice to continue taking the medicine. Also, it is easy to imagine that more days of dosing are apt to improve outcomes. To deal with these issues, an injection providing effective doses of naltrexone for a month has been developed and approved by the FDA, in 2006. Extended release naltrexone (XR-NTX) is marketed under the brand name *Vivitrol* as well as others.

Now (circa 2014) there are studies assessing XR-NTX as a treatment for AAA. In addition to the side-effect profile of oral naltrexone (e.g., possibility of nausea), there is a small possibility for infection as the site of injections and some soreness associated with the injections.

The first large study of XR-NTX gave persons with a history of heavy drinking one of two doses of naltrexone (380 or 190 mg) or a placebo injection. Both doses of XR-NTX provide small doses of naltrexone for at least 28 days. Heavy drinking was defined as: "... a minimum of 2 episodes of heavy drinking (5 standard drinks/d for men and 4 standard drinks/d for women) per week during the 30 days before screening" (Garbutt et al., p 1618).[37] In brief, these patients were drinking at levels deemed to be hazardous. A feature of this study is described by the authors: "Important selection features were that inclusion did not require intent to abstain and ongoing active drinking was not a cause for exclusion" (Garbutt et al., p 1619). Nevertheless, there was a group of patients who reported no drinking during a few consecutive days preceding the first dose of medication. Most designs of other studies of naltrexone required patients to be abstinent prior to dosing for a considerable period. In addition to treatment with naltrexone or placebo, all patients received low intensity, supportive psychotherapy. The planned dosing regimen was six intramuscular injections roughly one every 28 days which provided naltrexone for 24 weeks.

Did the dosing regimen with XR-NTX curb heavy drinking and lead to circumstances favorable for sustained abstinence? The brief answer is yes, but like oral naltrexone there were some who were not helped and some who stopped getting their planned monthly injections. Roughly, 64% of the patients of each of the three doses (2 of naltrexone and 1 of placebo) took all 6 of the planned injections. All patients were given an opportunity to participate in psychosocial therapy. The major finding is that naltrexone reduced the incidence of hazardous drinking. Also, the group entering treatment with some days of abstinence fared better than their counterparts who were drinking steadily with the beginning of treatment. It was shown that naltrexone would be effective with some who were troubled by their excessive drinking but were not abstinent at the time they began the regimen of long-acting naltrexone. A striking feature of the results is the remarkable reduction in all measures of drinking compared to preinjection-levels of drinking by placebo-treated patients as well as naltrexone-treated. All patients received some psychotherapy. The placebo-treatment involved injections and psychotherapy and that combination was effective in comparison to pretreatment levels of use of alcoholic beverages. This finding has some important implications. It suggests that results with long-acting naltrexone might be very effective in comparison with no treatment or placebo-treatment. It also indicates that psychotherapy that capitalizes on whatever mechanisms involved with the placebo-effect might be of benefit.

A further inspection of the available data of the first large trial of XR-NTX tabulated reports of quality of life of the alcoholic patients.[38] The data relevant to quality of life were from 414 individuals with a history of heavy drinking who had been randomly assigned to receive either 380 mg of naltrexone or zero mg per injection.

Quality of life was assessed by periodic administration of a health survey consisting of 36 items with questions about general health, vitality, social functioning and mental health which can be summarized as two measures: one supposedly indexing overall physical health and one supposedly indexing overall mental health. Despite exclusion from the study of those having severe physical and mental problems, the findings indicated the individuals presenting for treatment had indices of a lesser quality of life than the general population, an expected result. The dose of 380 mg of naltrexone produced improved increments in quality of life compared to pre dosing levels and compared to placebo controls. The improvements were significantly correlated with the reductions in drinking; an expected finding based on previous studies of quality of life and treatment outcomes.

One publication reported on the results of providing XR-NTX for 15 months.[39] Although a goodly number of those provided the opportunity to take XR-NTX for a prolonged period chose not to do so, those who did take the drug for the period very often profited from doing so. The opportunity to take the drug for the longer period did not involve much if any psychotherapy.

Many individuals convicted of drunk-driving are repeat offenders. Perhaps, those convicted of drunk-driving might profit from agreeing to take monthly injections of XR-NTX.[40] In one small study, twelve of those convicted of drunk-driving volunteered to receive XR-NTX. Seven received all three

150

injections of a planned course of treatments. The average drinks per drinking day decreased markedly as well as number of days in which drinking occurred. Although this report is of only a small number of individuals, it suggests that giving XR-NTX to persons who repeatedly drive after consuming hazardous amounts of alcohol could benefit from using the drug. A reasonable prediction: if XR-NTX were used widely with people who routinely drink and drive, then auto accidents would be reduced to the benefit of the drinker and others that may be a part of an accident.

In the context of a drug court, a study compared the effects of taking XR-NTX compared to a matched group who did not receive the drug. The summary of the study included the following: "In the principal end-point analysis of annualized number of new arrests, 26% of standard-care clients were rearrested versus 8% on XR-NTX" (Finigan et al., 2011, p 288).[41]

A small study tabulated the health care costs of those who were prescribed XR-NTX in comparison to other treatments for alcoholism. The finding was that those who engaged treatment by getting more than one injection of XR-NTX had "significant reductions in costs for alcohol-related hospitalizations, as well as total medical and total pharmacy costs" (Jan et al., 2011, p S210).[42]

XR-NTX does not benefit all who take it and compliance with continuing to take injections for months remains a problem. Although overall treatment with XR-NTX appears to have beneficial effects, there should be continued research with the goal of improving treatment outcomes.

We believe that the research with naloxone and naltrexone opened the way for research designed to develop new and better medicines for treating AAA, however, there is an interesting issue involved. A drug that completely blocked the urge to drink alcoholic beverages among those with a well-practiced drinking habit is apt to be a very harsh drug. Such a drug would also probably interfere with eating and nutrition and maybe even general motivation. There is also the issue of how to learn to resist temptation once the drug is no longer given. It is probably necessary to have some feature of the temptation to drink in order to develop habits that counter the conditioning inherent to the temptation. Muted, but not abolished, motivation to drink, might be the optimal setting condition for learning not to drink. It has been discovered, for example, that the treatment of phobias is optimal when there is some semblance of the fear present in order to countercondition the fear. A drug that was very good at muting the elicitation of the fear and anxiety that motivated the avoidance behavior did little to promote the learning that the fear and anxiety were irrational. As soon as the drug was no longer given, the phobia was immediately reinstated.[43]

The conclusion is that the prescription of naltrexone is a reasonable adjunct to other interventions to treat the habit of drinking hazardous amounts of alcoholic beverages. The mere prescription of naltrexone is not sufficient in many instances. It is probably necessary to focus treatment on creating a life-style that is generally recognized as healthy and involves total or near total abstinence from drinking alcoholic beverages. Merely telling patients to behave in healthy ways is not going to do much good, if any. Treatments have to be developed that counter the built-up habits of drinking. There are approaches that might foster better outcomes. Some of these approaches are discussed subsequently.

Theories of Alcoholism, an Up-dated Version

There are a number of competing ideas concerning alcoholism and related issues. Nevertheless, there does seem to be emerging a modern theory of alcoholism. The modern theory may be the simplest of the alternatives. The modern theory stresses that the habit of drinking alcoholic beverages is established in much the same way as any habit is established. The explanation for why drinking may be habit forming boils down to the rather simple fact that, for some, it can be pleasure-producing on a sufficient number of occasions; particularly, rather often, with the first few drinks of a day. Circulating ethanol is pleasure-producing for some and not so pleasure-producing for others (may even be somewhat nauseous). For individuals whose drinking is pleasure-producing, there is a good chance drinking will increase over time. For those whose drinking is not pleasant, there is a good chance that drinking will not increase over time. Accordingly, for those who do not markedly suffer hangovers with a night of drinking, there is a greater likelihood of more drinking than the individual that suffers considerably. Also, accordingly, for those that ethanol induces drowsiness or feelings of being tired are less likely to become habitual drinkers.[44]

The increment in pleasure associated with the development of any habit need not be great and need not be terribly consistent. The modern theory of AAA does not demand that drinking induces ecstasy. However, among those for whom drinking becomes habitual, modern theory holds that ethanol does induce an increment in positive emotion on a fairly consistent schedule. For some, they just feel a bit better after they start drinking than before. There may be competing opportunities to feel better that may limit any given individual's drinking. Or, certain social pressures may control an individual's drinking even when drinking is pleasurable.

The elicitation of a positive emotion does two salient things: (a) it reinforces any act perceived as inducing that emotion (increases the probability of the act being repeated) and (b) associates, by way of classical (Pavlovian) conditioning, features of the environment with the emotion. A detailed understanding of these two factors is much of what is modern learning theory. Modern learning theory is applicable to resolving AAA. One implication is that there should be a focus on the cues (secondary reinforcers) that sustain the full feature of the habit of drinking.

The broader system whose activity is positive emotional experiences involves the activity of the MFB system. The MFB's activity involves the actions of a number of neurotransmitters. Among those neurotransmitters are the endogenous opioids. The endogenous opioids are involved in the regulation of ingestion and seem to be particularly involved with sustaining ingestion once begun. Two kinds of disorders of behavioral regulation are characterized by ingesting too much, too often: (a) the eating disorders of binge eating and bulimia nervosa, and (b) alcohol use disorders. Intake of food and drink loaded with calories leads to becoming overweight. Drugs that mimic the actions of the endogenous opioid neurotransmitters, e.g., small doses of morphine, enhance ingestion of palatable food and drink. Naloxone and naltrexone decrease ingestion, particularly the tendency to continue to ingest once begun. Naloxone and naltrexone block the actions of the endogenous opioid neurotransmitters.

Ethanol, the active ingredient in alcoholic beverages, soon after being ingested reaches the brain. In the brain, it has multiple effects. One of those effects is to increase the usual activity of the endogenous opioid systems which, in turn, increments activity in the MFB. This kind of neural activity induces a pleasant emotional experience and tends to sustain ingestion once begun.

Alcoholic beverages, however, are no ordinary commodities. Ethanol, except for small doses, is toxic. Ethanol's ability to both positively reinforce its own ingestion and its toxicity represents the dilemma associated with alcoholic beverages.

Ethanol's short term toxicity is probably related to its ability to modify the receptors for the neurotransmitter (GABA) that produces neural inhibition. In so doing, it disrupts the usual coordination of neural processes and as such is manifest in reduced ability to plan. With increasing doses, ethanol eventually affects well-practiced behaviors manifest as staggering while walking and slurred speech. In larger doses, enhanced GABA activity produces tiredness and sleepiness. These short term toxic events can and often do precipitate irrational behavior and accidents.

When alcoholic beverages are taken regularly in what has been termed a hazardous amount, ethanol's toxicity induces a wide variety of toxic events. These toxic events are manifest in liver disease, malnutrition, and risk of a wide range of other diseases. In brief, habitual intake of alcoholic beverages is unhealthy.

One of the most serious complications of habitual intake of alcoholic beverages is a reduction in cognitive ability.[45] The reduction in cognitive ability is due to the direct toxic effects of ethanol on areas of the brain most involved with controlling impulsive behavior and planning.[46] The reduction of cognitive ability often retards the development of mature ways of dealing with life's challenges, particularly those involving complex interpersonal relations such as those involved with sustaining marriages, parenting, and work.

Modern Theories Lead to Improved Treatments.

If drinking involves regular episodes of hazardous drinking, the habitual drinker should stop drinking alcoholic beverages. This advice is made in recognition that continuing such drinking is unhealthy, often induces asocial behavior and can induce fatal complications. This is not news.

The first step toward stopping habitual drinking is managing withdrawal signs and symptoms. We have described modern treatment for intense withdrawal (Treatment for Withdrawal, p 125f). The withdrawal process should be made as easy and as trouble free as possible. An intensely aversive withdrawal merely sets the circumstances for fear of withdrawal which, in turn, sets the circumstance for negative reinforcement by relief of such fear by way of drinking. Concurrent with the management of withdrawal there should also be attention to medical conditions that may hinder cognitive performance such as thiamine deficiency and liver disease.

Psychotherapy following treatment for withdrawal should help the individual to change. The alcoholic needs to change from being a person who cannot stop drinking into a person who does not drink alcoholic beverages (no longer an alcoholic). The alcoholic needs to change to prevent further deterioration in health, including slowly, softly reducing cognitive abilities. The alcoholic usually needs to change to have better interpersonal relationships with respect to family, work, and being a better contributor to a happy, peaceful society. Becoming abstinent is usually a giant step toward meeting the needs for better health and improved interpersonal relationships. Given such, the focus should be on the behaviors associated with drinking alcoholic beverages. However, changing from a life-style focused on drinking to a healthier life-style involves changing a number of well-established habits which is, indeed, very difficult. It is so difficult that it will take time and considerable effort. Further, it is often so difficult that the recovering alcoholic needs help in order to sustain the effort. The recovering alcoholic often needs help in developing the ability, the skills, to make the necessary changes.

When practiced by trained professionals, modern psychotherapy is not haphazard. Modern psychotherapy is evidence-based, i.e., procedures, or something very similar, have been shown by scientific study to produce a desirable effect. Some form of cognitive behavioral therapy is the therapy of choice.[47] Such therapy will probably be directed toward systematically inspecting the cognitions and rationalizations that are voiced as reasons why an individual is addicted to alcoholic beverages. Depending on the co-morbidities presented, there may be instituted evidence-based therapies for specific anxieties. There might be activities directed toward modifying unhelpful behaviors and nudging more helpful behaviors (e.g., establishing good nutritional and sleeping habits). In addition to the usual help provided to a patient engaging psychotherapy, a recovering alcoholic can probably be helped by attending to damaging events associated with being drunk too often. (e.g., help filing late income tax forms, directing a patient to social services that might be helpful, searching for a job, etc.).

Changing enduring habits, as well as the accompanying beliefs that justified those habits, is an extremely challenging task for anyone, even for a person at their peak of cognitive abilities. In an almost direct relationship to the duration and extent of hazardous drinking, individuals presenting for treatment of their alcoholism will have suffered considerable cognitive decline.[12] The cognitive decline is most apparent with regard to the executive functioning, just the kind of skill necessary to make marked changes in one's life. Given the difficulty of the tasks at hand and given the reduced cognitive abilities, it is no wonder that treatment of alcoholism often fails. Nevertheless, there are reasons to be optimistic.

Previous theory advocated that once an adult's brain had been damaged, it will remain damaged for the balance of a person's life. Given this once prevailing idea, there was no reason to even try to repair a damaged brain. The only therapy was to teach the brain-damaged individual to cope with a handicap. We now know that this pessimistic theory is no longer an accurate prognosis. We now know that with systematic practice, many lost cognitive abilities can be regained. (Surely, if you are reading this book, any lost cognitive abilities can be restored. If you are reading this book to help a loved one, there are reasons to believe that they can be helped.) The brain is considerable more plastic than previously believed; a once degraded brain can be healed. This new understanding about the brain's capability to recover lost functioning has a label: brain plasticity or neuroplasticity.

The new ideas about the brain's capabilities to recover lost functioning took a considerable period of time to be verified by systematic, scientific research. There are a number of books directed toward persons not trained in neuroscience detailing this advancement in understanding.[48]

We have evidence to indicate that (a) persons with a history of regular drinking have degraded cognitive functioning (not as smart as they once were);[12,49] (b) if abstinence is achieved for a prolonged time (say months or years), there is evidence that usually there is recovery of the lost cognitive functioning due to alcoholism;[45,48] (c) there is every reason to believe that achieving a life-style sustaining abstinence is a very difficult task probably made more difficult due to reduced cognitive abilities, and (d) importantly, we now know of ways that might speed the recovery of cognitive functioning among recovering alcoholics, thereby enhancing the recovering alcoholic's *ability* to adopt a new life-style free of alcoholism.

It takes sustained practice at cognitive tasks to restore lost cognitive functioning. Sustained practice at relevant cognitive tasks is made easier by the development of modern computer technologies made manifest by the development of video games. Computer-assisted game-like programs have been developed specifically to treat degraded cognitive functioning.[50] This development has important implications for improving the treatment of AAA. There are scattered reports in the scientific literature of how sustained, programmed practice at cognitive activities can improve the treatment of alcoholism.[51]

Posit Science[52] is a company providing computer-assisted game-like programs that have been verified to restore lost cognitive functioning. The process is not magical; it takes practice at the "game" (actually "games") to achieve success. Nevertheless, it just makes sense for the newly abstinent alcoholic to engage such practice. A particularly nice feature of computer-assisted game-like programs is that they are inexpensive (about a hundred dollars will buy the opportunity to enhance cognitive skills) and that, once purchased, they can be used virtually any time by anyone with a modern computer and an internet connection for a long time without supervision by trained professionals. Although no one has tested the proposition: *If the habitual drinker continues hazardous drinking, it is highly likely that engaging computer-assisted game-like programs designed to restore lost cognitive functioning is not going to achieve the desired goal.*

Recall our previous discussion that NTX given orally and XR-NTX will reduce the instances of hazardous drinking among those seeking treatment for alcoholism. The good news is that the effects of naltrexone and the practice at computer-assisted game-like programs designed to rehab cognitive functioning will, most likely, interact favorably with one another.[53]

To be more specific, research[54] has indicated that there is a relationship between the alcohol's toxic effects on the orbital frontal cortex and the alcoholic's failures to stop drinking. Sustained alcohol-intake reduces the densities of neurons and supporting cells in the orbital frontal cortex. Reductions in the efficiency of the orbital frontal cortex are manifest as impulsive and preservative behaviors, just the kinds of behaviors that need to change if the alcoholic is to stop impulsively persisting in drinking. Research[54] has shown that naltrexone enhances activity in the orbital frontal cortex which, in turn, probably will make training with computer-assisted game-like programs more efficient than they would be otherwise.

Modern learning theory acknowledges that well-established habits are mostly the process of unconscious functioning. The fact that habits are executed with large elements being unconscious makes changing them difficult to modify by way of rational argument. These unconscious processes are triggered and sustained, almost automatically, by salient environmental cues. This is the nature of habits and development of habits is the way we mature our adaptive capabilities.

Think about the habit of going to a bar or tavern after work for a few drinks which is rationalized as treatment for the stresses of work and trying to manage complex interpersonal relations. This habit has probably been reinforced by both instances of pleasure and instances of relief (recall that positive and negative reinforcements need not be consistent or intense to sustain well-established habits). The cues sustaining this habit are many, ranging from noting the time of day to all the environmental cues that guide the movement (the motivation) for an opportunity to drink. Sometimes these cues are manifest as a craving for a drink and that craving will be the more intense the more the established cues signal an opportunity to drink (learning theorist call this propensity to be more motivated the closer to the goal as a gradient of reinforcement).

Modern learning theory tells us that habits do not extinguish with the passage of time. The cues that previously signaled the instigation of a habit will again instigate that habit when they appear, even if their appearance has not occurred for a prolonged time. The way one changes habits is to establish new habits that counter the old habits. If one set of cues for the habit of drinking is the end of the work day, then one has to associate end of the work day with new behaviors that induce some small measure of pleasure or relief to modify the habit of drinking after work.

There are data to indicate that naltrexone will mute the motivational effects of cues guiding the behavior toward drinking.[12] The effect is not large, but may be helpful in combination with other therapies, particularly cognitive behavioral therapy.

If an individual has been in a place where drinking is not allowed, such as an inpatient clinic, they probably, in this novel environment are not strongly tempted to drink. If nothing is done in that new environment to establish new habits that will counter the old habits and if little is done to enhance the ability to resist temptations and develop new behaviors, then the prediction is that when the newly abstinent individual returns to the previous environment where drinking was habitual, relapse is likely. Advanced cognitive behavioral therapy often addresses these issues. Further, new computer-assisted game-like programs are being developed that will facilitate the counter conditioning of cues motivating the movement toward drinking.

The recently abstinent individual must eventually return to living in a world of many opportunities to drink alcoholic beverages and, eventually, with only limited support of treatment-providers. Further, it is in the interest of many people to have the recovering individual return to buying large amounts of alcoholic beverages. These enablers of relapse actively promote their financial interests over those of a recovering individual.

Recently abstinent individuals can, however, get help as they engage their daily life trying to sustain abstinence without much, if any, professional counseling. They can be provided naltrexone which is known to help (curb craving and reduce instances of hazardous drinking). They can engage computer-assisted game-like programs designed for cognitive rehabilitation which will help in furthering the skills and abilities that will be useful in making the necessary changes in life-styles. They can join an AA group whose beliefs are concordant with their beliefs as a means of getting some social support for maintaining sobriety. Each of these individual evidence-based therapies provides a continuance of treatment beyond post withdrawal that is beneficial. Collectively, these three activities (taking naltrexone, doing brain training and joining an AA group) will provide help that will increase the chances of not relapsing.[53]

Every day of sustained abstinence provides an opportunity to establish new habits that will counter the habits of regularly drinking. The rewards concurrent with abstinence may not be particularly forthcoming with early abstinence but will almost assuredly emerge with continuance of abstinence as new habits will be developed. Eventually, taking naltrexone can be stopped, one might engage other brain improvement activities such as developing a new skill (e.g., learn to tango, develop a new hobby), and provide help to those trying to recover from alcoholism.

In summary, in addition to well-managed withdrawal, treatment should involve psychotherapy that will encourage life-style changes that will sustain sobriety (an empty generalization unless there are instituted specific practices that can facilitate healthy life-styles). The prescription of naltrexone, either oral doses or XR-NTX, can be a setting condition for the psychotherapy (note: as a setting condition it is thought to be useful for a limited amount of time, say months, not years). Training designed to restore lost cognitive functioning and training to desensitize the cues that usually sustained a habit of drinking will increase the success of treatments for AAA.

The best team for treating AAA involves a group of problem-solvers each applying their honed skills to resolve the issues presented by an individual needing help.[55] The team needs medically trained individuals (e.g., physicians and nurses) that can manage intense withdrawal and have skill in providing services like managing the injections of XR-NTX.[56] The team should involve those skilled at providing cognitive behavioral therapy. The team should involve those with skills to help the recovering alcoholic deal with social services that might be helpful. There are reasons to believe that the larger society, particularly in the USA, is already spending sufficient amounts to cover the costs of providing optimal treatment. However, the available money is often not well-spent.

Getting help when you need it.

We have stated two perspectives. One, the usual treatment-programs, provided in many prosperous nations, have not and do not provide adequate treatment for relapse prevention, i.e., given such, alcoholism will remain a chronically relapsing "disease." Two, recent research has developed new evidence-based treatments that can provide improved rates of relapse prevention. Related to both of these perspectives, many treatment-programs have not modified their treatments and continue to deliver less than optimal treatments. This subsection provides some information that might help in choosing a treatment program.

We have written this book[57] with smart young women in mind as well as those who love them. We hope that those treating women alcoholics will also read this book. Among the reasons for doing so will become even more apparent in the next chapter.

Providing treatments for alcohol and drug abuse (alcoholism and drug addictions) is a large enterprise consisting of individual practioneers (physicians, nurse practioneers, psychologists, social workers, and councilors of various strips), government sponsored treatment programs, and private clinics. Some programs and clinics are advertised as not-for-profit (be wary of the statements about not for profit, they may pay their managerial and professional staffs very high salaries and hence are "for profit"). Others clearly exist for delivering treatment while making a profit. Planned treatments can vary from a brief interview to a many months stay in a special clinic. Some private clinics offer luxurious accommodations in nice surroundings. If one uses Google for information about alcoholism, using virtually any related word, the seeker will get a wide array of ads for private clinics. There will be sites claiming that their staff will help you select a treatment program with the idea that they will provide the exact program that you need (probably, the most expensive program that you can afford).

In most states of the USA and in other prosperous nations, the government pays for treatment for alcoholism and drug addictions for those who obviously cannot afford treatment, yet need it. In the USA, health insurance can cover cost of treatments, and recently the Affordable Care Act (Obama care) mandates that all medical insurance programs cover treatment for alcoholism and other drug addictions.

There is, of course, no issue with people being paid for delivering needed services (nearly all working adults have monthly bills to be paid). Further, there is no issue for paying some people more than others, if higher paid people have special skills and their work involves demanding responsibilities. The issue boils down to whether the paid-for services deliver what is promised. Relatedly, are the programs ultimately paid for by tax-derived monies cost-effective? Also, related to cost-effectiveness issues: are government or insurance programs sufficiently funded to actually be successful?

For individuals with a prolonged history of regularly consuming hazardous amounts of alcoholic beverages, medically supervised management of withdrawal signs and symptoms is the optimal choice. With the beginning of abstinence, the most dangerous time is during the first week or so of withdrawal; therefore, the optimal choice for initial treatment is with a program that has the capacity for handling intense withdrawal and, in general, medical emergencies. Your usual physician is a source of information concerning medical management of withdrawal. There is likely a state agency (USA) that oversees programs providing medically managed withdrawal (sometimes called crisis centers). Those agencies provide ways of contacting the appropriate service provider. Often local hospitals have an established program for medically managed withdrawal.

Prior to discussing choice of treatment for relapse prevention, this is as good a place as any to restate the rather obvious fact: Treatment for habitual drinking is optimal prior to needing medical management of withdrawal. Usually, problems associated with regularly drinking become apparent before intense withdrawal is a consequence of initial abstinence. Many are successful in controlling the extent of their drinking without professional help. For some, professional help (some form of therapy) will surely help toward developing a life-style conducive of happiness without the habit of drinking.

The internet provides plenty of advice on how to manage life's problems. Some are useful, some are deceitful, some just plain wrong, and some are actually dangerous due to preventing getting better advice. Helpguide.org provides free advice on a number of mental health issues; Helpguide.org is a non-profit source. The authors of this book have no relationship with the workers at Helpguide.org; their advice just seems a bit more sensible than a number of other sites we inspected.

Treatments occur in two contexts: inpatient (hospitalization or residential treatment) or outpatient (counseling centers). Within these contexts, therapy can be any of a number of forms, not all of which are evidence-based. Programs developed in the past decades, and have not changed much if any, are apt to get the "usual rate of relapse" (see, Figure 6.1), i.e., not a satisfactory rate. These programs can often be identified by the fact that they advertise a rather prolonged stay in their facility, a 12-step program and intense group therapy.

There are those that say they provide evidence-based treatments. Before engaging them, one might ask specific questions such whether the evidence-based practices are cognitive behavioral therapy and whether they encourage the use of naltrexone. You might ask about the level of training of those who will provide counseling (Ph.D. trained clinical psychologists have the most extensive and relevant education).

Every state in the USA has an agency licensing alcohol and drug treatment programs and these agencies usually provide help in matching a person to treatment. For general knowledge, the National Institute on Alcohol Abuse and Alcoholism's site contains considerable useful information.

Usually, general medical practioneers or family physicians are those who are seen first for help with their alcoholism. These individuals often refer patients with unhealthy life styles to places where they might get specialized help[58]. There is a movement to include in a general medical practice, clinical psychologists who can help with disorders such as alcoholism and depression. These are advanced practices and have been shown to be effective and less costly than the alternatives.[55]

If you can go a week without drinking while struggling with craving for a drink and can avoid engaging in a life-style associated with "partying on," you might engage your own advanced treatment. You might request a prescription for naltrexone (ask your doctor for help and if she does not provide it, go to one that will). You might buy a program for enhancing cognitive skills and practice it regularly (we recommend those from Posit Science). You might consciously avoid the people and places associated with drinking while striving to engage in new activities (in brief, try not to put yourself in places where you will experience strong temptations to have just one more).

We hope these few hints will help you find the help you might need to develop a life-style nurturing a generally happy day-to-day existence free of habits that are contrary to a generally happy day-to-day existence.

Prevention of AAA

Given that AAA are costly and once established difficult to modify, it seems prudent to prevent the development of AAA. For many, the habit of drinking appears to be established early, for example, among those of middle and high school age as well as during young adulthood (college age and just beyond). It seems, therefore, that teaching about the problems of habitual drinking, even in schools, might be something that might prevent the development of habitual drinking. Our society has tried that, at least on a limited basis, without much success. The messages of abstinence and temperance are rather easily countered by the public relations and advertising of Big Booze. The current messages of abstinence and temperance just seem empty compared to "party on." Curbs on Big Booze's advertising have been done (e.g., no ads encouraging drinking of hard liquor on TV for long periods) and those were effective as evidenced by Big Booze's constant push to not conform to even their own self-regulatory policies.

There is a direct relationship between indices of the amount of alcohol sold in a locality and all easily measured medical and social ill effects associated with drinking. As per capita consumption increases, dire consequences increase. Conversely, when per capita consumption decreases from a plateau-level of consumption, ill effects decrease.[59] Understanding this relationship, virtually every government in the world regulates the sale of alcoholic beverages differently than it regulates the sale of groceries. With respect to the USA, every state of the Union has the legal right (Constitutional right) to regulate the sale of alcoholic beverages. Furthermore, local governments regulate such matters as zoning and licensing of outlets for the sale of the beverages. Generally speaking, the modern issue is not whether to treat alcoholic beverages as a special commodity, but what is the optimal balance between strict regulation and unfettered marketing of the beverages.

From a public health perspective, there are policies that can effectively nudge temperance. Further, these policies have been tried and found to be effective. Because these polices have been effective (i.e., reduce sales, hence reduce mayhem), they are strongly opposed by Big Booze. The following policies reduce sales: (a) high taxes on the beverages, (b) limiting the number of outlets selling alcoholic beverages, (c) limiting the time to sell alcoholic beverages, (d) shaming managers of Big Booze into not selling their products to children and very young adults, and (e) enforcing the laws already on the books such as not selling to minors and not driving while intoxicated.

One group of epidemiologists led by the distinguished Professor Alexander C. Wagenaar, U. of Florida, have combed data from numerous sources and applied advanced statistical methods to determine what would happen if there was a doubling of the tax on alcoholic beverages. Here is the conclusion of their 2010 article: "Our results suggest that doubling the alcohol tax would reduce alcohol-related mortality by an average of 35%, traffic crash deaths by 11%, sexually transmitted disease by 6%, violence by 2%, and crime by 1.4%" (p 2270).[60] Predicting the future is always hazardous. Even if their conclusions would turn out to be not as rosy as predicted, it is surely likely, given the considerable evidence available, that a great deal of misery would be prevented by merely doubling the tax on alcoholic beverages. Also, the US government could use the money.

Within 2010, the Federal tax (USA) on a can of beer was $.05, a 750 ml bottle of wine (with less than 14% ethanol by volume) was $.21, and a bottle of distilled spirits (80 proof, 750 ml bottle) was $2.14. More concentrated wines and distilled spirits were taxed at higher rates. This level of taxation yielded $9.7 billion in Federal excise tax in 2012.

The separate states also taxed alcoholic beverages and generated considerable revenue. The intake from Federal taxes is barely sufficient to offset the direct health-care related costs (last carefully tabulated in 2006 and much higher now) induced by excessive intake of alcohol, let alone the entire health and social costs of excessive drinking.[61] The last increase in Federal excise tax on alcoholic beverages was 1991. Inflation in the buying power of the dollar has made the current rate of taxation of alcoholic beverages at historically low levels.[62] At local grocery stores in our area, beer is often cheaper to buy than soft drinks. Doubling the tax on alcoholic beverages would be useful; however, trebling the tax may be even more useful.

Big Booze would like to see a bar, a tavern, or a cocktail lounge on every street corner because they know that such will increase sales (the equivalent of a tactic of Starbucks). Such establishments can be limited and the licenses to operate them very expensive. Various localities have imposed various sanctions on when alcoholic beverages can be sold with small beneficial effects in terms of public health.

It just makes sense to enforce existing laws vigorously; for example, the society is just better off when we do not have young drivers of cars (drivers without sustained practice) driving drunk.

Further, every one of the listed ways of nudging better public health is within the purview of governments to enact. The issue: Who will prevail? Will local citizens enact policies that promote public health or will the managers of international companies of Big Booze relentlessly, slowly, softly encourage more sales to make more money than they already make?

In addition to advertising that drinking is fun and even healthy, spokespersons for Big Booze promote certain *ideas* that protect their goal of selling more alcohol. The people of Big Booze maintain that responsible drinking can be learned and that this should be the cornerstone of public policy. Spokespersons for the industries, however, do not specify who should do the teaching (and who should pay for such teaching) and how to teach such skills. The industry also promotes the idea that alcoholism is a disease that affects only a few. They do not seem to be troubled by the inconsistency of saying on the one hand that responsible drinking can be and should be learned and on the other hand that the diseases of AAA are characterized by lack of control.

Summary

A goal of this and previous chapters was to provide sufficient information to support the following conclusions: (a) AAA are prevalent and often induce serious health and social issues; (b) most current prevention programs are not working as well as hoped (c) most current treatment programs outside of research centers are hardly more effective than no treatment or self-directed treatments and (d) we are developing knowledge and practices that will improve the success rates of treatment programs. Improved treatments will be a significant step toward better prevention of the many dire consequences of habitual drinking.

A primary goal of Big Booze is to increase sales and, thereby, increase profits. Women and girls are a potential source of new customers for Big Booze. An important goal of this book is to provide information that allows women and girls to assess the cost-benefit ratio of drinking alcoholic beverages: Are the potential pleasures that the industries' advertisements tout worth the risks inherent to using their products? Information relevant to answering that question is contained in the next chapter. Also, the question is addressed why one might consider men and women separately when it comes to prevention and treatment of alcoholism.

Chapter 7. Women and Alcohol

Alcoholism used to be considered a man's problem. Here, we are going to make the case that in the near future there will be more alcoholic women than alcoholic men. Here are some of the topics used in making that case:

The incidence of alcoholism among women is increasing at a rather alarming rate.

Alcoholic beverages are more toxic to women than men.

Alcoholic beverages may be more appealing to women than men.

Related to the last topic, estradiol (the "female hormone") may enhance an appetite for alcoholic beverages.

After reading this chapter, we hope women will recognize that their physiology increases their risk of alcoholism and its attendant problems. Further, we hope women will recognize that medications with estrogenic features should be taken with a great deal of caution.

Two popular movies have depicted women as alcoholics, one a bit older than the other and both well worth viewing. They are "Days of wine and roses" and "When a man loves a woman." Both depict nice women who have become alcoholic and their struggles with their addiction. Both movies have notable songs associated with them.

There are a number of books relating the struggles women have had and are having with drinking. For example, journalist Ann Dowsett Johnston has written a book with the title *Drink: The intimate relationship between women and alcohol.*[1] She relates how she and other successful women have developed alcoholism, have suffered accordingly, and have recovered from alcoholism. She asserts that women are particularly vulnerable to alcoholism. Her well-written book is a nice adjunct to this one.

Women's Drinking is Increasing at a rather Alarming Rate.

There are clear social norms related to drinking alcoholic beverages. Furthermore, most people are aware of those norms, endorse them and many, many people abide by them. For most of America's history, there were social norms that limited drinking among women. For example, public drunkenness was and is not condoned in men and particularly not condoned in women. Unruly public drunkenness is barely tolerated in men and is surely scorned when exhibited by women.

Previously, a woman drinking in public, particularly without a man as an escort, was not condoned in America. There were women addicted to alcoholic beverages, but those beverages were drunk at home. In the early days of the Republic, her drinks might be hard cider, home brews, and patent medicines (which often contained considerable alcohol and sometimes opium or cocaine). The social sanctions concerning women and alcohol prevented a high incidence of sustained drinking in large amounts and, therefore, prevented large incidents of alcoholism among women.

A man attending college might walk into a bar close to campus and proceed to drink, say a couple or more beers, without aversive consequences. He would not violate norms of that community and could easily engage in conversation with other men. On the other hand, until recently, a lone women walking into a tavern would be met with considerable negativity. Most likely she would experience unwanted sexual advances.

Across the last few decades, the social norms that constrained women's drinking have waned. Today women, usually not alone but with a women friend or two, can without undue social dispersions, walk into a college-bar and drink considerably. Women are also valued customers in trendy bars catering to the after-work crowd that populate the major cities of the USA. One consequence of this social change has been a rapid increase in the incidence of alcoholism among women. Young women feel free to drink and are encouraged to do so by the people of Big Booze (see Chapter 2).

An example of how cultural norms can affect propensity of women to drink is provided by the research of Dr. Sarah Zemore.[2] Her research reported the results of a rigorous survey of Latino women. The results verified that immigrant and first generation women who had become more acculturated to the dominant norms of the United States drank more than those who had not become as acculturated. Further, among drinkers who were more like the average of the greater population (e.g., using English as the language at home) drank more and reported being drunk more frequently. There were no associations between amount and incidents of depressive symptoms. Also, there was no association between the stress of trying to "fit in" to the dominant culture and drinking. In brief, when the social sanctions that previously dampened Latino women's frequency of drinking were weakened, drinking increased. Latino women drank less than Latino men, but if the current trends continue, the expectation is that these women will drink as much or more than comparison groups.

Time magazine in 2009 sent a group of reporters to discern the status of women and girls drinking in the USA. They interviewed academic researchers, college women, and college counselors among others. They found that women and girls are drinking at rates that were previously unheard of. Perhaps their most disturbing finding was that a relatively high percentage of middle and grade school girls were drinking regularly and binge-drinking. The data on drinking among very young girls is particularly troubling, because there is ample evidence to indicate that the earlier one starts drinking the greater the likelihood of sustaining and further developing problematic drinking.[3]

A co-ed at a major New York university is quoted by *Time* as saying that the goals of her senior year in college were to "Learn how to drive a stick shift, and drink a guy under the table." ... "You don't want to be that dumb girly girl who looks wasted and can't hold her liquor. I know it's juvenile, but I've had boys comment how impressed they are at the amount of alcohol I've consumed. To be able to drink like a guy is a badge of honor. For me, it's a feminism thing" (*Time*, 2002, p 35).[4] Most of us would sincerely prefer that college seniors have more uplifting goals.

What is particularly troubling to us is her conclusion that her aspiration to drink a "guy under the table" is "a feminism thing." It is not; the feminist movement is about empowering women. Her goals will not empower her and will likely (actually, almost assuredly) do the opposite.

Using information from interviews, the article reported that women who drink a lot are more prone to having unintended sex with its concomitant increase in venereal diseases. Co-eds who drink a lot increase their risk of being abused and raped.

The Centers for Disease Control and Prevention of the US government do monthly surveys to ascertain the state of disease in the Nation. In a supplement to the Centers' *Morbidity and Mortality Weekly Reports* dated January 14, 2011, Dafna Kanny, Ph.D., and colleagues reported strong relationships between incidents of drinking and incidents of problems.[5] Based on their correlations, the conclusion was drawn that a binge drinking episode is a risk factor for unintended injuries (e.g., auto accidents), sexually transmitted diseases and unintended pregnancy. Frequent binge drinking is a risk factor for depression, suicide, and hypertension-related heart attack and stroke. There are risks for liver and brain diseases (more later). In brief, binge drinking is risky business for women.

Telescoping is a term used to describe an accelerated progression from the start of alcohol-use to the onset of so many problems as to deserve the first admission into a formal treatment program. When surveys are done, they consistently indicate that women show faster telescoping in comparison to men.[6] Women enter treatment with more medical, behavioral and social problems than men.

A 2009-report, from the Center, provides estimates of the incidence of binge drinking by all women of America 18 years and older.[7] They defined binge drinking as consuming 4 or more standard drinks on an occasion of drinking (see Chapter 2 for definitions of a drink). The best estimate is that slightly over 10% of women have at least one instance of binge drinking a month with an average of three instances during the month.

Survey-results such as those reported in the last paragraph are subject to error. There are a number of reasons to suppose that this reported rate of binge drinking by women under estimates of the actual rate. The sample is large (over 400,000), but it was compiled by way of standard telephone lines. It excluded all institutionally housed individuals, including those in college dormitories, and those with cell-phones. Other data suggests that the excluded will drink more often and when they do drink, drink more. The numbers are reports from memory which may be faulty and women may be hesitant to report high rates of drinking. Further, the data do not mesh well with the amounts of alcoholic beverages sold. The conclusion is that the reported numbers are a very conservative estimate of the rate of binge drinking among American women.

On average, binge drinking is more prevalent among men than women. Nevertheless, a rate of binge drinking among women is sufficiently high to be problematic, particularly when considering the rate of drinking among younger women.

A question is: "Is it so bad to get drunk on a Saturday night?" The short answer is probably no, but if done regularly the answer is assuredly yes. Regular episodes of getting drunk are particularly problematic if you are a woman, and even worse, if you are a girl. In terms of liver disease, one night of drinking is not problematic; being drunk, however, is a risk factor for such events as accidents and violent encounters. The extent of toxic effects of drinking is generally dose-related. Being drunk is more intoxicating (i.e., more toxic) than merely getting a small amount of ethanol to the brain on a daily basis. Doing both, say having a drink a day with dinner most days and drinking 4 to 6 drinks on a Saturday night is toxic. If this rate of drinking is sustained, it can be very toxic to a female (more on toxicity of binge drinking is given subsequently).

Girls' Binge Drinking has been High Since, at least, 1993.

Please study the following graphics. They present data that should alarm anyone interested in public health. The first is pictorial representation of rate of binge drinking among women and girls. The second is a comparison among groups.

During 2009, young women and girls had a higher incidence of hazardous drinking than mature women and men and nearly the same incidence as boys. Among girls in the 12th grade attending public high schools, over 30% of them had one or more episodes of hazardous drinking in the previous month.[8] If a young person drinks extensively, there is an increased risk of excessive drinking subsequently. A reasonable prediction: As the current cohort of young women mature, they will continue to exceed men's rates of binge drinking. The incidence of binge drinking is a sign of problematic drinking and a predictor of full blown AAA and its attendant problems. With few social sanctions governing females' drinking and given that women might be more prone to AAA than men and given that girls are binge drinking at high rates, the prediction is, in the near future, there will be more alcoholic women than men.

Binge Drinking
A Serious, Under-Recognized Problem
among Women and Girls

1 in 8   1 in 5

Nearly 14 million US women binge
drink about 3 times a month.   1 in 5 high school girls binge drink.

6 ɣɣɣɣɣ

Women average 6 drinks per binge.

Source: CDC Vital Signs, January 2013

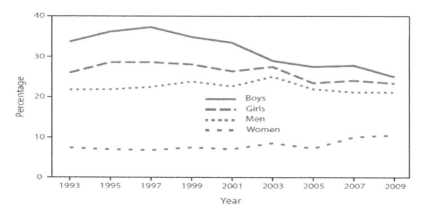

Figure 7.1. The figure depicts an estimate of the incidents of binge drinking among *high school students* (grades 9 through 12) in comparison to adults. Incidents were defined as having at least one binge drinking episode during the month before the survey. The data are based on responses to the Youth Risk Behavior Survey (YRBS) and Behavioral Risk Factor Surveillance System questionnaires, both large scale surveys sampling throughout the USA. Notice the marked difference in binge drinking among girls in comparison to women. YRBS defined binge drinking for boys and girls as "five or more drinks within a couple of hours," not the "four drinks on an occasion" in most other surveys since 2006. The estimate of prevalence of binge drinking among girls would have been higher if the four-drink definition had been used throughout. From Kanny et al. (2010).[8]

During 2009, young women and girls had a higher incidence of hazardous drinking than mature women and men and nearly the same incidence as boys. Among girls in the 12th grade attending public high schools, over 30% of them had one or more episodes of hazardous drinking in the previous month.[8] If a young person drinks extensively, there is an increased risk of excessive drinking subsequently. A reasonable prediction: As the current cohort of young women mature, they will continue to exceed men's rates of binge drinking. The incidence of binge drinking is a sign of problematic drinking and a predictor of full blown AAA and its attendant problems. With few social sanctions governing females' drinking and given that women might be more prone to AAA than men and given that girls are binge drinking at high rates, the prediction is, in the near future, there will be more alcoholic women than men.

The data of Figure 7.1 are from data collected before 2009. A more recent report (data of 2011) using similar methods as those used in the figure indicates that the situation has not changed much if any. The following is a summary of the main results of that tabulation. The 2013 report is subject to the same limitations as the earlier report.

"Among adult women, the prevalence of binge drinking was 12.5%, and among those who binge drank, the frequency of binge drinking was 3.2 episodes per month and the intensity was 5.7 drinks on occasion. Binge drinking was most prevalent among women aged 18–24 years (24.2%) and 25–34 years (19.9%), and among those from households with annual incomes equal to or greater than $75,000 (16.0%). Among those who binge drank, women aged 18–24 years had the highest frequency (3.6 episodes) and intensity (6.4 drinks) of binge drinking." (Kanny et al. 2013. p 1).[9]

How did we go from the low incidence of drinking, particularly binge drinking, among girls (say in the 1950s) to the considerably higher incidence currently? The social movement that promoted women's equality also led to a reduction in social conventions that guided women's drinking behavior. Drinking became more socially respectable, particularly for young women. The sophisticated advertising and public relations campaigns of Big Booze used the aspirations of the movements for women's equality very effectively (please, recall similar comments in Chapter 2). The advertising was aimed at making drinking a sign of rejection of subjugation to second class citizenry and a sign of liberation, fun, and happiness (and occasionally a sign of power, of sexual attractiveness that men were apparently helpless to resist). The industries lured girls to drink by providing beverages that tasted less like ethanol and more like desserts and beverages with the palatability of fruit juices and ice cream. Once drinking began, the advertising and public relations campaigns were designed to make being slightly intoxicated socially acceptable. Big Booze continued to mask the dire consequences of drinking often.

Alcoholic Beverages are More Toxic to Women than Men.

Ethanol can be toxic both in the short run (e.g., at a party) and, in the long run (e.g., when considered in terms of years of even moderate drinking). When alcohol is studied in the laboratory, the amount of alcohol drunk is often measured as grams of pure ethanol per kilogram of body weight. This provides a degree of precision. Even more precision is achieved when the amount of ethanol in blood is measured. The amount of ethanol in blood is directly related to amount circulating in brain. When, however, we discuss issues such as how much a person has drunk, we often speak of the number of drinks consumed. No matter how the degree of drinking is tabulated, it turns out that the degree of toxicity is related to degree of drinking.

Almost all authorities consider the following as the standard for hazardous or binge drinking: five drinks for a man and four drinks for a woman per occasion. Why five for men and four for women?

A number of factors contribute to the conclusion that the index of hazardous drinking should be a smaller for women. Each of the factors, however, is related to the amount of ethanol circulating in the brain which differs following a standard drink between men and women.

The average weight of women in the USA is about 155 pounds; for men, about 180 pounds. So, if the average women and an average man drink an identical 12 ounce can of Budweiser, the women will have a greater blood ethanol level as indexed by dose per pound which, of course, means greater ethanol circulating in brain. This difference in weight, however, is not the only reason that an average man can drink *an average woman "under the table."*

In the liver, ethanol is broken down into parts to be used or excreted (i.e., ethanol is metabolized in the liver). There are, however, enzymes (alcohol dehydrogenase) in the stomach that also metabolize ethanol. These stomach enzymes can process up to 15% of ingested alcohol. In the stomach, women process about 50% less ethanol than men, (due to less alcohol dehydrogenase in their stomach). The blood ethanol concentration is, therefore, increased by about 7% in women compared to men. This and other factors make a standard commercial drink more intoxicating and more toxic to women than men.

It follows that if men begin to incur health problems when they drink an average of three drinks a day, then women, particularly trim, small women, will incur health problems at an average of two drinks a day. Note that achieving an average of two drinks a day can be achieved by binge drinking on the weekends plus only one drink a day during the week (a glass of wine with the evening meal plus three drinks on Friday night and four on Saturday). A half bottle of wine with the daily evening meal may not be unusual, yet for a small woman that amount meets the criterion for hazardous drinking. To the novice drinker, this seems like a lot of drinking, even excessive drinking. For the typical alcoholic, however, the average of 14 drinks a week is a small amount. A truism: Alcoholics drink a lot.

As will be discussed when the topic is liver disease, breast cancer and alcohol-intake, for women even an average of a single drink a day may increase the risk of enduring health problems. Also, the habit of drinking small amounts of alcoholic beverage is clearly a large risk factor for escalating the amount drunk to truly toxic levels.

One estimate indicated that English and American women who went from being modest drinkers to heavy drinkers reduced their life-span an average of 15 years.[10] Recall the study reported in a previous chapter which followed a group of Swedish women as they aged. On average, they died sooner than their more temperate "sisters."

Alcohol Intake among Women and Diseases of the Liver

Ethanol is toxic in proportion to the amount of ethanol that is circulating in blood. If a woman drinks what might be considered a modest amount for a man, she is drinking at levels that can surely induce toxicity. This circumstance is manifest in incidences of liver disease in young women.

The following is a quotation from Dr. Gray Smith-Laing, an English physician specializing in diseases of the liver: "Until about 10 years ago, my patients with alcoholic liver disease were mostly middle-aged men. But women now make up about half of my caseload." He goes on to say, "it used to be that patients were in their forties and fifties when I first saw them. But I'm seeing sizeable and rising numbers of women in their twenties. Some have irreversible liver damage." He reported that, on his unit, a 26 year old woman had died from cirrhosis of the liver, an almost unheard of cause of death for a young woman.[11]

From what we know from surveys of drinking habits among the women of northern Europe, northern North America, and Australia and general knowledge, we can picture the following situation. There are a considerable number of young women who have the discretionary income to spend money on alcoholic beverages. Many of these women have developed careers that provide plenty of "beer-money" and more. They have money for expensive wines and can easily go to trendy, expensive bars after work to meet with friends and fellow workers. Often they have delayed marriage or have recently been divorced. They have a life-style that includes, if not focused on, periods of daily or weekly drinking. They could easily be fashionable in many ways, e.g., in dress, in supporting "green causes," or whatever other young sophisticates engage. They are often well-traveled and think of themselves as sophisticated. They rarely show marked drunkenness (e.g., they have learned to walk while intoxicated, because it has become a practiced behavior) and surely do not think of themselves as alcoholics and surely not drunkards. Unfortunately, among women, drinking a half bottle of wine on a regular basis with dinner and a glass occasionally at lunch, *or* a few cocktails after work, *or* regular heavy drinking on party-night is a serious risk factor for diseases of the liver including cirrhosis. Liver disease can progress without marked signs of the progression until there is serious organ damage. By the time these young women feel persistent pain in upper right portion of their belly; they have already incurred considerable damage to their liver.

For a variety of reasons, the conclusion is that women develop severe alcohol-related injury to the liver with lesser amounts of intake of alcohol and fewer years of exposure. After 25 years of study of the effects of ethanol on sex hormones, Professor (U of Pittsburgh School of Medicine) Patricia Eagon contends that estradiol's ordinary functionality is disrupted by the presence of ethanol. This in turn is related to the fact that the liver is also involved in the metabolism of steroids such as the sex hormones. Alcohol's presence on a regular basis can increase the levels of estradiol which, in turn, has a number of effects which may include enhanced appetite for alcohol and palatable foods (see below) and inability to get pregnant. She concludes her major review article with the following advice: "...women should exert caution by limiting their alcohol intake to one drink or less per day to avoid the complications of alcohol induced liver injury" (Eagon, 2010, p 1382).[12]

There are indications that single women drink more than their married counterparts and hence are more likely to suffer liver disease. An interesting study was done in Finland.[13] The investigators obtained information on 80% of all Finns who died between 2000 and 2007. This period is particularly interesting. During the first four years, Finland had a high tax on alcoholic beverages and during the last four a much lower tax. The tax-reduction was an average of 33% and particularly large for distilled spirits. The lowering of taxes in Finland was to make the tax on alcoholic beverages nearly equal across Europe.

The researchers were interested in death-rates and in investigating the relationship between living alone (compared to being married or living with someone) and drinking's effects. Previous findings suggested that living alone was related to an increase in drinking which, in turn, was related to increased alcohol-related adversities that ultimately were fatal.

Of the Finns between the ages of 15 to 79 years of age during the study-period, 18,246 of them died of alcohol related causes. The tabulated cause of death for 46% of the sample was liver disease or similar organ failures that were clearly related to excessive alcohol intake. The other portion of the sample died of events such as alcohol-related accidents, violence, or diseases that alcohol probably contributed to the death such as heart failure. Two-thirds of them lived alone (perhaps, a proxy for experiencing loneliness). The finding that those who lived alone made up the bulk of those dying did not reveal whether living alone was a result of drinking or living alone led to increased, problematic drinking.

The results with respect to level of alcohol taxes were "...a marked increase in alcohol-related mortality after the price reduction for those living alone and aged 50-69 years, but not for married or cohabiting persons (all ages)." "For liver disease, which is the most common fatal alcohol-related disease, the age-adjusted risk ratio associated with living alone versus being married or cohabiting was 3.7 before and 4.9 after the reduction in alcohol prices among men. The corresponding relative risks were 1.7 and 2.4 among women" (Herttua et al., 2011, p 5).[13] These data are a further indication that high alcohol taxes would promote health; indications contrary to what advocates for Big Booze tell us.

In summary, the increased drinking among women of prosperous nations has increased the incidence of liver disease. Among the factors linked to the increase in liver disease is more drinking among girls and young women which contribute to sustained drinking subsequently. Another factor: Big Booze is actively marketing their products to young women using highly sophisticated practices. Another risk factor is living alone and having the money to spend on leisure-time activities that involve considerable drinking. Ethanol is more toxic to women than men.

In the near future, there will be a marked increase in the number of young women who will suffer liver disease that is sometimes fatal.

Alcoholic Beverages and the Incidence of Breast Cancer

Cancer of the breast is common among women in America. Current estimates are that one in eight women will develop breast cancer sometime in their lives.[14] In 2007 (the most recent year complete numbers are available), 202,964 women in the United States were diagnosed with breast cancer. In that same year, 40,598 women in the United States died from breast cancer. Further, the incidence-rate has been rising. With the available evidence (circa 2011), the incidence for cancer in 2010, when finally tabulated, is expected to be 207,090. There is good news: treatments for breast cancer have been improving so that many more women are surviving the cancer.

Some risks for getting breast cancer are not under a person's control such as getting older. There are other things that are under a women's control including: (a) not taking estrogenic medicines such as those prescribed for birth control or as hormone replacement therapy for problems associated with menopause, (b) notably not drinking alcoholic beverages,[15] and (c) generally doing things that maintain good health such as preventing obesity.

Recall that one in eight women in the United States is apt to get breast cancer.[14] That estimate is based on the incidences for all women, nondrinkers as well as drinkers. Let us presume, for this discussion, that the rate for women who do not drink alcoholic beverages is say one in ten, rather than one in eight. That value (1 in 10) is a supposed baseline for us to calculate the risks of drinking alcoholic beverages for a nondrinker who starts drinking. As estimated by epidemiologists, the risks of drinking, on average, a single drink a day increases the risk of getting breast cancer by 9% and each additional drink by another 9% up to five drinks a day. The cumulative risk is presented in the accompanying table.

Drinks per Day	Risk of Breast Cancer
0	10%
1	11%
2	12%
3	13%
4	14%
5	16%

Please note that intake of 5 drinks a day, most days but not every day, sounds like a great deal to those who have not developed the habit of drinking. However, it is not an unusual amount for those with an intense habit of drinking. One set of data indicates that alcoholics on average drink that much or more on 125 days out of the year.[16]   Please note, once again, that an intense habit of drinking is a condition that begins with light social drinking.   Would you fly on commercial airlines, if airplanes crashed 16% of the time they flew? Why not? Most of the time, they wouldn't crash.

When these kinds of estimates are presented to a college class, there is inevitably a woman who will ask "does it count if you have 4 or 5 drinks on the weekend"? The answer is yes, it counts; and further binge drinking (i.e., massing your drinks) is more toxic than low steady drinking even when the number of drinks is equal across both instances. Although the data are not as strong as we might like to draw a conclusion, a reasonable conclusion is that risks increase as a function of the number of drinks across a life-time.   We might question the last assertion because we do not know why that might be the case.   What mechanism might account for the increase in risk of the excessive intake of alcohol during the college years that might span many years of abstinence? We do not know the answer. It may be some general effect similar to an overall amount of stress leading to a general weakness that, in turn, makes illness more likely (a general "weathering effect").

In a recent article from investigators working at the NIAAA, it was suggested that ethanol may be a carcinogen in its own right with respect to breast cancer.[17] Given the association between alcohol, estrogens and breast cancer, the prevailing idea is that alcohol increases estrogen levels which, in turn, increase the risk of cancer.[18] High levels of estrogens are probably carcinogenic and if ethanol is also carcinogenic, than the drinking of alcoholic beverages could be carcinogenic in two ways: by increasing estrogens and by its own actions.

One might find support for the conclusion that drinking increases the risk for breast cancer if you could find a group that did not drink as much as others but are comparable on many other variables and, then, tabulate their incidence of breast cancer. The Mormon religion prescribes against drinking by its adherents and presumably many, if not most, Mormon women do not drink alcohol. Mormons constitute a larger percentage of the populations of Utah and Arizona than almost all other states. Interestingly, the incidences of breast cancer rates in Utah and Arizona rank as 49th and 50th among the various states of the Union. The women of Utah do not drink as much as the women of other states and they do not get breast cancer at the same high rates as other states. Good for them!

From both the animal laboratory and epidemiological data, we have data to support the idea that drinking during adolescence is a strong risk factor for heavy drinking during womanhood.[19] In brief, it is more dangerous to begin drinking at the ages of 12 to 16 than from 21 to 27. Given that there are legal and other societal sanctions that support the idea that underage girls should not have the opportunity to drink alcoholic beverages; and given that it is desirable to reduce the incidence of breast cancer, it would seem wise for the sanctions to be enforced.

Other Manifestations of Ethanol's Toxic Effects

Previously and here, we did not feel the need to list all of the manifestations of alcoholic beverages' toxic effects. It just seems that the increased risk of breast cancer and liver disease are sufficient to make the point that the habit of drinking alcoholic beverages is risky. Nevertheless, it is worthwhile to reiterate that ethanol when taken regularly is toxic to the brain.

Recently, a group of scientists from Boston University, using sophisticated brain scanning technology, studied twenty-one women who previously evidenced alcoholism.[20] This group of currently abstinent women had an average of 10.6 years of abstinence after an average of 14.2 years of steady drinking. There was a matched group of women who were social drinkers. Both the previously alcoholic women and the controls provided brain scan data indexing the amount of white matter in brain (amount of white matter indexes healthy connections within areas of the brain). The scans indicated that the previously alcoholic women had reduced white matter in both the frontal and temporal lobes of the brain. The former alcoholics also had larger ventricular space in the brain than the controls. In general, the more years of heavy drinking, the smaller the white matter and, further, the longer the period of abstinence, the greater the amount of recovery of white matter volume. These data provide further confirmation that ethanol is toxic to brain and that the effects can be particularly long-lasting. All of our information about brains indicates that brain damage, even in relatively small amounts, will clearly be manifest when individuals are placed in cognitively challenging situations.

There are a number of psychological and social problems that are seemingly incurred by women drinking toxic amounts of alcohol. These include some of the same effects as seen in men such as increased propensity for violence, lack of social responsibility in terms of employment and family, an increase in impulsiveness and criminal activity. Many of these problems follow from ethanol's toxic effects on the brain and hence the reduced ability to plan and appreciate the consequences of behavior. Women have often prided themselves as being the gender that sustains moral behavior and controls the drinking of men. If women drink like men, will they have that same ability?

Alcoholic Beverages may be More Appealing to Women.

The fact that more ethanol reaches the brain when a woman drinks a standard alcoholic beverage supports the conclusion that alcoholic beverages may be more appealing to women than men. This is because the high (the pleasant effect) is related to the initial impact of ethanol reaching the brain in a sufficient amount. For women, that sufficient amount is more apt to be the amount associated with the first drink of the day. Stated differently, the fact that a woman can get high quicker from a standard serving of an alcoholic beverage makes it more likely that she will find drinking pleasant. There may be other reasons women might find alcoholic beverages more appetizing. Some research with female rats provided some interesting perspectives.

The first time we studied the intake of an alcoholic beverage among female rats, we were surprised by the amount of alcohol they drank. These were the days in which you taught that alcoholism was a man's problem (a male problem) and was rare among women. We should not have been surprised, because when we searched for similar findings in the scientific literature, we found that others had observed the same: female laboratory animals tended to drink more than males.

Some of the reports of females drinking more than males came from those doing research showing that one can do selective breeding to eventually have a strain of rats that voluntarily drink large amounts of an alcoholic beverage while at the same time have another strain that drinks less than ordinary. The procedure is straightforward. Within a group of rats that are outwardly very similar, some rats drink alcoholic beverage more than others. If one mates males who drink a lot with females who drink a lot and concurrently mates males who drink little with females who drink little, eventually the result is two strains of rats that drink different amount of alcoholic beverage. In about nine generations, the offspring of the selective breeding program yields two strains of rats that breed true: one strain drinks more than the strain that began the selective breeding and one that drinks less. The scientists who did these experiments uniformly reported that females drank the most, generation after generation. Scientists who have measured intake of alcoholic beverages among monkeys also report females drink more.[21]

The conclusion one can draw from the observations that some mammalian females drink more than males is that there is nothing inherent to being a female that can account for the fact that across many decades of the American experience AAA were predominantly male problems. It is likely that the social norms restricting women's drinking account for women's historically low incidence of alcoholism rather than some feature of a female's physiology.

The reductions in social conventions that previously reduced women's drinking may not be sufficient by themselves to put women at greater risk for hazardous drinking. There are likely other reasons at issue. One thing that differs between men and women is the difference in circulating levels of hormones; women have greater amounts of estradiol than men. Perhaps female's production of estradiol might be related to an enhanced appetite for alcoholic beverages when there are no strong environmental constraints on how much is drunk. The next section is relevant to that issue.

Prior to that discussion, this is a good place to point out that those who are searching for a relationship between genetic endowment and AAA may have overlooked the obvious differences in the genetic endowment: females versus males.

The scientific literature indicates that doses of the female hormone, estradiol, reduced rats' intake of food.[22] Since some of the same neurotransmitters and neuro-modulators, had been shown to be involved with intake of food and alcoholic beverages, we decided to directly test the idea that large doses of estradiol would reduce female rats' intake of palatable alcoholic beverages.

We provided a sweetened alcoholic beverage to rats along with their ordinary food and water. After they regularly took enough alcohol to produce signs of drunkenness during the 2 hr that alcohol was available, we then injected half of them with estradiol valerate and the other half with a placebo. A single injection of estradiol valerate produces high levels of estradiol for many days. The amount obviously varies with the size of the dose. We injected a large dose at first just to get some idea of what might be appropriate doses for further study.

When we injected placebos, they had no discernible effect on intake of alcoholic beverage. When we injected estradiol valerate, we got what was expected, a reduction in intake.[23] Our colleague at McGill University, Prof. Christina Gianoulakis, and a graduate student working with her, Mr. Peter Marinelli reported that they too had tested the effects of estradiol valerate, but found that, surprisingly, they saw increases in intakes. As we continued providing the females with the opportunity to take alcoholic beverages, under the influence of the long-acting estradiol-producing drug, we observed that the females after a few days slowly began taking more and more alcohol and eventually were taking more than the placebo-treated rats and more than before their injections of estradiol valerate. The researchers at McGill and our university continued to study the effect.[24] The idea that estradiol might enhance intakes of alcohol was very interesting and our results were unexpected.

Further research confirmed that just after the injections of estradiol valerate, that intakes of alcohol were less than before the injections. If, however, testing was continued for a number of days, alcohol-intake was larger than before and larger than females getting placebo. In fact, under the influence of continuous dosing with estradiol, we saw some of the largest amounts of intake ever reported for female rats during a brief period.[25]

Scientists generally do not trust conclusions derived from one or two experiments. Perhaps, the general results (estradiol can enhance intake of alcohol) would not be found if the procedures of the experiment were changed slightly. For example, perhaps the effect would fade when smaller doses were used. Perhaps, the particular preparation of the injection (the valerate part of the compound rather than the estradiol part) was responsible for the results. There were other features of the experiment that may have accounted for the results, for example, we tested the rats during the day (a time when rats usually sleep) and maybe that was what increased the females' drinking. We engaged what scientists call replication and extension. We continued to test the idea that continuous circulation of an estrogenic drug in experiment after experiment, but the experimental procedures differed somewhat. We tested the idea with a different form of estradiol injection (estradiol benzoate). Estrogenic drugs increased intakes of alcohol, when different strains of rats were the subjects and when different kinds of alcoholic beverages were used. We tested smaller doses. In brief, with each test, it was found that after the initial effects of injections of estradiol, that continuous dosing with estradiol enhanced intakes of alcoholic beverage, particularly sweetened alcoholic beverage.[26]

Figure 7.2 depicts results when we provided female rats 24 hr a day to take a palatable alcoholic beverage after they had received a moderate dose of estradiol valerate some days before the procedure. These were females who had a history of taking some alcohol before the experiment. Please notice that the females getting placebos drank a lot of alcohol, enough to make them tipsy during some portion of the day. The females under the influence of estradiol, however, drank considerably more. During some portions of the day, some of these females drank to the point of not being able to right themselves or to walk without staggering. This team of females probably holds the world's record for amount of intake of ethanol during a day.

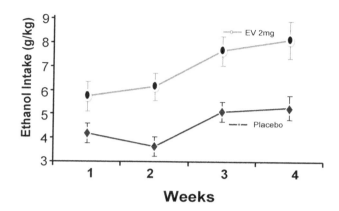

Figure 7.2. The figure depicts the amount of ethanol of two groups of female rats that previously had been given a palatable alcoholic beverage to drink for 24 hr a day. One group was then given a dose of estradiol valerate that produces nearly continuous high levels of estradiol for the days of the experiment. The other group received a placebo. The data are presented as mean daily intake for each of 4 weeks. Notice that the intake of the group getting placebos is large, large enough to produce obvious signs of drunkeness (e.g., slowed ability to right themselves when put on their backs) during some portions of a day. When the females also had continuous estradiol, their intakes became much larger. Intakes of over 7 grams of ethanol per kilogram of bodyweight induces obvious signs of drunkeness. The data of the figure is from a poster presented at a meeting in Argentina and authored by Meta, Larry and our son who helped collect the data.[25] The data used in making the figure is from Reid, M.L., et al. (2003).

Dr. Sofía Ledesma de la Teja, working in the laboratory of Professor Roberto Prado-Alcalá, demonstrated that the persistently high daily intake of a palatable alcoholic beverage disrupted the usual estrous cycle in female rats. Although not tested directly, the induced conditions would have made it impossible for the females to become pregnant. Among women, alcohol consumption also affects fertility.[27] In an experiment designed to measure the amount of circulating estradiol after various injections of estradiol valerate, Sofía noticed that females that received the estradiol had developed enlarged nipples probably indicative that the injected estradiol induced some of the conditions of pregnancy. During pregnancy, estradiol levels are normally very high.

After we became convinced that both large and small continuous doses of estradiol led female rats to drink more alcoholic beverage, we asked whether providing continuous estrogenic stimulation also increased the intake of other palatable drinks. The accompanying figure depicts data to support the conclusion that the continuous estradiol stimulation enhances rats' intake of a palatable saccharin solution but not an unpalatable saccharin solution.[28]

The experimental arrangement associated involved four groups of young female rats. They were given the opportunity to take one of two kinds of saccharin sweetened water: (a) one had a low concentration of saccharin producing a fluid of which rats typically drank large amounts and (b) one with a high concentration of saccharin, a drink that we knew that rats did not favor and, in fact, only drank small amounts. Among humans, high concentrations of saccharin tastes bitter and we presumed that was the same for the female rats.

We gave one half of the group having the opportunity to drink the palatable solution a dose of estradiol valerate. We also gave one half of the group having the opportunity to drink the unpalatable solution the estradiol. The other half of each group received placebos. The rats always had water and food available. A summary of the results of the effects of estradiol valerate on female rats' intake of two kinds of saccharin solutions is presented in the accompanying figure. In brief, the continuous estradiol enhanced intakes of the more palatable saccharin solution, but decreased intakes of the less palatable solution.

The experiment with the two kinds of saccharin solution indicated that continuous estrogenic stimulation did not enhance intake of all kinds of beverages, only those that were palatable and provided a rewarding experience. The injections of estradiol actually reduced intake of the supposedly bitter solution. Notice that the effects of estradiol valerate were remarkably enduring.

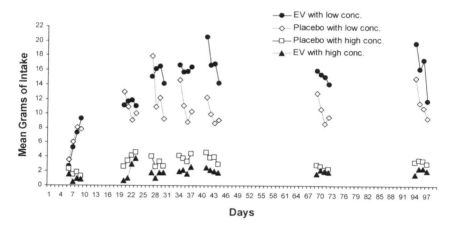

Figure 7.3. The figure depicts the data associated with the experiment testing the effects of injections of estradiol valerate on intake of two kinds of saccharin solutions. The filled data-points represent average intakes of those getting estradiol injections. The open data-points with represent average intake of those getting placebos. The main finding is that the large dose of estradiol enhanced for a prolonged time intake of the more palatable solution and actually decreased the intake of the less palatable solution. The data used in this figure is from Boswell et al. (2005).[28]

Doses of estradiol often do not enhance intake of ordinary rat food. We wondered if doses of estradiol valerate would enhance intakes of palatable food. Consequently, we fed female rats chocolate cake mix batter.[29] We expect that a reader, at this stage of our narration, is going to ask: "Why are you feeding female rats chocolate cake mix batter; isn't that bizarre?" We will grant you, it is unusual (maybe even weird). There is a reason; it makes sense in terms of just getting accurate measures of the amount of tasty food a rat will eat. Rats produce crumbs as they eat many of the foods that one might provide. In brief, rats are messy eaters and the crumbs they produce are usually mixed with their droppings and difficult, if not just unpleasant, to isolate and measure.

While thinking about a food that we could feed female rats would be taken avidly (was delicious) and that they would not spill (easy to measure), we learned about the advantages of using chocolate cake mix batter as food for assessing rats' propensity to take a palatable food. It was commercially available and easy to prepare. Rats usually ate a large amount of it, and because of its colloidal nature, they ate it without producing crumbs. It was the food of choice to test whether injections of estrogenic drugs might increase the intake of tasty food.

We gave two groups of female rats the opportunity to take as much of chocolate cake mix batter as they wished. We followed the directions for baking in terms of the amount of water to add to Duncan Hines chocolate cake mix to produce a batter. We put the batter in small glasses in their cages. They had all of their regular rat-food[30] they wished to eat as well as all of the water they wished. Within a few days, the rats ate large amounts of the batter while also eating some of their regular food and taking their regular amount of water.

The first thing to note is that young female rats really like chocolate cake mix batter. The placebo controls across all of our experiments with the cake mix, on average, took over 22 grams of the mix a day while weighing usually under 250 grams (or over 8% of their body weight; for the average women, that would be about 12.4 pounds of cake a day, day after day). Please notice the left graph of the figure. Across the first 20 days of measurement after injections, the average females getting estradiol ate 524 grams of the mix, 12% more cake batter than the placebo controls who were already taking very large amounts. The 524 grams of intake is more than twice their body weight in 20 days.

Others have also observed that continuous estrogenic dosing enhanced rats' appetite for palatable food and alcoholic beverage; for example, continuous estradiol enhanced intakes of Fruit Loops (a sweet commercial cereal), a favorite food of female rats.[31] Next we asked whether a food supplement of merely fat and sugar (no chocolate) would be taken avidly when female rats were given injections that produce high levels of estradiol for many days.

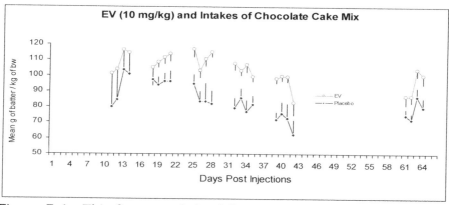

Figure 7.4. This figure and the following summarize the effects of doses of estradiol on intake of chocolate cake mix batter. The left graph depicts mean intake in terms of grams of batter taken per kilogram of the females' bodyweights. One of the groups received estradiol valerate (10 mg/kg) and the other group received placebos. Prior to injections, the females had opportunity to take the batter. After injections, we suspended presentation of the batter for a few days until the estradiol-treated group again was gaining weight regularly. Then, we presented the cake mix batter for a number of week-days, then stopped providing for a period (during our holiday) and then again presented it about 5 weeks after injections. You might notice that the intake of the batter seemed to go down with the passage of days. That apparent drop in intake is only when intake is measured as grams per bodyweight. The females were gaining weight, but their intakes in terms of grams eaten remained nearly the same (they probably could not eat more because of limitations in size of stomach).

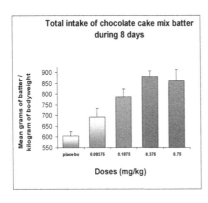

Figure 7.5. This graph depicts, using similar procedures, assessments of smaller doses of estradiol valerate. Measurements were taken some days after the injections and for a period of 8 days. Notice that the smallest dose given (0.09375 mg/kg) induced the females to take significantly more cake mix batter than those given placebos. From Boswell et al. (2006).[29]

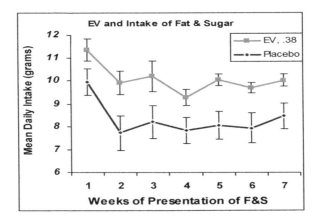

Figure 7.6. The figure depicts a summary of the results reflecting the effects of estradiol valerate on female rats' daily intake of a mixture of fat and sugar. The data points are means of daily intake of the two groups of rats averaged across the seven days of a week. In other words the females that received estradiol ate about 10 grams of fat and sugar daily for seven weeks after the fat and sugar was presented while those getting placebo ate about 8 grams. The bars extending from the data points are standard errors of the mean, a statistical measure. When error-bars' extent does not overlap, the conclusion is that the differences seen are very unlikely to be due to chance and are a product of some recognizable event (in this case whether the females got estradiol or placebo).

We used nearly the same procedures as we used with the experiment using chocolate cake mix. A group of female rats was given a mixture of one portion of vegetable shortening to one portion of table sugar (similar to commercial icing for a cake) as a supplement to their ordinary food and water. The females readily learned to eat a lot of fat and sugar (Figure 7.6).

As one can easily predict, the females who ate the fat and sugar supplement gained weight at a greater rate than one would expect of young female rats. The subjects given the opportunity to eat as much fat and sugar under the influence of higher than normal estradiol valerate gained weight more rapidly than those got only placebos.

Estradiol valerate is a compound specifically designed to have long lasting estrogenic effects. Perhaps, the effects depicted in the figures are specific to estradiol valerate. Given that possibility, we assessed other estrogenic compounds, namely estradiol benzoate, 17 alpha-ethynylestradiol, and estrone 3-sulfate. Estrone is an estrogenic hormone and is a metabolic product of estradiol. The procedures and subjects of those tests were nearly the same as the tests of estradiol valerate on intake of chocolate cake mix batter. All three compounds are used as medicines or components of birth control pills. Estradiol benzoate, 17 alpha-ethynylestradiol enhanced females' intakes of the palatable food, but estrone did not produce significant increments in intake.

Our initial findings indicated that a preparation that provided estradiol over a long period produced some startling results. The results open the possibility that estrogenic effects might enhance a female's appetite for alcoholic beverages. We then found that estrogenic compounds actually enhanced intakes of palatable food and drink, a finding that was just the opposite of the general conclusion derived from many other experiments.[32] The common conclusion was that estradiol reduced food intake, a correct conclusion if, and only if, you only take into account the initial effects of estradiol as a drug. When one tests for the long term effects of estradiol as a drug, one finds just the opposite of the commonly held conclusion that estradiol reduces food intake.

The conclusions and the implications that can be derived from these studies can be controversial; controversial because they conflict with the rationale for the sales of estrogenic medicines which can be highly profitable; controversial because they provide rationale that conflict with the sales of alcoholic beverages; controversial because they conflict with other scientists' research showing that estrogenic drugs reduce appetite for food and drink; and, controversial because they are generally novel. A controversial implication of these findings is that women probably have a heightened appetite for alcoholic beverage due to their physiology. The studies from our laboratory, although reasonably extensive, are probably not sufficient to fully support the implication. Fortunately, there are other observations, scattered throughout the literature, that support the contention that high levels of circulating estrogenic compound enhance appetite for palatable food and alcoholic beverages.

Using female rats, further research at the laboratory of Professor Gianoulakis, McGill University, and research from a laboratory at the Universidad de Guadalajara, directed by Professor Juárez, have shown that prolonged administration of estradiol enhanced alcohol consumption.[33,34] From multiple laboratories using different strains of rats, different alcoholic beverages, different preparations for administration estradiol, and slightly different procedures, the experiments indicate that rats can be induced to take more alcoholic beverage than ordinarily by giving pharmacological doses of an estrogenic drug. The effect is not seen just after the administration of doses of estrogens, but emerges with prolonged dosing. The effect is not due to a small procedural variable of any one experiment, but rather the results are seen across a number of experimental variables. Given the multiple experiments, it is reasonable to conclude: the proposition is strongly supported that estrogenic stimulation can significantly enhance female rats' voluntary consumption of alcoholic beverages.

The question is: Do the findings have any relevance to women and their potential appetite for alcoholic beverages? There are relevant data.[35] A study by the distinguished professor Dr. Paola Muti and her colleagues at Italian National Cancer Institute is an example.[36] What they did was to measure women's amount of circulating estradiol at two separate times one year apart during the morning and during the luteal phase of the menstrual cycle (period just after ovulation, the beginning of which is the best time to conceive). They then separated the women's data into three groups. One group that produced consistently high values of circulating estradiol; one group that produced consistently low values of circulating estradiol; and a third group whose values were variable. They then looked at the women's reported use of alcoholic beverages.

Dr. Muti and her colleagues found that women who consistently had large amounts of circulating estradiol (375.5 pmol/liter) drank, on average, 92.8 grams of alcohol a week, whereas those who consistently had low amounts of circulating estradiol (353.3 pmol/liter) drank, on average, 31.6 grams of alcohol a week. Women who abstained from drinking alcoholic beverages had 332.0 pmol/liter of circulating estradiol whereas women who drank alcoholic beverages (91.4 grams a week) had 391.9 pmol/liter. Dr. Muti and her colleagues concluded "...these findings suggest that alcohol consumption is associated with consistently higher serum concentrations of estradiol in premenopausal women. If alcohol consumption causes breast cancer, its action could be mediated, at least in part, through an effect on estrogen metabolism" (Muti et al. 1998, p 193).

Are there any indications that estradiol might affect the systems of the brain associated with the rewards of ingestion? Relevant to the issue is the understanding that circulating estradiol acts on multiple areas of the brain by way of specific receptors and that estrogenic neuromodulators are synthesized in areas of the brain. The endogenous opioid systems of the brain are part of the larger system that controls the rewards of eating and drinking.

Given this broad perspective, it is surely possible that estrogenic molecules could have effects on the neurons of the endogenous opioid system which, in turn, would have effects on the neural system controlling ingestion.

The findings and conclusions that estrogenic effects are salient to appetite for palatable alcoholic beverages, palatable food and nonalcoholic beverages are compatible with findings and conclusions that estrogenic effects are salient to addictive drug use, for example, cocaine use. A review of the available findings by the distinguished Professor Marilyn Carroll and her colleagues from the University of Minnesota led to the following conclusion: "...females seem to be more sensitive to the rewarding effects of drugs than males, and estrogen is a major factor that underlies these sex differences..." (Carroll et al., 2004, p 273).[37]

During the normal menstrual period, the levels of estradiol vary; the levels are not constant. With onset of pregnancy, estradiol levels remain high and continue to increase, that is, pregnancy is a state of large, escalating levels of estradiol. It is adaptive for pregnancy to be a period during which the pregnant woman has a large appetite for nourishing food and drink in order to sustain the nutritional demands of a growing baby. At the same time, it would be adaptive for a pregnant woman to be picky eater in order to avoid food-related poisons that in low doses might interfere with the development of a healthy baby. Toxic substances are often bitter. Notice that in our experimental arrangements large levels of circulating estradiol decreased intake of a bitter substance and increased intakes of high calorie substances such as fat and sugar, chocolate cake mix batter, and sweetened alcoholic beverages. This concordance with the features of pregnancy and the outcome of our rather simple experiments, leads to the following idea. Any event which might lead to large levels of continuous estradiol would instigate a process of normal pregnancy; that is, a large appetite for palatable food and drink, particularly food and drink that was clearly palatable and produced ready calories (sweets, starches and some alcoholic beverages).

In our book, *Women, alcoholism and feminism*, we have a rather lengthy discussion on issues associated with older women and alcoholic beverages.[38] At one time, the giving of estrogenic drugs was touted as reducing some of the problems of ageing, including vascular and heart diseases. We pointed out that recent research indicates that the use of estrogenic drugs to treat problems of ageing may not be as good of an idea as previously believed.

Fetal Alcohol Syndrome

Pregnant women who drink alcoholic beverages risk poisoning their babies.[39] Chemicals that can cause malformations in a developing baby before the baby is born are called teratogens. Ethanol is a teratogen. Ethanol readily crosses cellular membranes, including those protecting the baby and those of the developing baby itself. Consequently, any ethanol in the mother's blood gets to the baby. Also, mother's milk has the same ethanol content as her blood.

Ethanol seems to be particularly, but not exclusively, toxic to neural tissue. One of the main consequences of ethanol's toxicity is limited cognitive capabilities in children of women who drink when pregnant.

We have labeled the most severe cases of injury as the fetal alcohol syndrome. Other labels have been used to describe the less severe cases. The syndrome is manifest by low birth weight, tendency for retarded rates of growth, small head size, certain features of the face (see Figure 7.7), kidney malfunctioning, poor cognitive functioning and a general lack of robust health. With the most severe forms, the level of cognitive functioning may not reach levels required to successfully complete elementary school. The most severe cases are incapable of functioning independently and must be cared for throughout their lives.

As with a number of disorders, the approach is to conceptualize the toxic effects of ethanol on developing babies as a continuum and that continuum is called the fetal alcohol spectrum disorders (FASD). FASD varies from those of fetal alcohol syndrome with its multiple manifestations to mild cognitive impairment.

In general, we have substantial data on children showing the more severe cases of damage. The average incidence of severe cases (i.e., those of fetal alcohol syndrome) in the United States is likely to be between 0.5 and 2.0 per 1,000 births.

If we tabulate the incidence of the most obvious rates of ethanol poisoning with the less obvious, the rate of ethanol poisoning is about 10 per 1,000 births or about 1%. Given that this is an average, some groups might have considerably higher rates than others.

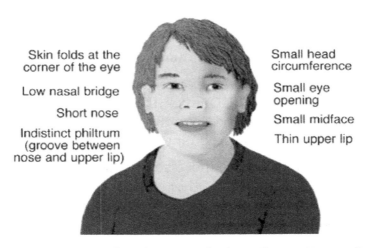

Skin folds at the corner of the eye

Low nasal bridge

Short nose

Indistinct philtrum (groove between nose and upper lip)

Small head circumference

Small eye opening

Small midface

Thin upper lip

Figure 7.7. The drawing depicts the pattern of facial features associated with fetal alcoholism syndrome. Source: Warren, K.R. & Foudin, L.L. (2001). Alcohol-related birth defects—The past, present, and future. *Alcohol Research & Health,* **25,** 153–8.39

Obviously, groups showing the highest rates of alcoholism also have the highest rates of FASD. Certain tribes of Native Americans, but surely not all tribes, may have rates as high as 9 to 10% of their children evidencing alcohol-induced cognitive problems. It also follows that other groups that drink considerably have high rates of FASD. This includes 35 to 44 year old, white, college educated and employed women, who are known to drink too much too often and, therefore, have a higher incidence of FASD than their counterparts. It is a myth to conclude that FASD is a problem limited to poor minority groups.[1]

Figure 7.8 presents some interesting data. It indicates, for example, a high incidence of binge drinking during the first trimester of pregnancy, a period in which women may not know they are pregnant. It also includes data of drinking after the baby was born. These data compared to previous data indicate that there has been some progress in terms of prevention of drinking during pregnancy. Despite some signs of progress, far too many women drank heavily during pregnancy.

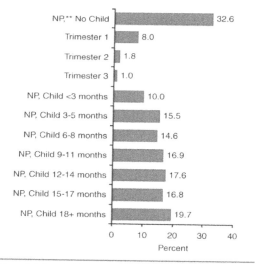

* Binge alcohol use is defined as drinking five or more drinks at the same time or within a couple of hours on at least 1 day in the past 30 days.
**NP = Nonpregnant
Source: 2002 to 2007 SAMHSA National Surveys on Drug Use and Health (NSDUHs).

Figure 7.8. Women's (Aged 18 to 44 Years, data of USA) past month binge alcohol-use-rate by pregnancy trimester and age of the youngest child in household: 2002 to 2007. Although these data are somewhat dated, there is no reason to suppose more recent data, when finally tabulated, will be much different than these tabulations. These data were published in May, 2009.

Since women often do not know they are pregnant during the first month or more of pregnancy, women who drink moderately (and we do mean moderately; for a woman, probably only 1 drink during a party) during this period are apt to worry that they have caused great damage to their developing baby. The risk is small and probably need not cause great anxiety. Once again, the risk is greater the greater the dose of ethanol. Conversely, a woman who consistently binge drinks before learning she is pregnant (and especially one who continues to do so) is apt to suffer the severe hardships of raising a severely cognitively challenged child.

Recently, investigators monitored a large group of women.[40] They tabulated the number who drank heavily during their pregnancy and those that did not. They also tabulated drinking after children were born. From these and other data, the conclusion was that 44% of drinking women had children with "functional central nervous systems abnormalities." The abnormalities were manifest in the maturing children as language problems and as attention deficits. The tabulation of "functional central nervous systems abnormalities" yielded a higher incidence of toxicity than tabulating the more obvious physical signs of the fetal alcohol syndrome.

There is a consensus that binge drinking is more toxic to a developing baby than spaced drinking of the same number of drinks. Please notice that the definition of binge drinking in the accompanying figure is five drinks in a short period. This is larger than the definition more frequently used for women, i.e., four drinks.

There are multiple events that might interact with a dose of ethanol. A concept called *weathering* is a summary of effects that increase the chances that doses of ethanol might be toxic to a developing baby. Weathering includes cumulative effects of poor living conditions, poor nutrition, and high levels of stress including those of multiple child bearings. The early age of starting regular drinking is said to enhance the risk of weathering as well as enhancing the chances of becoming a habitual drinker, and, therefore, increasing the risk of FASD.

The consensus of the medical and academic communities that has studied the risks of alcohol's potential to damage a developing baby is that pregnant women should not drink any alcoholic beverage during pregnancy. The advice of "no alcohol during pregnancy" is based on our limited knowledge of exactly when damage can occur and our limited knowledge of exactly how alcohol might affect a given individual (either mother or developing baby).

If you prefer living in a community that prospers, it is reasonable to also prefer the reduction of instances of FASD. It follows that you would also prefer programs that limit the use of alcoholic beverages among those most apt to become pregnant. Since we already have laws designed to restrict drinking among those under the age of 21 in the USA, it also seems to follow that we should strictly enforce these laws in the interest of decreasing the risks of unwanted pregnancies and pregnancies that are apt to be sullied by alcohol toxicity. It is of interest to note that mothers who exposed their children to ethanol during their pregnancy more often started drinking at ages less than 18 years and this was earlier than mothers who did not drink during pregnancy.[41]

There are a small number of studies indicating that the father's drinking increases the risk of having a child that is less than healthy.[42] The idea is that drinking may induce modifications in the sperm that, in turn, modifies the genetic code subtly (not sufficiently to prevent full term pregnancies but sufficiently to produce changes that are less than optimal).

A couple planning on having a child should control their drinking, if they prefer to reduce the chances of having a sickly child, or stated conversely, if they prefer to increase their chances of having a healthy child.

Summary

Well-regulated ingestion is the hallmark of a healthy, happy life-style. Ingestion that is not well-regulated is manifest as alcoholism (frequent intoxication), obesity, and other eating disorders, which in turn contribute to the early onset (sickness) of deadly diseases (commonly, diabetes, depression, liver disease, cardiovascular diseases or cancer). AAA increase propensity for accidents and asocial behavior. In some fundamental ways, well-regulated ingestion is an issue of regulating our immediate pleasures for long-term gains. Due to differences in physiology, for some people, regulating ingestion is easier than for others. When nutritional needs are probably met, for some the pleasures of eating and drinking are more salient than for others. Nevertheless, we must all regularly eat and drink to live and, therefore, regularly face temptations regardless of whether the immediate opportunity for pleasure is great or not so great. In modern industrialized worlds, most citizens face many choices about what to ingest. Those marketing food and drink relentlessly urge more consumption of their products. Since most of our eating and drinking habits are well-engrained, our eating and drinking behaviors are nearly automatic (unconsciously controlled) and not subject to much deliberate thought.

There are reasons to believe that throughout history, the issue of resisting temptation to achieve immediate comfort and pleasure in order to achieve long term opportunities for enduring comfort and pleasure has been paramount. We are just built that way; brains have limited capacity to fully account for probable delayed pleasures and pain. The focus on the immediate is probably adaptive (you need to avoid that looming truck in your path rather than dwell on what you might have for dinner). Despite an inherent bias toward focusing on the possibilities for immediate pleasure and pain, habits can be established that provide for the behaviors of resisting multiple pleasures to achieve long-term goals but those kinds of habits are often difficult to develop. Into these age-old conundrums, we have foods, drinks, and drugs that have the effect of making the resistance to temptations more difficult.

There are a number of drugs designed to treat psychological disorders that have the effect of increasing bodyweight. A number of drugs used for recreational purposes increase appetite. We have increased our knowledge of how to make food more palatable without regard to its nutritional value. There is a possibility that by manipulating the hormonal state of women that we have increased the appetite for palatable food and drink. We have on the market highly palatable alcoholic drinks and a whole cadre of bartenders competing in how to best mask the harsh taste of concentrated ethanol. Further, we are learning that even moderate alcohol consumption, by modern standards of what is moderate, may erode the brain areas most responsible for impulse control. Such circumstances combine to support the prediction that in the near future there will be more alcoholic women than now and more alcoholic women than men. There will be more mothers and grandmothers who are alcoholics.

More specifically, alcoholic beverages contain a compound that is toxic in high doses. But what is a high dose? A high dose differs between men and women. There is a good chance that even a small number of drinks, taken across say a week, can be highly toxic. Although the risk is applicable to all drinking women, the risks are higher for lean women, small women, women taking a variety of medicines including estrogenic ones, women of some ethnic groups, and to women who believe that they can hold their liquor (e.g., a large women of Northern European extraction who can have a *few* without a hangover or undue reduction of decision-making capabilities).

Alcoholic beverages can easily establish the habit of regularly drinking them and regularly drinking large amounts of them. Concurrent with the establishment of the habit, people come to love their drinks (they have, at least, in the past provided a measure of comfort and pleasure). The habitual drinker defends their behavior and often acts as love-struck teenagers who become incensed when someone tells them that the object of their affection is not good for them.

Based on recently collected scientific evidence there is a good chance, really a very good chance, that women's physiology promotes an appetite for alcoholic beverages. Relatedly, estrogenic hormones that might promote an increased appetite for alcohol are regularly sold as medicines almost exclusively to women. Because of alcohol's unique effects (no ordinary commodity) a woman can "marry" drinking; and, as even with a bad marriage, find divorce is difficult.

The managers of Big Booze are well aware that women can become their very good customers; they promote the sale of alcohol in a women-friendly, girl-friendly manner and mask the dangers of drinking. These managers probably prefer young women as customers; they can become lifelong customers even though some of them are apt to have a shorter life than otherwise. They know that moderate, socially acceptable drinking is likely to establish a profound habit (a prolonged love affair) with an agent whose toxicity increases as a function of the duration of its use. To get young women to drink often, they pair their product with fun and romantic sex. They pair their products with independence and, ironically, particularly independence from men making decisions for them. Big Booze, by way of public relations, masks the dire consequences of habitual drinking. They even portray those who would regulate their activities as <u>undemocratic, heavy handed, corrupt government</u> hacks having the ulterior motives of just wanting to be bossy; rather than men and women who just want their daughters and granddaughters not to be manipulated unduly.

We are living in a time when it seems to be acceptable for a company, any company, with obligations to share holders and its employees to make profits by any means. The end here (making increased profits) supposedly justifying any means (e.g., getting girls to become habitual drinkers). When young women become habitual drinkers they increase their risk of breast cancer and liver disease to mention only two hazards. Do we really have such a social contract (profit by any means)? Does any established business have the unfettered right to make money despite the long-term costs to a large group (even a very small group) of people? We believe that the answer is: No, emphatically No. It is good to make money by doing good, not by any means.

Notice how we speak about companies. We endow these organizations with person-like characteristics in terms of having financial obligations, but not in being responsible for what else the company does. In fact, companies are run by people and it is those people who make the decisions. Managers and directors of companies make choices, but the rationale for and the consequences of those decisions are attributable to disembodied companies. Companies can suffer consequences of poor decisions by their managers. However, seldom do managers suffer consequences of their choices, particularly if sales are up.

It strikes us as particularly atrocious to have magazines and Web sites designed for women and often managed by women to be in love with alcoholic beverages (or in the pay of Big Booze) to the point that they feel comfortable promoting life-styles emphasizing "sophisticated, romantic" drinking. They promote a life-style that puts women at risk for alcoholism, depression, general unhappiness and poor health in contrast to life-styles that sustain health and happiness.

Chapter 8: Making Smart, Right, Good Choices

When writing about the cover-up of child molestation that occurred at Penn. State, commentator Maureen Dowd used the term *moral dystopia*.[1] Such a term might describe people's actions that are rationalized as acceptable; but when inspected closely, are found to be disgustingly morally unacceptable. At Penn. State, an honored assistant football coach was somewhat regularly sexually molesting young boys. Some folks who knew something about the sexual misbehavior, decided to do nothing, to not become involved in such messy circumstances. We suppose that they rationalized that others would handle the situation. Nevertheless, their behavior was sort-of-cowardly.[2] Leaders of the university, who had some information about what was happening, did little or nothing with the idea that it was better all-round to not do much, if anything. Supposedly, they acted in what they thought were "the best interests" of the institutions (football, the university) and the reputation of the truly honorable head coach. Also, the assistant coach was generally a good guy (except, of course, he engaged sex with young boys).

The people of the university presumed that they were doing good, being moral and if not these, then sensible and pragmatic. Eventually, however, the truth became public and what seemed to actors of this drama as being sensible, turned out to be judged by many others as unsavory, excessively selfish, and not good for the university, for the head coach, and especially for a number of boys. It is interesting to point out that the circumstances allowing the assistant coach's misbehavior to continue did not do a favor for the assistant coach. He now resides in prison. Some citizens of this well-established university by their lack of caring did nothing for the better good. The choices guided by so-called pragmatism turned out to not be pragmatic. The circumstances seem to be an instance of moral dystopia.[3]

Perhaps, the following situations are further examples of moral dystopia: (a) the promotion of the sale of alcoholic beverages to girls and young women, (b) the marketing of certain drugs as both safe and efficacious when the sellers knowingly have data to indicate that the practice is at best problematic and at worst dangerous and (c) the discontinuance of nearly all therapies for mental disorders except prescription of marginally effective drugs and electroconvulsive therapy by American psychiatry while also claiming that the treatment of all mental disorders should be under the supervision of psychiatry. All of these are in the service of people of esteemed companies and institutions.

Prof. Marcia Angell, M.D., is an American physician, author, and the first woman to serve as editor-in-chief of the prestigious *New England Journal of Medicine.* She has been a critic of the practices of the pharmaceutical companies. She has said at various times and places something like this: "I suppose that you cannot blame them (the decision-makers of drug companies), they are charged with making money by selling drugs in *any way they can.*"[4] We sincerely disagree. Our honored traditions do not condone making money *any way anybody can.* To make the point that making money anyway you can is *not* a beneficent moral imperative, we point out that it is not O.K. to poison your spouse in the service of collecting insurance money, which is, making money any way you can. The social contract is for companies to make money by doing good (more good, more profit) not by making money *anyway they can.*

Issues of considerable importance: How do you know, if a choice is "smart, right, and good?" Of course, you need truthful, useful information to make smart, good choices. Who can you trust to provide truthful information? How do you avoid being swindled by the people who run institutions that condone making money "anyway they can"? These issues, of course, are not simple. These issues have, in one way or another, been before us since the beginning of civilization.

The issues of how to assess propositions for their truth value, and for their utility in guiding choices, are perhaps more difficult to resolve now than ever before. Here we are concerned with propositions about a group of products, namely alcoholic beverages and certain drugs, but the issues are germane to many choices. Among other things, those of us that live in prosperous nations have many more choices than previously. Further, many products that are for sale are "new," for example, old products made new by slight modifications in contents and new branding (witness the cereal aisle in any large food market). The slight modifications might not be noticeable, but yet they are significant. Some products are so novel that there has not been time to assess their long term impact.

Further, we are constantly bombarded by advertisements and by messages that are advertisements disguised as authoritative information. Further, these advertisements and messages are for the products of large transnational corporations who have been shown, at least in a few instances, to sell dangerous products. Furthermore, these marketers are particularly adept at countering potential regulations and avoiding responsibility. There is very little person to person accountability. You will probably never come into contact with the persons working at a large transnational corporation who authorized the sale of a harmful product; or even have a way of knowing their names.

Being Smart

In brief, to increase your chances of being happy for many years, you have to be smart in order to navigate the complexities of the modern world. This brings up first principles. Any choice that reduces your ability to think well is apt to lead to less than wholesome choices. Psychotropic drugs can be toxic to brain processes. Known toxins include the ethanol in alcoholic beverages, drugs that are prescribed to supposedly make you happier and a large number of drugs that are touted by your local illegal drug dealer. Brains that do not work as well as they might are brains that produce behaviors that are not as smart as they might be. *Therefore,*

213

first principle: nurture your brain and conserve its integrity. At a public policy level, the healthy society also promotes policies nurtures and conserves the integrity citizens' brains.

As used here, the concept of smart does not mean the same thing as measured IQ. The usual intelligence tests measure readiness to take advantage of further education. The scholarly skills measured by standard IQ tests are useful, but they may not, for example, equip one to deal with a variety of temptations. In this context, smart refers to the ability to make good choices during day-to-day living (we will get around to dealing with what are *good* and bad choices!). It boils down to this: Being smart involves having a well-functioning brain. The status of brains can vary from being well-organized by the individual's circumstances or disordered, that is, not functioning well enough for good adaptation to the circumstances. Well-functioning brains, for example, usually protect the individual from being swindled, being beguiled, being taken advantage of, etc. Well-organized brains, using usual words, usually do not produce stupid behavior.

Notice in the previous paragraphs that we used the term well-functioning rather than healthy and did not use terms such as diseased, ill, and unhealthy to describe a brain not functioning as well as it might. True enough, during common discussions, the concept of a well-functioning brain carries the same information as the concept of a healthy brain. However, the connotation of health also connotes medical resolutions for nurturing the functionality of brains and, when not functioning well, fixing them. Sometimes a poorly functioning brain needs a medical intervention to restore well-functioning and sometimes not. Defining a brain that is not functioning well as unhealthy (or diseased) biases the decision as to whether the individual needs a medicine, a medical procedure or other kinds of help.

Before we go further, know this: We used to believe that being smart was limited to only a few people; we now know that many, many people can become smart. Once it was common to believe that a person's intelligence was limited by the intelligence of their father and mother, by race, ethnic group, gender, early education, intelligence-level at 25 years of age, and by social class. We now have enough solid evidence to conclude that, although there are relationships between the factors mentioned and measures of intelligence that those same variables do not specify, either alone or in combination, the limits for becoming smarter and smarter.

There are real limits to developing highly serviceable cognitive ability, particularly the cognitive ability to develop a happy life. Severe starvation of nutrients, for example, is a real limit. Some opportunities to develop cognitive ability are surely better than others. If one has, however, a well-functioning brain the limits on becoming smarter and smarter are surely not as limited as previously believed. You can develop your smarts throughout your life. We now understand that even physically traumatized brains can be rehabilitated provided there is an attempt to do so. *In brief, a well-supported contention is that nearly everyone can become smart enough to develop a happy, productive life, provided that they have a well-functioning brain. And even further, well-functioning brains can be developed by nearly everyone, when such is nurtured by a society. One can develop a well-functioning brain provided that others do not block the opportunity to do so.* An example of a cultural practice that is an impediment to a well-functioning brain: the practice and the accompanying rationalizations that it is O.K. to make money *any way legally possible* even if the practice poisons brains. To belittle practices that reduce cognitive functioning and take no responsibility for acts that reduce cognitive functioning is to engage moral dystrophy.

Moral Choices

Judgments about what is moral and immoral involve choices as to what is right and what is wrong, respectively. Judgments about what is right and wrong eventually get translated into statements of "ought to do" and "ought not to do" and similarly statements of "should do" and "should not do." Moral imperatives are usually distinguishable from advice such as "you *should* dress conservatively" when interviewing for a job having considerable responsibility. When one speaks of moral behavior, the issues in question are usually very serious; when rules of morality are breached, there is often sanctioned punishment.

Different societies have different rules, cultural practices, customs, norms and ways of facilitating social interactions. These different ways of regulating social behavior evolved supposedly to promote the well-being of the society. Nevertheless, an outsider to a society might find a particular practice to be very strange and hardly practical. From an outsider's perspective, some common practices of a society may seem morally reprehensible. Of course, within a society, there can be bitter strife about the various rules devised to regulate behavior.

Distinguished cultural anthropologist, Marvin Harris made the case in books such as "Cows, Pigs, Wars and Witches (1975)[5] that cultural practices, including morals, came about because they were practical when they were established. Harris argued that cultural guidelines, when established, were useful, and helped a culture to adapt to the prevailing circumstances. He inspected practices that to outsiders seemed particularly weird or just plain wrong. Considering what he found, he concluded that such practices were in fact not wrong or even weird, if you took into account the circumstances in which the society operated when the rules were adopted. Circumstances change, but often rules governing behavior do not change in step with the changing circumstances. Consequently, once clearly sensible customs may not only become obsolete, but they may hinder successful adaptation to changing circumstances. Nevertheless, it is helpful to understand that many customs that now seem to be useless or even problematic may have been a smart way of dealing with the circumstances at hand.

The scope of this book is limited to the cultural practices and moral issues surrounding women and their relationship to alcoholic beverages. It is not about everything moral and just. Nevertheless, the issues are serious, even rising to the level of being moral issues. The previous chapters of this book made a lot of declarations, stated a number of propositions, and boldly stated that features of the American society were bad, wrong, and indefensible while others were good and should be practiced more. Further, at the beginning of this chapter, we accused a fairly large number of our fellow citizens of being a party to *moral dystopia*.

Epistemology Made Simple

How does one evaluate the truth value of any proposition, including those in this book? There is a branch of academic philosophy that deals specifically with the issue of the "truth of propositions," it is called epistemology.

A professor of mine (Larry) condensed epistemology by delivering the following summary.[6] There are a number of ways of arriving at the truth. They are:

by way of *authority*,

by way of *intuition*,

 by way of *empiricism*,

by way of *logical reasoning*, and

by way of *science*, a combination of empiricism and logical reasoning.

Truth by way of *authority* is exemplified by such statements as "I know it (a proposition) is true because God said it was true." "I know God said it is true because the Bible says it is true." "I know the Bible is the true delivered word of God because my religious leader said the Bible was God's word." There are authorities other than religious leaders, hence: "I know it is true because my professor said it was true." And a child might say, "I know it is true because my mommy said it was true."

When God, or his representative on earth who claims total fidelity to God's word, delivers a proposition it is fixed; not subject to change. Recently for example on a nightly T.V. news program, we saw the public execution of a woman for adultery based on the truth-value of the assertion that such is the proper way to deal with an incidence of adultery. If a true prophet of God said execution was the just desserts for adultery, it must be so and, if God is all powerful and omniscient, there is no way to challenge the proposition and the behavior that follows from that belief.

Of course, different authorities have different beliefs. Consequently, the truth-value of an authoritarian conclusion boils down to the argument of who is the "real" authority. Since there is no way to negotiate among fixed beliefs (often supposedly God-given), except to challenge the authority of a competing authority figure, the only way to have an actor's truth to prevail is by way of force (suppression of an alternate view). An epistemology based in authority gives way to "might makes right."

One can supposedly derive truth by way of *intuition:* I know a proposition is true because it feels as if it is true; my intuition says it is true; any alternative proposition just does not feel right. Sometimes this is characterized as being inherently true. The problem with this avenue to the truth is that anything can be true. There is no way of disputing such truth; how can you challenge what someone feels; they supposedly know their feelings better than anyone else. If a proposition is *felt* to be true by a large number of people, there is a sort of verification of truth of the proposition. It is true because it is popular is a common manifestation of relying on feelings as a guide to the truth.

If the criterion for truth is one's feelings, there is no demonstrable difference between every proposition as long as someone believes it; all beliefs are true if the prevailing epistemology is based on how *one* feels. An obvious difficulty with intuition as an avenue to the truth is that some intuitions, even if widely held, are clearly wrong (e.g., the earth is flat) and some intuitive propositions when popular can lead to inordinately horrible events (e.g., ethnic massacres). Also, it elevates the beliefs of even the most disturbed individuals to the same level as the most well-thought-out ideas.

The phrase, "I will believe it when I see it" exemplifies *empiricism* as a method of arriving at the truth. This has an advantage over intuition because many persons can observe the same event and, thereby, verify the truth-value of an observation. The major limitation to empiricism is that for many propositions of interest there is no way to observe the object of the proposition (e.g., it is difficult to see viruses and atoms). For another example, if an observer notices that every cow he has ever seen has a black and white coat-color, he is likely to assert that all cows have black and white coats. When an empiricist is told that a brown calf was born to a white and black cow, as a true empiricist, he will respond "I will believe it, when I see it" and retain the belief about all cows and their coat-color. Rank empiricism limits knowledge.

Some believe that a truth can be arrived at by following the rules of logic or rules of *reason*, as exemplified by a well-established system of logic or math. The problem here is that the initial proposition that is to be verified by logic and formal reasoning can be arrived at by a variety of means including intuition, authority, or limited experience. Given that *all* cows are black and white, and the fact that a cow-like animal is observed to be brown, it follows logically that the observed animal is not a cow. If one might mention that the brown animal was born of a black and white cow, it would matter little because logic proved otherwise. Reason, logic, and their extension into mathematics are often useful, but not by themselves.

Science is a combination of empiricism and reasoning. It is, however, more than that simple formulation. Science has evolved into a culture. The acceptance of both empiricism and reasoning is exemplified in the various experiments and descriptions appearing in scientific journals. Modern science involves such elements as experiments explicitly designed to falsify a proposition in question (which is heresy from an authoritarian point of view). Science is bolstered by professional ethics, peer review, and open disclosure of the methods used in obtaining data. Interestingly, adoption of the scientific method has built into it a tolerance for ambiguity. The history of scientific progress is marked by questioning the scientific dogma of the day (if there are scientific heroes, e.g., Galileo, Copernicus or Darwin, it is probably those who have successfully challenged the accepted scientific and scholarly truths).

The first step toward resolution of the issues associated with conflicts that emerge from the intersection of equal rights for women and differences between women and men is the understanding that "the truth will make you free." The next step is to realize that there are significant differences in the way truth is derived. When truth of a proposition is derived by way of mere authority, intuition, empiricism, and logic, such truth may or may not be the circumstances for freedom. When truth of a proposition is derived by way of science, that truth may or may not be the circumstances for freedom, but the scientific way has significant advantages over the alternatives. The truth derived by way of science is stable, but changeable. The truth-value of the proposition that alcohol is more poisonous to women than to men is stable, i.e., there is considerable evidence to support it and that evidence stands until further research provides alternative ways of conceptualizing the issues. The advantage is that further research, further systematic observation, can change the truth-value of a scientifically derived conclusion.

Scientifically derived knowledge has some other advantages. A major advantage: science is inherently compatible with democracy, i.e., ideas are open to debate, open to inspection of the methodology used to derive a conclusion, subject to a test of logic, and a built-in way of checking on cheating--the test of verification by replication. There are, of course, critics of the way science is practiced in any given instance and those critics are often justified in their opposition. Like democracy, science is not perfect, but superior to the alternatives.

There is a compatible point of view to the idea that scientific methods are more apt to yield truth than alternatives. There is the idea that the truth-value of a proposition is based on whether it works, whether the proposition is functional and pragmatic. The approach is often labeled functionalism or pragmatism. The truth-value of the idea that fixed winged devices can fly was tested by the Wright brothers; their plane flew (albeit, only a short distance) and led to the development of modern airplanes. The idea that one can treat common phobias (e.g., fear of flying in airplanes) by way of systematic deconditioning, as described by Dr. Joseph Wolpe and his followers, is to practice systematic deconditioning to test the idea.[7] It turns out that simple phobias can be treated effectively by way of systematic deconditioning. This colloquial phrase captures the idea of functionalism: "the proof of the pudding is in the eating" (not in the particular recipe, not in an authority making an assertion about the pudding, not in an advertisement, etc., but in whether it tastes good and does not make you sick). Americans have embraced and continue to embrace pragmatism, which is the idea that the truth of theories or beliefs is in terms of the success of their practical application.

The test of a proposition might be two-fold: (a) is the proposition supported by research using scientific methods and (b) further testing, i.e., when a proposition is applied in somewhat less than the ideal conditions of the laboratory did that application verify the proposition.

This book is littered with definitive statements, i.e., testable propositions. Here are four examples.

1. Ethanol is more toxic to women than men.

2. Substantial increases in taxes on alcoholic beverages will reduce buying alcoholic beverages even among heavy drinkers.

3. The asocial and unhealthy consequences of drinking alcoholic beverages are dose-related; the more the drinking, the more negative consequences.

4. Hazardous drinking of alcoholic beverages, as well as what many believe is moderate drinking, increases the risk of breast cancer among women.

Each proposition is supported by considerable scientifically collected data. From a scientific perspective, each of these is ultimately a tentative conclusion because that is the nature of science. To acknowledge that science does not provide absolute truths, however, does not detract from the truth-value of each of the listed, well-supported propositions. In some grand abstract sense, all human knowledge is not absolute. To apply the idea that all human knowledge is not absolute and, therefore, all propositions are (or can be) equally false is to leave us with no knowledge, or else knowledge only based in authority or intuition. The issue is not whether a proposition is absolutely true, but whether it is supported sufficiently to be accepted as true, to be a basis of action.

It is popular in some academic circles to point out that the practice of science can be biased by the hopes of those funding the research (a reasonable proposition; for example, those who distain breast cancer are apt to direct research toward breast cancer rather than another troubling circumstance such as income inequality). It is probably accurate to assert that individual scientists are apt to favor their own ideas and, therefore, chose to do some kinds of experiments rather than others. More problematic, there have been cases where statistical manipulations of the data can obscure the most obvious conclusions of an experiment, particularly when the conclusion contradicts a vested interest (e.g., the sales of some antidepressant drugs). There are cases of faked data and faked tabulations of data. Given the broad swipe of the history of knowledge, we assert that an inspection of such mishaps leads to the conclusion that the antidote to biased, poor scientific practices (and lies cloaked in the assertion that they are scientifically derived) is more science; surely not less science. Given many institutions who whole heartedly embrace the culture of science and diversity of interests inherent to modern science, the continuance of modern science will correct the mistakes of a small fraction of the total science being produced.

There are potentially more substantial criticisms of the four listed propositions other than the obvious, but vacuous, conclusion that science has limitations. A critic of the truth-value of the proposition linking drinking to breast cancer might dispute the definition of hazardous drinking. The critic might concede that there is an increased risk, but indicate that the degree of risk is so small as to be meaningless. There is apt to be a dispute over the definition of "substantial increases in taxes" and "heavy drinkers." There are disputes over the shape of the dose-response curves linking amount drunk to undesirable consequences. Nevertheless, given the amount of evidence available today (from both scientific and functionalist perspectives), the burden of questioning the truth-value of each of the propositions dissolves to (a) quibbling about definitions (sometimes an important issue) and (b) the necessity to do more scientific research whose results might yield contradictory data.

Given that the four listed propositions stand as being sufficiently true, can one extrapolate to generate reasonable laws, social norms, moral imperatives, etc.? In other words, knowing that the propositions stand as being true (if you want to be picky, true enough), can one devise useful statements of "should and should not," and "ought and ought not." For example: Women *should not* drink alcoholic beverages in quantities similar to those characteristic of drinking men.

Many epistemologists come to the conclusion that among the various avenues to the truth that science is superior to all others. They also conclude that science cannot and should not come to a conclusion about what are the moral and the right things to do (the should- and ought-propositions). Said differently, the critics say that a proposition such as "women *should not* drink alcoholic beverages..." (or the contrary) is to be left to those who use other epistemologies than science. They often further assert that scientific methods applied to social and psychological issues are really not science. Yet, we find that the application of scientific methods have failed to support a goodly number of social and psychological propositions that sounded O.K., but upon inspection were merely someone's intuition and the reasoning supposedly supporting the proposition were merely rationalizations.

Although a case can be made that "should" and "ought" statements can be tested scientifically by inspecting the consequences of applying those values inherent in should and ought statements, there are some troubling features to using propositions similar to those listed to devise should and ought statements. For example, given that women are in danger when they drink alcoholic beverages, one might conclude that a law should be put in place which states that women's possession of alcohol beverages *ought to* be a crime punishable by severe means. Another example: Any person providing alcoholic beverages to a woman *should be* punished severely. These examples point out the problematic features of extrapolating potential facts into social actions. Given these problematic features, is there a way of taking into account other observations to allow our social policies to be driven by well-supported propositions? A discussion of ideas germane to that question is the topic of the next section.

Should- and Ought-Admonitions

The professor that supervised Larry's doctoral dissertation, Prof. Paul B. Porter, was a highly respected physiological psychologist, or behavioral neuroscientist. In light of his reputation, he was elected to the presidency of the Rocky Mountain Psychological Association. Shortly thereafter, he was asked to provide a title for his presidential address that would be given at the next annual meeting of the Association. His response was "the title will be '*Mrs. Brigham Young*'." Prof. Porter was professor of psychology at the University of Utah. Utah is the primary home of the Mormon Church. Among the founders of the Church was Brigham Young. Brigham Young was a polygamist with many wives. So, when asked why he titled his presidential address as "Mrs. Brigham Young," Paul replied that he had not decided

224

on a topic and figured that he could chose among those that interested him. "Mrs. Brigham Young" conveyed the idea that there was likely to be more than one in consideration.

The lecture Prof. Porter delivered was never published. It addressed the issue of how to make scientific statements into ought and ought not and should and should not statements. I did not hear that lecture, but Paul did provide me with a written copy. Much of what is said here is similar to what Paul said many years ago.

The idea that the scientists who study alcohol and its effects on females (and related topics) should be respected "authorities" on the topic seems to be an O.K. conclusion. The idea that scientists are in the best position to determine what to do with that knowledge, however, angers many people, such as moralists of a religious persuasion. It invades their turf and they do defend their turf with tenacity. It angers some secular philosophers (ethicists) for the same reason. It angers politicians and political commentators because it constrains their judgments (law-making would defer to the scientific evidence rather than to lawmaker's intuition and reasoning or to their representation of vested interests). It angers many scientists because they find it uncomfortable to be professionally engaged in making moral judgments. Also, some scientists fear that being involved with controversial issues endangers the funding that sustains their work.

The idea that science is the best arbiter of the truth of many propositions is scary to many people who did not like, or succeed in, courses such as chemistry and physics. The scientific way of thinking, however, differs considerably from a single course in chemistry. Science is a useful way of thinking and useful thinking can be "surprisingly" applied to all kinds of issues. Scientific thinking is something everybody can engage and can learn to use.

Scientific thinking is democratic. It strips away special privilege. It reduces authoritarian rule to authoritative rule and, when used, reduces the power of priests in all of their guises. Scientific practices (exemplified by studied experimentation, tests of logic, and other customs of modern science) are also a way of learning about mysterious events (think the cause of a disease, the knowledge of precise nature of the physical world that will allow the development of new materials, etc.).

The thinkers who become angry at the idea that scientific facts should be the basis for establishing the rules of a society have an important point. We made that point a few paragraphs back. The scientifically derived fact that women can easily be poisoned by regularly drinking alcoholic beverages might be used to establish rules such as women should be severally punished if caught drinking. It becomes apparent that just any extrapolation of apparent facts is not sufficient to establishing customs of a society including moral values. Other considerations must be taken into account.

Some considerations are more compatible than others in benefitting from a scientific way of thinking. Under authoritarian regimes, certain technologies can flourish; but if science should also provide information that is contrary to the regimen's rationale for being in power, then scientists and their ideas are usually harshly squashed. Given that the academic disciplines of psychological science, economics, sociology, modern historical research and political science are likely to produce "truths" not in the interest of authoritarian regimes; under such regimes, these disciplines are not fostered.

Professor Pinker, after surveying the historical facts of the incidence of violence both personal (e.g., wife-beating or murder) as well as institutional (e.g., police brutality or war), came to the conclusion that (a) taken over a long period, violence has subsided, and (b) violence has been reduced, because a new conception of morality has emerged.[8] The new morality is less centered on subservience to state or religious authority and more centered about a respect for laws of fairness and equality. The new morality is more centered about public health and ideas that the rules of governance and morality should be guided by "the greatest

226

happiness of the greatest number" (Cesare Beccaria in 1764) and "the greatest good to the greatest number" (Jeremy Bentham in 1785). The new morality takes into account people's preferences, ideas that were put into practice by founders of the USA's government such as Jefferson, Franklin, and Madison.

How does one determine the "the greatest good"? An approach is to determine the preferences of citizens. When I (Larry) poll individuals as to whether they prefer to be chronically in pain, or chronically nauseated, they respond by saying, in one form or another, emphatically No! (They also wondered why I am asking questions with such obvious answers.) When a scientifically derived set of observations indicate that procedure X reduces pain with only minor side-effects, it follows that the application of procedure X is a *good* thing to do, something we *ought to do,* when performing surgery. Why? Because citizens prefer such and Procedure X has been demonstrated to provide surgery without pain by verifiable methods.

To the point of coming to the conclusion that women *should* (ought to) greatly temper their consumption of alcoholic beverages, we can ask questions of women such as: Do you prefer to reduce your risk of disease of the liver? Do you prefer to reduce your risk of breast cancer? Do you prefer to *not* reduce your cognitive ability? When asked, the answers to these questions are emphatically: Yes. Do you prefer to be an alcoholic? The answer is emphatically: No. One can be even more direct: Do you prefer to have liver disease and breast cancer and get the expected answer.

Scientifically derived results support the proposition that, dose-relatedly, taking alcoholic beverages increases the risk of liver disease, breast cancer, cognitive decline and alcoholism, with the dose-response curve being steeper among women. Nearly all women will assert that they prefer not to develop liver disease, breast cancer, cognitive decline and alcoholism. Given women's increased risk associated with drinking alcoholic beverages, the proposition is supported that women *ought to* temper their drinking if they *prefer* not to increase their risk of disease. The scientifically derived conclusion of ethanol's enhanced toxicity among women and women's preferences lead to the conclusion that women *should* temper their drinking of alcoholic beverages. Preferences also exclude unpopular, excessively harsh laws restricting women's choices.

A critic of this line of reasoning (scientific facts plus knowledge of preferences allows should and ought statements) might make the argument that preferences are the same as intuitions and you have just criticized intuitions as not being a sound avenue to the truth. We counter that many preferences are highly reliable and almost universal. When individuals are asked why they engage behavior X, they often have an answer, but the answer differs from time to time (i.e., it is unreliable). When asked about preferences, the answers are usually reliable. We have yet to have someone sincerely assert that they prefer to be an alcoholic and to have breast cancer over the contrary. Preferences can be reliable, and nearly universal preferences are useful in translating scientific facts into should and ought statements. When preferences are not reliable and not held nearly universally, then they become less useful and should- and ought-propositions become more open to debate.

Scientific investigations can also reveal not only an association between an event such as a habit of hazardous drinking and developing a disease but also the degree of that relationship. The added precision is helpful in making choices.

Not everyone has the means, and surely no one has the time and expertise, to do experiments to test the reliability of a scientifically derived conclusion that might be of interest at any given time. Citizens can, however, learn to recognize when a scientific method has been used to either support or not support relevant conclusions. Also, a democratic society that supports universities doing scientific research, has the ability for a variety of ideas to be assessed scientifically and consequently to make those assessments available to the citizenry. Thomas Jefferson recognized that universities were valuable, even essential, assets for sustaining a democracy.

228

Propositions that are strongly supported by way of scientific investigations appear in review articles. Authors of textbooks use review articles to provide a bulk of the content of textbooks. Widely used textbooks are reviewed by classroom instructors as well as experts before and after their publication. There are errors in widely used texts, but generally they present a consensus view of the state of knowledge (the widely accepted theory on topic X). For example, when different college-level textbooks on drug abuse, sociology, developmental psychology, and abnormal psychology all state that there is a strong association between intake of alcoholic beverages and the incidence of domestic violence, there is a very good chance that such a conclusion is based in systematic study of that issue. Further, there is apt to be converging evidence: for examples, someone counted court records, someone investigated whether former alcoholics who previously engaged domestic violence continue to do that even after they were no longer drinking, whether heavy drinking populations also have higher incidences of domestic violence, etc. The converging evidence supports the general proposition that alcohol-use is highly related to domestic violence; hence the truth-value of the proposition is strongly supported. The converging evidence does not support the proposition that all who drink alcoholic beverages become violent in the home. The converging evidence does support the conclusion that there is a strong relationship between habitual drinking of alcoholic beverages and domestic violence. Such a conclusion is knowable to the public by way of relevant scientific textbooks and their equivalent.[9]

The issues become more controversial when the conclusion is reached that a set of scientifically derived data lead to the conclusion that policy X leads to the greater good for the most people. If the preference is for there to be fewer alcoholics in the society, and the systematically collected data indicate that increasing the taxes on alcoholic beverages will reduce the number of citizens who develop alcoholism, then it appears that there is support for the conclusion to raise taxes on alcoholic beverages (we *ought to* raise the taxes). Advocates for Big Booze do not dispute the preference for fewer alcoholics, they do dispute the data indicating that increasing taxes will lead to less drinking, hence less alcoholism. The issue, therefore, becomes whether the relevant data are derived scientifically or otherwise. The research supports the proposition that raising taxes on the sale of alcoholic beverages will reduce alcoholism. The conclusion: we ought to raise taxes on the sale of alcoholic beverages is a relatively easy decision to make because the germane data are easily extrapolated from the research and known nearly universal preferences. Those who do not want higher taxes on alcoholic beverages (due to their preference for drinking large amounts of the beverage and the marketers who wish to continue to escalate their profits) must either challenge the available evidence or try to defend their callousness with respect to public health. In brief, they have to argue that high incidences of alcoholism are in the greater good. Or, they exert authoritarian power to have their preferences instated rather than the preferences of the many.

Scientists are not smarter than nonscientists. Also, often there is insufficient scientific data to resolve individual and societal choices. The contention is that scientific data and scientific reasoning should not be excluded from the decision-making process. The contention is that a combination of the available scientifically derived conclusions and democratic institutions expressing people's preferences can be effective guides to what ought to be done, what should be done.

Women are not going to prefer harsh penalties for drinking or punishment for people who provide alcoholic beverages for them. They may, however, opt for higher taxes on alcoholic beverages if it leads to less alcoholism and its inherent consequences. They might conclude that there "ought to be higher taxes on alcoholic beverages" based on their preference for a healthier society and the data indicating that increasing taxes is preferable to not doing so.

By accepting the idea that women's preferences should be an integral part of decisions affecting public policy, women are empowered; something women prefer. Many men have similar preferences.

Scientifically derived data support the conclusion that women are extraordinarily vulnerable to alcoholism. The scientifically derived data support the conclusion that habitual drinking increases the risk of a wide variety of diseases. Women prefer not to become an alcoholic; women prefer to be healthy. It follows that women should dramatically temper their drinking and that is the right choice, the good choice, and the smart choice.

A Nasty Issue Concerning Moral Decision-making

The proposition that humans have a bias towards being morally good has been put forth recently by a number of scholars.[1] This conclusion is in concordance with certain ancient Greek philosophers' ideas.[10] They concluded that what was pleasurable was good and striving toward long-term pleasure was the essence of morality. The idea is bolstered by the idea that our evolution selected, in general, the right behavior, the adaptive behavior by the very fact that we survived. Also, the contention is that since we are highly social animals, we are biased toward consideration of the group's welfare as well as our own. There are observations that fit with the conclusion that we are biased toward being good by our inherent preferences. For example, almost everyone finds babies appealing and tends to protect them. Along a similar line, there are some circumstances that are nearly universally disgusting. The idea is that what we consciously perceive as pleasure and pain (behaviorally, acceptance and avoidance) is an inherent guidance system that is biased toward directing our behavior to be morally appropriate, to be doing the right thing, to be doing good.

No one contends that humans are inherently so good that we cannot do horribly bad things. The contention is that we are biased toward being good and that the guidance system directing us toward goodness is the same, or nearly the same, as the system that accounts for pleasure and pain.

Across the last half century, we have learned a great deal about the pleasure system of the brain. We have discovered the major anatomical parts of the system whose activity is manifest as pleasure; we have discovered chemicals in the brain that are important for the functionality of the system. We know that major addictive drugs mimic or exaggerate the actions of the system that is pleasure.

Important for the issue at hand is the discovery that addictive agents, for examples, cocaine, heroin, nicotine and, yes, ethanol, achieve the ability to sustain the behavior of taking them by activating the system of pleasure. There is a tendency for the scientists studying the systems under discussion to avoid the term pleasure for terms not so loaded with subjective meaning (i.e., reward, incentive motivation, etc.). Nevertheless, it is an increment in positive emotion (i.e., pleasure or some very close variant of such) or the increment in positive emotion (or some very close variant of such) that comes from reducing pain (aversive stimulation) that guides addictive behaviors just as it guides other classes of behavior.[11]

Pleasure and pain are the conscious manifestations of activity of the system that evolved for guiding behavior. When powerful euphorigenic agents such as cocaine and methamphetamine activate these areas by mimicking or exaggerating the actions of the guidance system, they reinforce the acts of taking the agents. These powerful euphorigens also provide false positives, e.g., snorting cocaine activates systems that in ordinary circumstances signals something adaptive, something good, something that is the right thing to do, a morally right thing is being done. This follows because the very system that evolved to provide guidance is the same system that provides signals that are manifest as pleasure or some variant of pleasure. Signals of pleasure evolved to provide guidance for adaptive behavior. For some, ethanol is a powerful euphorigen and, consequently, can provide the "false feeling of doing good."

When ethanol's effects are combined with ordinary behaviors that have a semblance of being adaptive (for examples, eating and engaging in social behaviors) they are apt to strengthen the experienced value of particular acts beyond their long-term adaptive value. For some, wine with dinner may enhance the hedonistic value of eating, hence may lead to more eating than is adaptive and a tendency to drink more and more often. This example may not be particularly contrary to people's preferences, but some ordinary behaviors such as driving fast (getting there quickly) combined with the ethanol-induced idea that it is O.K. to drive fast may not be particularly adaptive. Ethanol induced toxicity may seem to justify brutal punishment because it provides a false signal that doing so is doing good.

Providing false signals or exaggerating signals that ordinarily promote the execution of adaptive behavior induces noise in a system that evolved to bias us toward good, moral behavior. It is understood that the idea that pleasure is a signal for good as well as moral behavior is controversial. It has been controversial, at least, since the ancient Greek philosophers formulated the ideas linking pleasure with being moral. The idea that there is an extensive overlap among the behaviors that induce adaptation and induce pleasure is not controversial. Basic adaptive behaviors such as eating when hungry, drinking when thirsty, sleeping after an extensive time being awake, and other behaviors whose activity maintains stability of bodily functions (physiological homeostasis) are experienced as pleasure and are adaptive. Among social animals, being socially appropriate also induces pleasure. The idea is that efficient adaptation might be compromised by providing false signals induced by euphorigenic, recreational drugs. False signals are defined as those that induce pleasure but have little adaptive significance.

Although a good case can be made that we have an inherent bias toward being moral (socially fit), there is also a strong case that the propensity to be moral, if it exists, is fragile. It surely takes considerable nurturance from childhood and beyond to develop the habits of moral behaviors. The guess is that it takes some sustained practice to develop morality particularly in our complex, modern and often chaotic societies. Such sustained practice can be thwarted by the intake of pleasure-producing drugs during childhood merely by providing powerful signals that something good is happening when there is only a drug-high.

To put the ideas in slightly different terms, please note that from both an evolutionary as well as individual developmental points of view, behavior is guided by consequences. Consequences are made manifest by instances of pleasure and pain. If one experiences pleasure as a consequence of an act, that behavior is more apt to be repeated. If that act is taking a pleasure producing drug, the system is built to signal that such is a good thing, a morally correct thing. When modern cultures are able to devise powerful euphorigens whose only "value" is to be powerful euphorigens, the link between having pleasure and being adaptive is aborted.

Modern technology has enabled the production of nearly pure ethanol and the production of the flavors of delicious foods without anything else characteristic of food. When drinks are made with pure ethanol with almost any flavor by way of chemistry, we have been able to make an euphorigen that can pass as a food without much if any nutritional value, but nevertheless nutritional value is signaled by the system that evolved to guide eating. High ethanol-content drinks that tastes like desserts has the potential to induce emotionality that signals pleasure, goodness, and the right thing to do. Behavior in the service of powerful euphorigens does more than reinforce any particular act of taking the drug: it develops the concept that such is an example of goodness, of the correct thing to be doing. The concept of goodness can be sustained by the intake of such drugs in the face of what would otherwise be judged as aversive or just plain wrong.

The Really Nasty Issue

The idea that addictive drugs provide mixed signals to the very system that evolved to provide guidance for adaptive behavior seems to be relevant to making decisions about whether to develop the habits of taking addictive drugs. Perhaps, messing with the hedonic signaling system is apt to increase the risk of engaging in unadaptive behavior. That is not, however, the nasty issue in mind when this last section of the book was started. There is a possibility that some addictive agents can actually be toxic to the system of pleasure. If the system for pleasure suffers from toxicity, then it follows that there would be some degradation of a sense of morality.

The psychomotor stimulants such as cocaine, amphetamine, methamphetamine and ecstasy all have the capacity at large doses of producing damage to the systems of the brain whose activity is pleasure (in a previous chapter, it was pointed out that the medial forebrain bundle system was a critical part of the "pleasure system"). When taken with alcoholic beverages there are reasons to believe that there is an increased risk of toxicity. Abuse of multiple drugs at once (polydrug abuse) is surely problematic from a number of social and health perspectives.

Cognitive degradation is a probable outcome of hazardous intake of alcoholic beverages and polydrug-abuse enhances that risk of cognitive decline. If there is neural damage to the system of pleasure, there is also a risk of developing a blunted sense of what is right and wrong. In accord with what we generally know about neural toxicity, one would expect that the complex cognitive systems built with activity of the pleasure system, for example, moral principles, would be damaged first by toxicity. The more basic behaviors sustained by pleasure, for example eating, would be only hindered with considerable toxicity. To put the message bluntly, intake of hazardous amounts of pleasure-producing agents (euphorigens) stands a chance of enhancing immorality, not merely immorality while under the influence of the euphorigen but a general degradation of the ability to sense morality.

We know powerful euphorigens, in addition to the pleasure they produce, also decrease fear and enhance confidence often to the point of grandiosity. We know also that some euphorigens, for example ethanol, decrease cognitive capability as manifest as ability to think ahead. These two kinds of toxic effects (reduced ability to recognize what is good and inability to foresee consequences) can produce acute signs of immoral behavior. The really nasty issue: There are reasons to suppose that powerful euphorigens can produce a chronic condition of blunted moral sense.

Every complex society must have most of the adults engaging in moral behavior nearly all of the time to be well-functioning. It, therefore, benefits the citizens of a society to arrange the contingences for behaviors (the norms, the laws, the regulations, the standards for polite behavior, etc.) to be such that good habits are developed. Good habits are those that are productive while at the same time pleasure-producing. Good habits have the consequences that most people prefer. Good habits contribute to public health. Good habits yield for most citizens many years of happiness. These admonitions are more than saying good is good, because they involve the particulars of keeping the contingencies straight. Also, the flip side can also be made particular: it benefits the citizens of a society to arrange for circumstances that do not establish bad habits such as those involved with taking powerful euphorigens. For example, powerful, potentially toxic euphorigens should be very, very expensive.

A question of some interest is whether a damaged system for signaling what is right and wrong can be repaired. With respect to alcoholic beverages, we believe that the answer is: Yes, in many cases. With respect to the damage caused by polydrug abuse, we are not confident that the answer is yes.

In addition to biologic damage, there is damage to one's perception of what is right and wrong established by incoherent consequences. When there is biologic damage and the conceptual damage induced by prolonged, harsh imprisonment with few rewards and considerable fear and punishment, the damage induced will be very difficult to undo.

This last section of this book presents ideas that have the least amount of support from systematic studies. The ideas may be over blown and problematic from a number of points of view. It is theory in need of being tested. Nevertheless, for those who prefer living in a society in which nearly everyone is morally adept, the advice is that we should be cautious about the widespread use of pleasure-producing drugs that by their very nature blunt temporarily and maybe permanently our inherent guidance system.

Chapter 9: Summary

If you prefer to remain healthy and remain capable of developing a happy life, the advice, particularly for women, is to severely temper your intake of alcoholic beverages.

We end this book, like a previous one, with a variation of a Benjamin Franklin saying: Have fun, do good and be well; and the additional addendum, these need not be incompatible with each other.

References and Notes

Chapter 1

1. Pennock, P. E. (2007). *Advertising Sin and Sickness: the politics of alcohol and tobacco marketing, 1950-1990.* DeKalb, Illinois: Northern Illinois University Press.

2. Kanny, D., Liu, Y., Brewer, R. D., Garvin, W. & Balluz, L. (2010). Vital Signs: Binge Drinking Among High School Students and Adults --- United States, 2009. *MMWR* 59, 1274-79.

3. The generalization that women are different than men is controversial. See, for example, these references:

Fine, C. (2010). Delusions of gender: How our minds, society and neurosexism create difference. Norton, N.Y.

Halpern, D.F. (2010). How neuomythologies support sex role stereotypes. *Science*, 330, 1320-21.

Jordan-Young, R. (2010). Brain storm: The flaws in the science of sex differences. Cambridge, MA, Harvard University Press.

Barreca, C. (ed.) (2011). *Make Mine a Double: Why women like us like to drink (or not).* Lebanon, NH: University Press of New England. This book is a series of comments by women about their experience with alcohol. Although the experiences of the 29 authors are diverse, it is clear that they are troubled by the differences between the society's norms that seem to stipulate that men and women should drink differently.

Chapter 2

1. Ian Gately has written a comprehensive history on humans dealing with alcohol. I liberally used his book as a source for this chapter. Gately, I. (2008). *Drink: A cultural history of alcohol.* London, England: Gotham.

2. Dasgupta, A. (2011). *The Science of Drinking: How alcohol affects your body and mind.* New York: Bowman & Littlefield, 2011.

3. Babor, T., Caetano, R., Casswell, S., Edwards, G., Giesbrecht, N., Graham, K., et al. (2003). *Alcohol: No ordinary commodity.* New York: Oxford University Press.

4. Conrad III, B. (1988). *Absinthe: History in a bottle.* San Francisco, CA: Chronicle Books.

5. The restaurant *1833* in Monterey, CA, sells absinthe cocktails. See the *San Francisco Chronicle*, Sept. 18, 2011, "New talents in Monterey", P3-P5.

6. Mattingly, C. (1998). *Well-tempered Women: Nineteenth-century temperance rhetoric.* Carbondale: Southern University Press (see also: Gately 2008).

7. Rush is an interesting character. If you want to learn more, see: Brodsky, A. (2004). *Benjamin Rush: patriot and physician.* New York: St. Martin's Press.

8. For those interested in the history of the temperance movement in the USA, I recommend histories by Gately (2008, see above); Mattingly (1988, see above); and Fleming, A. (1975). *Alcohol: The delightful poison.* New York: Delacorte Press. There is also the book by Okrent, D. (2010). *Last Call: The Rise and Fall of Prohibition.* New York: Scribner. It focuses on the time of Prohibition.

9. "I make my money by supplying a public demand." The quotation is taken from Gately (2008, p 384). Gately took it from Booristin, D. J. (1974). *The American: The democratic experience.* New York: Vintage Book. I do not have the slightest idea of where Booristin got the quotation, but probably not from Capone himself. Regardless of whether or not Capone said it, it probably represents the sentiments of the illegal provider of alcoholic beverages.

10. Pennock, P. E. (2007). *Advertising Sin and Sickness: the politics of alcohol and tobacco marketing, 1950-1990.* DeKalb, Illinois: Northern Illinois University Press.

11. Information concerning MADD, its history and its programs can be found at www.madd.org.

12. Information concerning Ms. Lighterner's unhappiness can be found at www.ICAP.org.

Chapter 3

1. Pennock, P. E. (2007). *Advertising Sin and Sickness: the politics of alcohol and tobacco marketing, 1950-1990.* DeKalb, Illinois: Northern Illinois University Press.

2. Brandt, A. (2007). *The Cigarette Century*, New York: Basic Books, New York. The subtitle of the book is: "The rise, fall and deadly persistence of the product that defined America."

3. One can find all of the arguments for fewer restrictions mentioned here plus more by consulting the Web site for the International Center for Alcohol Polices (ICAP) at www.ICAP.org.

4. Daube, M. (2012). Alcohol and tobacco. *Aust N Z J Public Health*, 36, 108-10.

5. International Center for Alcohol Polices (ICAP) at www.ICAP.org.

6. Babir et al. (2003). *Alcohol: No ordinary commodity*. New York: Oxford.

Wagenaar, A. C., Tobler, A. L., & Komro, K. A. (2010). Effects of alcohol tax and price policies on morbidity and mortality: a systematic review. *American J of Public Health*, 100, 2270-8.

7. To see the advertisement, search "Pinnacle Ad" in any search engine or go to www.pinnaclevodka.com/advertising.

8. Much of the following few pages are taken from Pennock (2007). See also Pennock, P. (2005). The evolution of U.S. temperance movements since repeal: a comparison of two campaigns to control alcoholic beverage marketing, 1950s and 1980s. *The Social History of Alcohol and Drugs*, 20, 14-65.

9. Weiner, D. (2009). *Cosmopolitan.* Retrieved Nov 21, '11, from www.cosmopolitan.com.

10. Gekas, A. (2011, June 1). *Daily Buzz Americans are drinking more wine than the French!* Retrieved Nov. 22, 2011, from Womansday.com/news /daily-buzz:dailywd.

11. Buonomano, D. (2011). *Brain Bugs: How the brain's flaws shape our lives.* New York: W. W. Norton Company, Inc.

12. Plassmann, H., O'Doherty, J., Shiv, B., & Rangel, A. (2008). Marketing actions can modulate neural representations of experienced pleasantness. *Proceedings of the National Academy of Sciences*, 105, 1050-54.

13. Munching, P. V. (1997). *Beer Blast*. New York: Random House.

14. Barreca, C. (ed.) (2011). *Make Mine a Double: Why women like us like to drink (or not).* Lebanon, New Hampshire: University Press of New England.

15. Babor, T., Caetano, R., Casswell, S., Edwards, G., Giesbrecht, N., Graham, K., et al. (2003). *Alcohol: No Ordinary Commodity.* New York: Oxford University Press.

Kerr, W. C. & Greenfield, T. K. (2007). Distribution of alcohol consumption and expenditures and the impact of improved measurement on coverage of alcohol sales in the 2000 National Alcohol Survey. *Alcohol: Clin. & Exp Res.*, 31, 1714-22.

16. Johnston, A.D. (2013). *Drink: The Intimate Relationship between Women and Alcohol*, New York: HarperCollins. Johnston's words (p 69-70) reporting an interview by Johnston of Jernigan, April 2011.

Chapter 4

1. Mendelson JH & Mello NK (1985). *Alcohol: Use and abuse in America.* Boston: Little, Brown & Company (see page 269).

2. Hart CL & Ksir C (2013). *Drugs, Society, and Human Behavior.* New York: McGraw-Hill.

Levinthal CF (2014). *Drugs, Behavior, and Modern Society.* Boston: Pearson.

3. Ewing JA (1984). Detecting alcoholism. The CAGE questionnaire. *JAMA,* 14, 1905-1907.

4. Gifford M (2009). *Alcoholism.* Santa Barbara, CA.: Greenwood Press.

5. These quotations came to our attention in a book by Gene Cohen titled *The Mature Mind*, a book presenting the idea that we can live well for decades even the decades after we retire. So, we are apt to live a long time with our choices. Cohen, G. D. (2006). *The Mature Mind: The positive power of the aging brain.* New York: Basic Books.

6. Pinker S (2011). *The Better Angels of Our Nature: Why violence has declined.* New York: Viking Adult.

7. Larry has written elsewhere that the best distinction between habits we call addictions and other habit is to inspect the consequences of such. The habit of taking chocolate can be called an addiction, but why? It has little dire consequences. The habit of taking methamphetamine is a bad habit, an addiction, because it has dire consequences including not following democratically determined laws. The reference is Reid LD (2010). Delicious or addictive? In Bishop MR (ed), *Chocolate, Fast Foods and Sweetener: consumption and health*. NY: Nova Science. Pp 313-317.

8. The information in the balance of this chapter and the references for the basic science supporting that information is available in some popular textbooks. Two of them are listed here.

Hart CL & Ksir C (2011). *Drugs, Society & Human Behavior*. New York: McGraw-Hill.

Julien RM, Advokat CD & Comaty JE (2011). *A Primer of Drug Action*. New York: Worth Publishers.

Chapter 5

1. Bouchery E, Harwood HJ, Sacks JJ, Simon CJ & Brewer RD (2011). Economic costs of excessive alcohol consumption in the U.S., 2006. *Am J Prev Med*, 41, 516-24.

2. NIAA http://www.niaaa.nih.gov/alcohol-health/special populations-co-occurring-disorders/college-drinking.

3. Taylor B & Rehm J (2012). The relationship between alcohol consumption and fatal motor vehicle injury: high risk at low alcohol levels. Alcohol Clin Exp Res, 36, 1827-34.

4. Haver B, Gjestad R, Lindberg S & Franck J (2009). Mortality risk up to 25 years after initiation of treatment among 420 Swedish women with alcohol addiction. Addiction, 104, 413-19.

5. Dasgupta A (2011). *The Science of Drinking*. New York: Rowman & Littlefield Publishers, Inc.

6. Chikritzhs T, Fillmore K & Stockwell, T (2009). A healthy dose of scepticism: four good reasons to think again about protective effects of alcohol on coronary heart disease. *Drug Alcohol Rev 28*, 441-44.

7. Ronksley PE, Brien SE, Turner BJ, Mukamal KJ & Ghali WA (2011). Association of alcohol consumption with selected cardiovascular disease outcomes: a systematic review and meta-analysis. BMJ, 2011 Feb 22;342:d671. doi: 10.1136/bmj.d671.

8. Holmes MV, Dale CE et al. (2014). Association between alcohol and cardiovascular disease: Mendelian randomization analysis based on individual participant data. BMJ 2014;349:g4164 doi: 10.1136/bmj.g4164 (Published 10 July 2014)

9. Bagnardi V. et al. (2012). Light alcohol drinking and cancer: a meta-analysis. *Annals of Ocology*, advanced access, published August 21, 2012, doi:10.1093/annonc/mds337.

10. Hart CL & Ksir C (2011). *Drugs, Society, & Human Behavior* (14th ed.), New York: McGraw-Hill.

11. Substance Abuse and Mental Health Services Administration, Center for Behavioral Health Statistics and Quality. (July 2, 2012). The DAWN Report: Highlights of the 2010 Drug Abuse Warning Network (DAWN) Findings on Drug-Related Emergency Department Visits. Rockville, MD.

12. Lazarou J, Pomeranz BH & Corey PN (1998). Incidence of adverse drug reactions in hospitalized patients: a meta-analysis of prospective studies. *JAMA 15*, 1200-5.

13.http://rethinkingdrinking.niaaa.nih.gov/IsYour DrinkingPatternRisky/WhatsYourPattern.asp. Read 7/28/2012.

14. Garnier LM, Arria AM, Caldeira KM, Vincent KB, O'Grady, KE & Wish ED (2009). Nonmedical prescription analgesic use and concurrent alcohol consumption among college students. *Am J Drug Alcohol Abuse 35*, 334-38.

15. Bala S, Marcos M, Gattu A, Catalano D & Szabo G. (2014). Acute binge drinking increases serum endotoxin and bacterial DNA levels in healthy individuals. PLoS ONE 9(5): e96864. doi:10.1371/journal.pone.0096864

16. Kopelman MD, Thomson AD, Guerrini I & Marshall EJ (2009). The Korsakoff syndrome: clinical aspects, psychology and treatment. *Alcohol Alcohol* 44, 148-154

17. Aserinsky E & Kleitman N (1953). Regularly occurring periods of eye motility, and concomitant phenomena, during sleep. *Science* 118, 273-74.

18. Mayers AG & Baldwin DS (2005). Antidepressants and their effect on sleep. *Hum Psychopharmacol 20*, 533-59.

19. A more detailed version of this section appears in Reid LD (2013). *Women, Alcoholism and Feminism*, Brunswick, NY: Hexagon.

Susan Nolan-Hoeksema addresses the issues of women, alcoholism and depression. For examples: Nolen-Hoeksema S (2003). *Women who think too much: How to break free of overthinking and reclaim your life.* New York, Henry Holt.

Nolen-Hoeksema S (2006). *Eating, drinking, overthinking: The toxic triangle of food, alcohol, and depression--and how women can break free.* New York, Henry Holt.

Also valuable is Lambert K (2008). *Lifting Depression: A Neuroscientist's Hands-on Approach to Activating Your Brain's Healing Power.* New York: Basic Books.

20. Kessler RC, Berglund P, Demler O, Jin R, Merikangas KR & Walters EE (2005). Lifetime prevalence and age-of-onset distributions of DSM-IV disorders in the National Comorbidity Survey Replication. Arch Gen Psychiatry 62, 593-602.

Kessler RC, Chiu WT, Demler O & Walter EE (2005). Prevalence, severity, and comorbidity of 12-month DSM-IV disorders in the National Comorbidity Survey Replication. *Arch Gen Psychiatry 62,* 617-709.

Boschloo L, van den Brink W, Penninx BW, Wall MM & Hasin, D S (2011). Alcohol-use disorder severity predicts first-incidence of depressive disorders. *Psychol Med 26,* 1-9.

21. Diener E. & Biswas-Diener R. (2008). Happiness: Unlocking the Mysteries of Psycyological Wealth. Malden, Ma., Blackwell Publishing.

22. Shuchter, S. R., Downs, N. S., & Zisook, S. (1996). Biologically Informed Psychotherapy for Depression. NY: Guilford Press. They go on to say that the functioning of the medial forebrain bundle system of the subcortical midbrain and forebrain is the CNS system most salient to hedonic processes.

23. Maxmen, J. S., & Ward, N. G. (1995). Essential Psychopathology and Its Treatment. NY: WW Norton & Co. Inc.

24. Relevant data are available on the Web site of the National Institute of Mental Health. The Center for Disease Control tabulates for data on suicide. Data were obtained in 2014 by searching the CDC Web-site. To verify our reporting and to get updates, all that is necessary is to get data from the CDC which is easily accessed by way of any search engine.

25. Keller, M.C., Neale, M.C., Kendler, K.S. (2007). Association of different adverse life events with distinct patterns of depressive symptoms. *Am J Psychiatry 164,* 1521– 29.

Andrews, P. W., S. G. Kornstein, et al. (2011). Blue again: perturbational effects of antidepressants suggest monoaminergic homeostasis in major depression. *Front Psychol 2*, 159.

Andrews, P. W. and J. A. Thomson, Jr. (2009). The bright side of being blue: depression as an adaptation for analyzing complex problems. *Psychol Rev 116*, 620-54.

Andrews, P. W., J. A. Thomson, Jr., et al. (2012). Primum non nocere: an evolutionary analysis of whether antidepressants do more harm than good. *Front Psychol 3*, 117.

Pettinati HM, O'Brien CP & William D. Dundon WD (2013). Current status of co-occurring mood and substance use disorders: a new therapeutic target *Am J Psychiatry* 170, 23–30.

26. A publication of the United States Agency for Healthcare Research and Quality (US) (2007). There is a second publication: Second-Generation of Adult Depression: An Update of the 2007 Cpmarative Effectiveness Review (from the same agency). Free copies are available from AHRQ Publications Clearhouse at 800-358-9295.

Diener E. & Biswas-Diener R (2008). *Happiness: Unlocking the Mysteries of Psycyological Wealth*. Malden, Ma., Blackwell Publishing.

27. Weir K (2011). The exercise effect. *Monitor on Psychology 42*, 49-52.

Mata J, Thompson RJ. Jaeggi SM, Buschkuehl M, Jonides J & Gotlib IH (2011). Walk on the bright side: physical activity and affect in major depressive disorder. *J Abnorm Psychol 121*, 297-308.

28. Keller MC, Neale MC, Kendler KS (2007). Association of different adverse life events with distinct patterns of depressive symptoms. *Am J Psychiatry 164*, 1521– 29.

29. Boschloo L, van den Brink W, Penninx BW, Wall MM & Hasin, D. S. (2012). Alcohol-use disorder severity predicts first-incidence of depressive disorders. *Psychol Med,* 42, 695-703.

30. Graham K & Massak A (2007). Alcohol consumption and the use of antidepressants. *Canadian Medical Assoc J 176*, 633-37.

31. Parsons OA (1998). Neurocognitive deficits in alcoholics and social drinkers: a continuum? *Alcohol Clin Exp Res 22*, 954-61.

Volpicelli JR, O'Brien CP, Alterman AI & Hayashida M (1990). Naltrexone and the treatment of alcohol-dependence: Initial observations. In Reid, L.D. (ed.). *Opioids, Bulimia, and Alcohol Abuse & Alcoholism*. New York: Springer-Verlag.

32. Julien RM, Advokat CD & Comaty JE (2011). *A Primer of Drug Action.* New York: Worth Publishers.

34. Parsons OA (1998). Neurocognitive deficits in alcoholics and social drinkers: a continuum? *Alcohol Clin Exp Res 22*, 954-61.

35. Beck A, Wüstenberg T, Genauck A, Wrase J, Schlagenhauf F, Smolka N, Mann K & Heinz A. (2012). Effect of brain structure, brain function, and brain connectivity on relapse in alcohol-dependent patients. *Arch Gen Psychiatry, 69*, 842-52.

Chapter 6

1. A recent book details the problems associated with laws remaining on the books without regard to their consequences. The recommendation of that book is to have every law expire at the end of 15 years, thereby, bringing the law's utility to the fore. The book is very compelling and is recommended: Howard, P.K. (2014). The rule of nobody: Saving America from dead laws and broken government. New York: Norton.

2. Tatarsky, A., Marlatt, G.A., (2010). State of the art in harm reduction psychotherapy: an emerging treatment for substance misuse. J. Clinical Psychology, 66, 117-22.

Mendoz N.S., Walitzer K.S., Connors G.J. (2012). Use of treatment strategies in a moderated drinking program for women. Addict Behav. 37, 1054-7.

3. Vaillant, G.E. (2003). A 60-year follow-up of alcoholic men. Addiction, 98, 1043-51.

4. Zindel, L.R., Kranzler, H.R. (2014). Pharmacotherapy of alcohol use disorders: seventy-five years of progress. J. Stud Alcohol Drugs Suppl, 17, 79-88

5. Hart, C. L., & Ksir, C. (2013). Drugs, Society & Human Behavior (15th ed.). New York: McGraw-Hill.

6. Helzer J. E., Badger G. J., Searles J. S., Rose G.L., & Mongeon J. A. (2006). Stress and alcohol consumption in heavily drinking men: 2 years of daily data using interactive voice response. Alcohol Clin Exp Res, 30, 802-11.

7. Voss, E., Mejta, C., & Reid, L. D. (1974). Methods of deconditioning persisting avoidance: Response prevention and counterconditioning after extensive training. Bulletin of Psychonomic Society, 3, 345-47.

Julien, R., Advokat, C.D., & Comaty, J. (2014). *Primer of Drug Action* (13th ed.). Richmond, England: Worth Publishing Ltd.

8. See Julien et al. (2014), item 7 above.

9. Hunt, W. A., Barnett, L. W., & Branch, L. G. (1971). Relapse rates in addiction programs. *J Clin Psychol* 27, 455-56.

Miller, W. R., Walters, S. T., & Bennett, M. E. (2001). How effective is alcoholism treatment in the United States? *J Stud Alcohol,* 62, 211-20.

O'Brien, C. P. (1994). Treatment of alcoholism as a chronic disorder. *Alcohol, 11*, 433-437.

Miller, W. R., & Wilbourne, P. L. (2002). Mesa Grande: a methodological analysis of clinical trials of treatments for alcohol use disorders. *Addiction 97*, 265-277.

Cutler, R. B. & Fishbain, D. A. (2005). Are alcoholism treatments effective? The Project MATCH data. *BMC Public Health, 5*, 75. doi: 10.1186/1471-2458-5-75

Dow, S. J. & Kelly, J. F. (2013). Listening to youth: Adolescents' reasons for substance use as a unique predictor of treatment response and outcome. *Psychology of Addictive Behaviors, 27*, 1122-1131. doi: 10.1037/a0031065. Epub 2012 Dec 31

Polich, J. M., Armore, D.J. & Braiker, H. B. The course of alcohoholism: Four years after treatment. San Monic,Ca.: Rand (R-2433-NIAAA).

10. See McLellan, A.T., Lewis, D.C., O'Brien, C.P. & Kleber, H.D. (2000). Drug dependence, a chronic medical illness: implications for treatment, insurance, and outcomes evaluation. *JAMA.* 284, 1689–95.

11. The figure was redrawn from a similar figure appearing in Hunt et al. (1971) and Miller et al. (2001). See above, item 9, for full references.

12. Boschloo, L., Vogelzangs, N., van den Brink, W., Smit, J. H., Beekman, A. T., & Penninx, B. W. (2012). Predictors of the two-year recurrence and persistence of alcohol dependence. *Addiction*. doi:10.1111/j

Polich, J. M., Armore, D.J. & Braiker, H. B. The course of alcohoholism: Four years after treatment. San Monic,Ca.: Rand (R-2433-NIAAA).

13. Stehman, C. R. & Mycyk, M. B. (2013). A rational approach to the treatment of alcohol withdrawal in the ED. *American Journal of Emergency Medicine*, 31, 734-742.

Holbrook, A. M., Crowther, R., Lotter, A., Cheng, C., & King, D. (1999). Meta-analysis of benzodiazepine use in the treatment of acute alcohol withdrawal. *Canadian Medical Association Journal*, 160, 649-655.

14. Mendelson, J. H. & Mello, N. K. (1985). *Alcohol: Use and Abuse in America*. Boston, MA: Little, Brown & Co.

Monte, R., Rabunal, R., Casariego, E., Lopez-Agreda, H., Mateos, A. & Pertega, S. (2010). Analysis of the factors determining survival of alcoholic withdrawal syndrome patients in a general hospital. *Alcohol and Alcoholism, 45*, 151-158.

15. Ignjatovic-Ristic, D., Rancic, N., Novokmet, S., Jankovic, S. & Stefanovic, S. (2013). Risk factors for lethal outcome in patients with delirium tremens - psychiatrist's perspective: a nested case-control study. *Annals of General Psychiatry, 12*, 39. doi:10.1186/1744-859X-12-39

16. Pennington, D. L., Durazzo, T. C., Schmidt, T. P., Mon, A., Abé, C. & Meyerhoff, D. J. (2013). The effects of chronic cigarette smoking on cognitive recovery during early abstinence from alcohol. *Alcoholism: Clinical and Experimental Research, 37*, 1220-1227.

17. Dean, R., Bilsky, E.J. & Negus, S.S. (Eds.). *Opioid receptors and antagonists: from bench to clinic.* Humana Press, 2009.

18. B. L. Smith & J. D. Lane (Eds.), *The Neurobiology of Opiate Reward Processes* (pp. 147-174). New York: Elsevier Biomedical Press.

19. Naranjo, C.A., Sellers, E.M. (1992). Novel Pharmacological Interventions for Alcoholism. New York, Springer-Verlag.

20. Wardell, J. D. & Read, J. P. (2013). Does cue context matter? Examining the specificity of cue-related activation of positive and negative alcohol expectancies. *Exp Clin Psychopharmacol.* 21, 457-66.

21. Reid, L.D., Gibson, W.E., Gledhill, S.M., & Porter, P.B. (1964). Anticonvulsant drugs and self-stimulation behavior. *J Comp Physiol Psych,* 58, 353-56.

22. Olds established a laboratory of his own that pursued his original observations and his ideas explaining them. A group of young scientists, most of whom were graduate students at the time, became intrigued with the findings that direct electrical stimulation of the brain could reinforce behavior. They (namely George Koob, Bart Hoebel, Jaak Panksepp and I) each established research programs of our own that contributed to the ongoing research germane to Olds' original observations. Other senior scientists became involved, including Elliot Valenstein. This relatively small group of behavioral neuroscientists produced results that supported the theory that the brain had a well-organized system the activation of which induced positive emotionality that was capable of rewarding behavior, hence could be a mechanism for habit formation. Each of the various possible explanations listed by Professors Hilgard and Bower of why rats might be pressing bars for brain stimulation were tested. None of them were supported by the evidence. The only explanation that was supported by the evidence was that certain brain stimulation induced behavior that was very similar to the behavior induced by presentation of ordinary rewards.

The research disputing the idea that the stimulation induced seizures and somehow that could account for why rats pressed was proven inadequate by the research cited in item 21.

23. Olds, J. (1962). Hypothalamic substrates of reward. *Physiol. Rev.*, 42, 554-604.

24. Bush, H.D., Bush, M.F., Miller, M.A., & Reid, L.D. (1976). Addictive agents and intracranial stimulation: Daily morphine and lateral hypothalamic self-stimulation. *Physiological Psychology 4,* 79-85.

25. Rossi, N.A. & Reid, L.D. (1976). Affective states associated with morphine injections. *Physiological Psychology 4,* 269-274.

26. Wise, R. A. & Bozarth, M. A. (1987). A psychomotor stimulant theory of addiction. *Psychol Rev.,* 94, 469-92.

27. Reid, L. D. (Ed.). (1990). *Opioids, Bulimia, and Alcohol Abuse & Alcoholism*. New York: Springer-Verlag.

Altshuler, H. L., Philips, P. E. & Feinhandler, D. A. (1980). Alteration of ethanol self-administration by naltrexone. *Life Sciences, 26,* 679–688.

28. Reid, L.D. Opioid antagonists and ethanol's ability to reinforce intake of alcoholic beverages: Preclinical studies. In: Dean, R., Bilsky, E. J. & Negus, S. S. (eds) Opioid receptors and antagonists: from bench to clinic. Humana Press, 2009. Pp. 335-369.

29. Hubbell, C.L., Abelson, M.L., Burkhardt, C.A., Herlands, S.E. & Reid, L.D. (1988). Constant infusions of morphine and intakes of sweetened ethanol solution among rats. Alcohol, 5, 409-15. Also see Reid, L. D. (2009) cited above, item 28.

30. Gianoulakis, C., Angelogianni, P., Meaney, M., Thavundayil, J. & Tawar, V. (1990). Endorphins in individuals with high and low risk for development of alcoholism. In Reid, L.D. (ed.) *Opioids, Bulimia, and Alcohol Abuse & Alcoholism*. New York: Springer-Verlag.

31. Garnier, L. M., Arria, A. M., Caldeira, K. M., Vincent, K. B., O'Grady, K. E. & Wish, E. D. (2009). Nonmedical prescription analgesic use and concurrent alcohol consumption among college students. *Am J Drug Alcohol Abuse*, 35, 334-38.

32. Volpicelli, J.R., O'Brien, C.P., Alterman, A.I. & Hayashida, M. (1990). Naltrexone and the treatment of alcohol-dependence: Initial observations. In Reid, L.D. (ed.). *Opioids, Bulimia, and Alcohol Abuse & Alcoholism*. New York: Springer-Verlag.

33. O'Malley, S. S., Jaffe, A. J., Chang, G., Schottenfeld, R. S., Meyer, R. E., & Rounsaville, B. (1992). Naltrexone and coping skills therapy for alcohol dependence. A controlled study. *Arch Gen Psychiatry*, 49, 881-87.

34. Volpicelli, J. R., Alterman, A. I., Hayashida, M. & O'Brien, C. P. (1992). Naltrexone in the treatment of alcohol dependence. *Arch Gen Psychiatry*, 49, 876-80.

35. Rösner, S., Hackl-Herrwerth, A., Leucht, S., Vecchi S., Srisurapanont M. & Soyka, M. (2010). Opioid antagonists for alcohol dependence. Cochrane Database of Systematic Reviews. Dec 8;(12):CD001867. doi: 10.1002/14651858.CD001867.pub2

36. Kiefer, F., Helwig, H., Tarnaske, T., Otte, C., Jahn, H. & Wiedemann, K. (2005). Pharmacological relapse prevention of alcoholism: clinical predictors of outcome. Eur Addict Res 11, 83-91.

37. Garbutt, J. C., Kranzler, H. R., O'Malley, S. S., Gastfriend, D. R., Pettinati, H. M., Silverman, B. L., Loewy, J. W. & Ehrich, E. W. (2005). Efficacy and tolerability of long-acting injectable naltrexone for alcohol dependence a randomized controlled trial. J Am Med Assoc, 293, 1617-25.

38. Pettinati, H. M., Gastfriend, D. R., Dong, Q., Kranzl, H. R., & O'Malley, S. S. (2009). Effect of Extended-Release Naltrexone (XR-NTX) on Quality of Life in Alcohol-Dependent Patients. Alcohol Clin Exp Res, 33, 350-56.

39. Lee, J. D., Grossman, E., Huben, L., Manseau, M., McNeely, J., Rotrosen, J., . . . Gourevitch, M. N. (2012). Extended-release naltrexone plus medical management alcohol treatment in primary care: findings at 15 months. *J Subst Abuse Treat,* 43, 458-62.

40. Lapham, S. C. & McMillan, G. P. (2011). Open-label pilot study of extended-release naltrexone to reduce drinking and driving among repeat offenders. *J Addict Med,* 5, 163-69.

41. Finigan, M. W., Perkins, T., Zold-Kilbourn, P., Parks, J. & Stringer, M. (2011). Preliminary evaluation of extended-release naltrexone in Michigan and Missouri drug courts. *J Subst Abuse Treat,* 41, 288-93.

42. Jan, S., Gill, P. & Borawala, A.S. (2011). Utilization patterns of extended-release naltrexone for alcohol dependence. *Am J Manag Care,* 17, S210-2.

43. Thyer, B.A., Baum, M. & Reid, L.D. (1988). Exposure techniques in the reduction of fear: A comparative review of the procedure in animals and humans. *Advan Beha Res Ther,* 10, 105-27.

Taub, J., Taylor, P., Smith M., Kelley, K., Becker, B. & Reid L.D. (1977). Methods of deconditioning persisting avoidance: Drugs as adjuncts to response prevention. *Physiol Psych,* 5, 67-72.

44. Holdstock, L., King, A.C. & de Wit, H. (2000). Subjective and objective responses to ethanol in moderate/heavy and light social drinkers. *Alcohol Clin Exp Res.* 24, 789-94.

Morean, M.E. & Corbin, W.R. (2010). Subjective response to alcohol: a critical review of the literature. Alcohol Clin Exp Res. 34, 385-395.

Reed, S.C., Levin, F.R. & Evans, S.M. (2012). Alcohol increases impulsivity and abuse liability in heavy drinking women. *Exp Clin Psychopharmacol* 20**,** 454-465.

45. Parsons, O. A. (1998). Neurocognitive deficits in alcoholics and social drinkers: a continuum? Alcohol Clin Exp Res. *22,* 954-961.

46. Chanraud, S., Martelli, C., Delain, F., Kostogianni, N., Douaud, G., Aubin, H-J., Reynaud, M., & Martinot, J-L. (2007). Brain morphometry and cognitive performance in detoxified alcohol-dependents with preserved psychosocial functioning. *Neuropsycho-pharmacology, 32,* 429-438.

Crews, F. T., & Nixon, K. (2009). Mechanisms of neurodegeneration and regeneration in alcoholism. *Alcohol and Alcoholism, 44,* 115-127.

Loeber, S., Duka, T., Welzel, H., Nakovics, H., Heinz, A., Flor, H., & Mann, K. (2009). Impairment of cognitive abilities and decision making after chronic use of alcohol: the impact of multiple detoxifications. *Alcohol and Alcoholism, 44*, 372-81.

Beck, A., Wüstenberg, T., Genauck, A., Wrase, J., Schlagenhauf, F., Smolka, M. N., Mann, K., & Heinz, A. (2012). Effect of brain structure, brain function, and brain connectivity on relapse in alcohol-dependent patients. *Archives of General Psychiatry, 69*, 842-852.

Elofson, J., Gongvatana, W., & Carey, K. B. (2013). Alcohol use and cerebral white matter compromise in adolescence. *Additive Behaviors, 38*, 2295-2305.

47. Hugh, R.K. & Barlow, D.H. (2010). The dissemination and implementation of evidence-based psychological treatments. *Am Psychologist, 65*, 73-85.

Barlow, D.H., Boswell, J.F., & Thompson-Hollands J. Eysenck, Strupp, and 50 years of psychotherapy research: a personal perspective. *Psychotherapy (Chic).* 2013, 77-87.

48. There are books written to introduce these new perspectives:

Stein, D.G., Brailowsky, S. & Will, B. (1995). *Brain Repair.* New York: Oxford Univer. Press.

Doidge, N. (2007). *The Brain that Changes Itself: Stories of Personal Triumph from the Frontiers of Brain Science.* New York: Penguin Books.

Begley, S. (2008). *Train Your Mind, Change Your Brain.* New York: Ballantine Books.

Merzenich, M. (2013). *Soft-wired: How the New Science of Brain Plasticity Can Change Your Life.* San Francisco: Parnassus Publishing.

49. Bates, M. E., Darry, D., Labouvie, E. W., Buckman, J. F., Fals-Stewart, W., & Voelbel, G. (2004). Risk factors and neuropsychological recovery in alcohol use disordered clients exposed to different treatments. *Journal of Consulting and Clinical Psychology, 72*, 1073-1080.

Bates, M. E., Buckman, J. F., Voelbel, G. T., Eddie, D., & Freeman, J. (2013). The mean and the individual: integrating variable-centered and person-centered analyses of cognitive recovery in patients with substance use disorders. *Frontiers in Psychiatry, 4*, 177. doi: 10.3389/fpsyt.2013.00177. eCollection 2013

50. Merzenich, M. (2013). *Soft-wired: How the New Science of Brain Plasticity Can Change Your Life.* San Francisco: Parnassus Publishing.

IOM: *Cognitive Rehabilitation Therapy for Traumatic Brain Injury: Evaluating the evidence.* Washington, DC: The National Academies Press, 2011.

51. Fals-Stewart, W., & Lam, W. K. K. (2010). Computer-assisted cognitive rehabilitation for the treatment of patients with substance use disorders: A randomized clinical trial. *Experimental and Clinical Psychopharmacology, 18*, 87-98.

Houben, K., Reinout, W. W., & Jansen, A. (2011). Getting a grip on drinking behavior: Training working memory to reduce alcohol abuse. *Psychological Science, 22*, 968-975.

Rupp, C. I., Kemmler, G., Kurz, M., Hinterhuber, H., & Fleischhacker, W. W. (2012). Cognitive remediation therapy during treatment for alcohol dependence. *Journal of Studies on Alcohol and Drugs, 73*, 625-634.

Kreusch, F., Vilenne, A. & Quertemont, E. (2013). Response inhibition toward alcohol-related cues using an alcohol go/no-go task in problem and non-problem drinkers. *Addictive Behaviors, 38*, 2520-8. doi: 10.1016/j.addbeh.2013.04.007. Epub 2013 May 7

52. There are other companies that sell programs advertised to improve cognitive ability. However, some of them do not have the sustained experience inherent to Posit Science to be good at anything but marketing a product. Note: none of the authors of this text have any financial relationships with Posit Science. We do admire the outstanding research that is the basis for the development of the programs that have been developed by the scientists of Posit Science.

53. Reid LD (2015). Improving treatment of alcoholism by using evidence-based practices and computer-assisted game-like programs. *Jacobs Journal of Addiction and Therapy,* 2015, 1, 015. (open access)

54. Moselhy HF, Georgiou G, Kahn A. Frontal lobe changes in alcoholism: a review of the literature. *Alcohol Alcohol*, 2001, 36: 357-368.

Reid, M.L., Hubbell, C.L., Douglas, A.V., Boedeker, K.L. & Reid, L.D. Research with rats germane to medications for alcoholism: Consequences of non-compliance. Alcohol, 2001, 24, 169-177.

Bates ME, Darry D, Labouvie EW, Buckman JF, Fals-Stewart W et al. Risk factors and neuropsychological recovery in alcohol use disordered clients exposed to different treatments. *J Consult Clin Psychol*. 2004, 72(6): 1073-1080.

Crews FT, & Nixon K. Mechanisms of neurodegeneration and regeneration in alcoholism. *Alcohol Alcohol*. 2009, 44: 115-127.

Crews F & Boettiger CA. Impulsivity, frontal lobes and risk of addiction. *Pharmacol Biochem Behav.* 2009, 93: 237-47.

Bates ME, Buckman JF, Voelbel GT, Eddie D & Freeman J. The mean and the individual: integrating variable-centered and person-centered analyses of cognitive recovery in patients with substance use disorders. *Front Psychiatry*, 2013, 4: 177.

55. There is good news. There is a movement toward integrated health care, i.e., a system that makes it easy to access and integrate the services of physicians, nurses, psychologists and other specialties in what is now called family medicine or primary care. The idea is to provide services that are helpful in establishing healthy life styles including the treatment of alcoholism. This movement is the topic of virtually an entire issue of *American Psychologist*, Specal Issue: Primary Care and Psychology May-June 2014, 69 with a number of separate articles. Also, the newly elected President (circa 2014) of the American Psychological Association has said he (Barry Anton) will concentrate his efforts on promoting integrated health care: see, Chamberlin J (2015). A focus on team care. *Monitor on Psychology*, 46, (No. 1), 24-5.

56. A publication provides information about how to do the injections of XR-NTX, thereby, avoiding making mistakes having adverse effects. Giving the injections is apparently not as easy as it might seem to be. See: Center for Substance Abuse Treatment. *Incorporating Alcohol Pharmacotherapies Into Medical Practice. Treatment improvement protocol (TIP), Series 49.* HHS Publication No. (SMA) 09-4380. Rockville, MD: Substance Abuse and Mental Health Services Administration, 2009. Note this booklet is available for free as a download or as a print version.

57. This book and a similar book *Women, Alcoholism and Feminism* published in 2013 are designed to bring new perspectives to the treatment of alcoholism with respect to women.

58. The typical physician has neither the time nor the skills to help modify unhealthy life-styles. The psychiatrists who merely prescribe drugs supposedly beneficial in treating psychological problems also do not provide treatment for changing life-styles. We have a chapter on the treatment of depression in Reid (2013, Women alcoholism and feminism) which address some of the issues associated with merely relying on psychopharmacology as a treatment for mental disorders.

59. Babor et al. (2003). *Alcohol: No Ordinary Commodity.* New York: Oxford University Press.

Herttua K, Martikainen P, Vahtera J & Kivima ki M (2011). Living alone and alcohol-related mortality: A population-based cohort study from F inland. *PLoS Med* 8(9): e1001094. doi:10.1371/journal.pmed.1001094

60. Wagenaar, A. C., Tobler, A. L. & Komro, K. A. (2010). Effects of alcohol tax and price policies on morbidity and mortality: a systematic review. *American J of Public Health*, 100, 2270-8.

61. Estimating the total costs of widespread use of alcoholic beverages is difficult. The CBO (http://www.cbo.gov/budget-options/2013/44854) cites one estimate of cost as $130 billion of external economic costs of AAA, a cost considerably greater than revenue derived by taxation.

62. Congressional Budget Office (Nov. 13, 2013). Options for the reducing the deficit: 2014 to 2013. http://www.cbo.gov/budget-options/2013/44854

Chapter 7

1. Johnston, A.D. (2013). Drink: The Intimate Relationship between Women and Alcohol, New York, NY: HarperCollins.

In particular, Johnston treats the issues of fetal alcohol syndrome with more nuance and personal testimony than our treatment. We recommend consulting her book.

2. Zemore, S. E. (2005). Re-examining whether and why acculturation relates to drinking outcomes in rigorous, national survey of Latinos. Alcoholism: Clinical and Experimental Research, 29, 144-53.

3. McCarty, C.A., Ebel, B.E., Garrison, M.M., DiCiuseppe, D.L., Christakis, D.A. & Rivara, F.P. (2004). Continuity of binge and harmful drinking from late adolescence to early adulthood. Pediatrics 114, 714-19.

DeWit, D.J., Adlaf, E.M., Offord, D.R. & Ogborne, A.C. (2000). Age at first alcohol use: a risk factor for the development of alcohol disorders. Am J Psychiatry 157, 745–50.

4. Morse, J. (2002, April 1). Women on a Binge. Time (Latin American Edition), 159 34- 39.

5. Kanny, D., Yong, L. and Brewer, R.D. Morbidity and Mortality Weekly Report Supplements v. 60 (1).Center Center for Disease Control and Prevention. Atlanta, Georgia : U.S. Government, 2011. pp. 101-104.

6. Greenfield, S. F., Pettinati, H. M., O'Malley, S., Randall, P. K., & Randall, C. L. (2010). Gender differences in alcohol treatment: an analysis of outcome from the COMBINE study. Alcohol Clinical and Experimental Research, 34, 1803-12.

7. Kanny, D., Yong, L., & Brewer, R. D. (2011). Morbidity and Mortality Weekly Report Supplements Binge Drinking --- United States, 2009 v. 60 (1). Center for Disease Control and Prevention. Atlanta, Georgia: U.S. Government.

8. Kanny, D., Liu, Y., Brewer, R. D., Garvin, W. & Balluz, L. (2010). Vital Signs: Binge Drinking Among High School Students and Adults --- United States, 2009. MMWR 59, 1274-79.

9. Kanny, D., Liu, Y., Brewer, R. D. & Eke, P. I. (2013). Vital signs: Binge drinking among women and high school girls—United States, 2011. MMWR 62, 1-5. http://www.cdc.gov/mmwr/pdf/wk/mm62e0108.pdf

10. Reichman, J. From the /web: MSNBC Health News

11. Campbell, D. (2008 Sat. 23 Feb). Women: the hidden risks of drinking, The Observer.

12. Eagon P.K. (2010). Alcoholic liver injury: Influence of gender and hormones. World J Gastroenterology 16, 1377-84.

13. Herttua K, Martikainen P, Vahtera J, Kivima¨ ki M (2011) Living Alone and Alcohol-Related Mortality: A Population-Based Cohort Study from Finland. PLoS Med 8(9): e1001094. doi:10.1371/journal.pmed.1001094

14. U.S. Cancer Stastics Working Group (2010). United States Cancer Statistics: 1999-2007 Incidence and Mortality Web-based Report. Centers for Disease Control and Prevention. Retrieved from http://www.cdc.gov/uscs.

15. Brooks, P. J., & Zakhari, S. (2013). Moderate alcohol consumption and breast cancer in women: From epidemiology to mechanisms and interventions. Alcohol Clin Exp Res, 37, 23-30.

16. Chen W.Y., Rosner, B., Hankinson, S.E. Colditz, G.S. & Willett, W.C. (2011). Moderate alcohol consumption during adult life, drinking patterns, and breast cancer risk. JAMA 306, 1884-90 doi:10.1001/jama.2011.1590.

17. Brooks, P. J. & Zakhari, S. (2013). Moderate alcohol consumption and breast cancer in women: From epidemiology to mechanisms and interventions. Alcohol Clin Exp Res. 37, 23-30

18. Hilakivi-Clarke L (1996) Role of estradiol in alcohol intake and alcohol-related behaviors. J Stud Alcohol 57, 162–70.

Purohit V (1998). Moderate alcohol consumption and estrogen levels in postmenopausal women: a review. Alcohol Clin Exp Res, 22, 994–97.

Sarkola T, Makisalo H, Fukunaga T, Eriksson CJ (1999). Acute effect of alcohol on estradiol, estrone, progesterone, prolactin, cortisol, and luteinizing hormone in premenopausal women. Alcohol Clin Exp Res 23, 976–82.

19. Squeglia, L. M., Schweinsburg, A. D., Pulido, C., & Tapert, S. F. (2011). Adolescent binge drinking linked to abnormal spatial working memory brain bctivation: Differential gender effects. Alcohol Clin Exp Res., 35, 1831-41.

20. Ruiz, S. M., Oscar-Berman, M., Sawyer, K. S., Valmas, M. M., Urban, T., & Harris, G. J. (2013). Drinking history associations with regional white matter volumes in alcoholic men and women. Alcoholism: Clinical and Experimental Research, 37, 110-122.

21. For examples: Lancaster, F. E., Brown, T. D., Coker, K. L., Elliott, J. A. & Wren, S. B. (1996). Sex differences in alcohol preference and drinking patterns emerge during the early postpubertal period in Sprague Dawley rats. Alcohol Clin Exp Res, 20, 1043-49.

Lancaster, F. E., & Spiegel, K. S. (1992). Sex differ-ences in pattern of drinking. Alcohol, 9, 415-20.

Li, T.K., & Lemung, L. (1984). Alcohol preference and voluntary alcoholintakes of inbred rat strains and the National Institutes of Health Heterogenous Stock of rats. Alcohol Clin Exp Res, 8, 485-6.

Juarez, J., Guzman-Flores, C., Ervin, F. R. & Palmour, R. M. (1993). Voluntary alcohol consumption in vervet monkeys: Individual, sex, and age differences. *Pharmacology Biochemistry and Behavior* 46, 985-88.

22. Eckel, L. A. (2004). Estradiol: a rhythmic, inhibitory, indirect control of meal size. Physiol Behav, 82, 35-41.

23. Reid, L. D., Marinelli, P. W., Bennett, S. M., Fiscale, L. T., Narciso, S. P., Oparowski, C. J., Reid, M. L., Merrigan, B. A., Moricone, J, Hubbell, C. L. & Gianoulakis, C. (2002). One injection of estradiol valerate induces dramatic changes in rats' intake of alcoholic beverages. Pharmacology Biochemistry & Behavior, 72, 601-616.

24. Marinelli, P. W., Quirion, R. & Gianoulakis, C. (2003). Estradiol valerate and alcohol intake: a comparison between Wistar and Lewis rats and the putative role of endorphins. Behav Brain Res, 139, 59-67.

Ford, M.M., Eldridge, J.C. & Samson, H.H. (2004). Determination of an estradiol dose response relationship in the modulation of ethanol intake. Alcohol Clin Exp Res 8, 20–8.

25. Reid, M. L., Hubbell, C.L. & Reid, L.D. (2003). A pharmacological dose of estradiol can enhance appetites for alcoholic beverages. Pharmacology Biochemistry & Behavior, 74, 381-388.

26. Quirarte, G. L., Reid, L. D., de la Teja, I. S., Reid, M. L., Sánchez, M. A., Díaz-Trujillo, A., Aguilar-Vazquez, A. & Prado-Alcalá, R. A. (2007). Estradiol valerate and alcohol intake: dose-response assessments. *BMC Pharmacol., 4*, 3.

Juárez, J., Vázquez-Cortés, C., & Barrios-De Tomasi, E. (2005). Different stages in the temporal course of estrogen treatment produce opposite effects on voluntary alcohol consumption in male rats. Alcohol, 36, 55-61.

Juárez, J., Camargo, G. & Gómez-Pinedo, U. (2006). Effects of estradiol valerate on voluntary alcohol consumption, beta-endorphin content and neuronal population in hypothalamic arcuate nucleus. *Pharmacol Biochem Behav.* 85, 132-9.

27. Quirarte, G. L., Reid, L. D., de la Teja, I. S., Reid, M. L., Sánchez, M. A., Díaz-Trujillo, A., Aguilar-Vazquez, A. & Prado-Alcalá, R. A. (2007). Estradiol valerate and alcohol intake: dose-response assessments. *BMC Pharmacol., 4*, 3.

Reid, L.D., Onksen, J.L., Schlosburg, J.E., Katz, R.A., Boswell, K.J., Diaz-Trujillo, A., Sanchez, M.A, Reid, M.L., Prado-Alcala, R.A. & Quirarte, G.L. Estrogens can enhance female rats' intake of palatable food. Current Topics in Steroid Research, 2009, 6, 33-47.

Jensen, T. K., Hjollun, N. H., Henriksen, T. B., Scheike, T., Kolstad, H., Giwercman, A., & Olsen, J. (1998). Does moderate alcohol consumption affect fertility? Follow up study among couples planning first pregnancy. BMJ, 317, 505-10.

28. Boswell, K. J., Reid, M. L., Fitch, J. V., Bennett, S. M., Narciso, S. P., Hubbell, C. L., & Reid, L. D. (2005). Estradiol valerate and intake of sweetened water. Pharmacology Biochemistry & Behavior, 80, 1-7.

29. Boswell, K. J., Reid, L. D., Caffalette, C. A., Stitt, K. T., Klein, L. A., Lacroix, A. M., & Reid, M. L. (2006). Estradiol increases consumption of a chocolate cake mix in female rats. Pharmacol Biochem Behav., 84, 84-93.

30. Yes, there are commercially produced rat-foods just as there are commercially produced food for dogs and cats. Rats are the subjects of choice for a lot of medical research and there is a need for a healthy food for these research-subjects and a few companies fulfill that need.

31. Gamaro, G. D., Prediger, M. E., Lopes, J. B., & Dalmaz, C. (2003). Interaction between estradiol replacement and chronic stress on feeding behavior and on serum leptin. Pharm Biochem Behav, 76, 327-333.

32. There are many papers demonstrating that doses of estradiol will reduce intake of food and produce weight loss. They only measure intakes shortly after the injections. One of those papers was cited above, item 22.

33. Marinelli, et al. (2003) see item 24.

34. Juárez et al. (2005), see item 26.

35. Purohit, V. (1998). Moderate alcohol consumption and estrogen levels in postmenopausal women: a review. Alcohol Clin Exp Res, 22, 994-997.

Hilakivi-Clarke, L. (1996). Role of estradiol in alcohol intake and alcohol-related behaviors. J Stud Alcohol, 57, 162-170.

Sarkola, T., Makisalo, H., Fukunaga, T., & Eriksson, C. J. (1999). Acute effect of alcohol on estradiol, estrone, progesterone, prolactin, cortisol, and luteinizing hormone in premenopausal women. Alcohol Clin Exp Res 23, 976-982.

36. Muti P, Trevisan M, Micheli A, Krogh V, Bolelli G, Sciajno R. (1998). Alcohol consumption and total estradiol in premenopausal women. *Cancer Epidemiol Biomark Prev* 7,189-193.

37. Carroll, M. E., Lynch, W. J., Roth M. E., Morgan, A. D. & Cosgrove, K. P. (2004) Sex and estrogen influence drug abuse. *Trends Pharmacol Sci.* 25, 273-9.

Elman, I., Karlsgodt, K. H. & Gastfriend, D. R. (2001). Gender differences in cocaine craving among non-treatment-seeking individuals with cocaine dependence. Am J Drug Alcohol Abuse, 27, 193-202.

Segarra, A. C., Agosto-Rivera, J. L., Febo, M., Lugo-Escobar, N., Menéndez-Delmestre, R., Puig-Ramos, A., & Torres-Diaz, Y.M. (2010). Estradiol: a key biological substrate mediating the response to cocaine in female rats. Horm Behav, 58, 33-43. Epub 2009 Dec 21.

38. Reid, L.D. (2013). Women, alcoholism, and feminism, Brunswick NY: Hexagon. Available from Amazon.

39. May, P. A., & Gossage, J. P. (2001). Estimating the prevalence of fetal alcohol syndrome. A summary. Alcohol Res Health 25, 159–67.

May, P.A., & Gossage J.P. (2011). Material risk factors for fetal alcohol spectrum disorders. Alcohol Res Health, 34, 15-24.

40. Kuehn D. et al. (2012). A prospective cohort study of the prevalence of growth, facial, and central nervous system abnormalities in children with heavy prenatal alcohol exposure. Alcohol Clin Exp Res. 36, 1811-19.

41. Kuehn et al. (2012). A prospective cohort study of the prevalence of growth, facial, and central nervous system abnormalities in children with heavy prenatal alcohol exposure. Alcohol Clin Exp Res. 36, 1811-19.

42. Weinberg, N. Z. (1997). Cognitive and behavioral deficits associated with parental alcohol use. *J Am Acad Child Adolesc Psychiatry* 36, 1177-86.

Chapter 8

1. Dowd, M. (2012). Moral dystopia. New York Times Sunday Review: The opinion pages. Published June 16, 2012.

2. Eleanor Roosevelt said, "To remain aloof is not a solution, it is but a cowardly evasion." Seen at the Eleanor Roosevelt Museum, Hyde Park, New York.

3. Recently it has come to light that universities in the USA are, perhaps, committing moral dystopia with respect to date rape and other instances of rape. The goal appears to be the protection of the reputation of the university by keeping quiet about instances of rape. Gang rape of a drunken girl is clearly a very serious matter and dealing with it in a manner that lessens the impact on the reputation of the university rather than the impact on the girl is just not good. Universities are obligated to work toward making their communities safe places including reducing the instances of sexual violence. Reducing the instances of drunken parties will also reduce the instances of sexual violence.

4. Dr. Angell is a distinguished physician and former editor of a prestigious medical journal. In speaking of Big Pharma, Dr. Angell said that "you cannot blame them because they are charged with making money anyway they can" (on a PBS program). The quotation, however, does not represent her full views. See: Angell, M. (2005). *The truth about the drug companies: How they deceive us and what to do about it.* New York, Random House. This is only one of a number of books whose contents are critical of Big Pharma. For an introduction the problems associated with Big Pharma see the books advertised on Amazon Books when you ask about Angell's book. There is some very interesting reading to be had among the listed books.

5. Harris, Marvin (1975). Cows, Pigs, Wars and Witches: The Riddles of Culture. London: Hutchinson & Co. 1975. ISBN 0-09-122750-X. Reissued in 1991 by Vintage, New York.

6. Prof. Baum surely simplified things. To see just how much check out: Steup, Matthias, "Epistemology," The Stanford Encyclopedia of Philosophy (Winter 2012 Edition), E.N.Zalta (ed.),<http://plato.stanford.edu/archives/win2012/entrie s/epistemology/>.

7. Wolpe, J. (1961). The systematic desensitization treatment of neuroses. J Nerv Ment Dis, 132, 189-203.

Wolpe, J. (1984). Deconditioning and ad hoc uses of relaxation: an overview. J Behav Ther Exp Psychiatry, 15, 299-304.

8. Pinker, S. (2011). The Better Angels of Our Nature:Why violence has declined. New York: Viking Adult Press.

9. Although disputed by some, Wikipedia is a source of reliable knowledge about many topics and often meets the standards of respected college-level textbooks and is free

10. For examples: Haidt, J. (2005). *The Happiness Hypothesis: Finding Modern Truth in Ancient Wisdom.* New York: Basic Books.

Harris, S. (2010). *The Moral Landscape: How Science Can Determine Human Values.* New York: Free Press.

McMahon, D. (2005). *Happiness: A History.* New York: Atlantic Monthly Press.

11. It is not necessary (and probably hopelessly complicated) to disentangle all of the semantic arguments associated with the discussion of pleasure and pain as guidance systems for adaptive behavior in order to make the last point of this book. For example, try to distinguish pleasure from rewarding, from incentivizing, from positive affect, from positively reinforcing, etc. If you attempt to make better sense of the semantic tangle, I (Larry) believe that you will come to the conclusion that the concepts of pleasure and pain are very serviceable.

Appendix 1

The Alcohol Use Disorders Identification Test (AUDIT) was developed by the World Health Organization in 1982. It consists in the following ten multiple choice items. It has been shown to be very effective in detecting hazardous drinking.

The Alcohol Use Disorders Identification Test

1. How often do you have a drink containing alcohol?

> (0) Never (Skip to Questions 9-10)
> (1) Monthly or less
> (2) 2 to 4 times a month
> (3) 2 to 3 times a week
> (4) 4 or more times a week

2. How many drinks containing alcohol do you have on a typical day when you are drinking?

> (0) 1 or 2
> (1) 3 or 4
> (2) 5 or 6
> (3) 7, 8, or 9
> (4) 10 or more

3. How often do you have six or more drinks on one occasion?

> (0) Never
> (1) Less than monthly
> (2) Monthly
> (3) Weekly
> (4) Daily or almost daily

4. How often during the last year have you found that you were not able to stop drinking once you had started?

> (0) Never
> (1) Less than monthly
> (2) Monthly
> (3) Weekly
> (4) Daily or almost daily

5. How often during the last year have you failed to do what was normally expected from you because of drinking?

> (0) Never
> (1) Less than monthly
> (2) Monthly
> (3) Weekly
> (4) Daily or almost daily

6. How often during the last year have you been unable to remember what happened the night before because you had been drinking?

> (0) Never
> (1) Less than monthly
> (2) Monthly
> (3) Weekly
> (4) Daily or almost daily

7. How often during the last year have you needed an alcoholic drink first thing in the morning to get yourself going after a night of heavy drinking?

> (0) Never
> (1) Less than monthly
> (2) Monthly
> (3) Weekly
> (4) Daily or almost daily

8. How often during the last year have you had a feeling of guilt or remorse after drinking?

> (0) Never
> (1) Less than monthly
> (2) Monthly
> (3) Weekly
> (4) Daily or almost daily

9. Have you or someone else been injured as a result of your drinking?

> (0) No
> (2) Yes, but not in the last year
> (4) Yes, during the last year

10. Has a relative, friend, doctor, or another health professional expressed concern about your drinking or suggested you cut down?

> (0) No
> (2) Yes, but not in the last year
> (4) Yes, during the last year

Add up the points associated with your answers above. A total score of 8 or more indicates harmful drinking behavior. See your doctor.

Acknowledgements

Meta and Larry Reid wrote the book. They also edited, designed, and proof-read the book with considerable help from Katelyn (Kitty) VanderClute. In brief, we did everything that was needed to be done before a book was ready for printing. Consequently, there are no acknowledgements to make with respect to the specifics of this book; we did it ourselves.

There are, however, others who provided that good help that allowed us to spend an inordinate amount of time thinking about the book's contents and producing it. We thank Rensselaer Polytechnic Institute, in its entirety, for providing the large infrastructure that allows professors the time and resources to do scholarly work. In particular, we thank Paula Monahan and Betty Osganian for almost daily efficient help in making sure that the professors and students of the Cognitive Science Department are organized. Professor Selmer Bringsjord has been extra ordinarily helpful in being a leader who trusts his fellow scholars.

On the home-front where most of the work on this project was done, we thank Letha and Lawrence for being supportive. Strong, happy homes are extraordinarily helpful in providing the cognitive space to think about complex issues. Letha and Lawrence contributed greatly to our home being a happy, loving place and we are sincerely appreciative of their contributions.

About the Authors

Meta and Larry Reid were a happily married couple. Sadly, Meta died recently. There were years during which Meta and I worked side by side in laboratories studying alcoholism and related issues. There were other years when we collaborated at home on a variety of projects while maintaining somewhat different daily activities (our home-life included a running discussion about the topics of this book). In addition to being a scientist, Meta was a children's librarian, a vocation she enjoyed. Larry has been a university professor for over 50 years. Much of that time he was a Professor of Psychology and Neuroscience at Rensselaer Polytechnic Institute, a vocation that he has enjoyed and continues to do so.

Meta decided that Larry's book *Women, Alcoholism and Feminism* needed to be rewritten to be more readable and more directed toward young women. This book is the product of that decision. During the summer of 2014, we enlisted the help of Katelyn (Kitty) VanderClute in the task of making what might be called a second edition of *Women, Alcoholism and Feminism*. Kitty, at the time, was an undergraduate student at RPI. Kitty was remarkably helpful and Meta and Larry sincerely appreciate her contributions.

Meta and Larry's yearly activities usually involved extended periods of hard work (often extremely enjoyable work complicated by only the ordinary chores and troubles of maintaining a household and putting up with usually nice bosses. Our hard work was punctuated by extended periods of travel. We have visited a lot of countries and cities. We took some time from academia to design and have built a house that we are appallingly proud of. In that house, we wrote this book. The house's design made the work of this book easier than it might have been. Larry Reid, 12/20/2017

Made in the
USA
Middletown, DE